Language Centres

Language International World Directory

The LANGUAGE INTERNATIONAL WORLD DIRECTORY is a series of international listings on subjects pertaining to language related practice such as language policy and planning, training, translation, modern tools for teaching, lexicography, terminology, etc.

The LANGUAGE INTERNATIONAL WORLD DIRECTORY is published under the auspices of *Language International: The magazine for language professionals.*

The following titles have thus far been published in this series:

1. *Language International World Directory of Sociolinguistic and Language Planning Organizations* compiled by Francesc Domínguez and Núria López, 1995.
2. *Language International World Directory of Translation and Interpreting Schools* compiled by Brian Harris, 1997.
3. *A Practical Guide to Software Localization* by Bert Esselink, 1998.
4. *A Practical Guide to Localization* by Bert Esselink, 2000.
5. *Language Centres* by D. E. Ingram

Volume 5

Language Centres: Their roles, functions and management
by D. E. Ingram

Language Centres
Their roles, functions and management

D. E. Ingram
Griffith University

John Benjamins Publishing Company
Amsterdam / Philadelphia

The paper used in this publication meets the minimum requirements of American National Standard for Information Sciences – Permanence of Paper for Printed Library Materials, ANSI z39.48-1984.

Library of Congress Cataloging-in-Publication Data

Ingram, David, 1944-
 Language centres : their roles, functions and management / D. E. Ingram.
  p. cm. (Language International World Directory, ISSN 1383–7591 ; v. 5)
 Includes bibliographical references and index.
 1. Language schools. 2 Title: Language centers. II. Title. III. Series

P53.455.I54 2001
407.1--dc21   2001037891
ISBN 90 272 1957 5 (Eur.) / 1 58811 094 X (US) (Hb; alk. paper)

© 2001 – John Benjamins B.V.
No part of this book may be reproduced in any form, by print, photoprint, microfilm, or any other means, without written permission from the publisher.

John Benjamins Publishing Co. · P.O. Box 36224 · 1020 ME Amsterdam · The Netherlands
John Benjamins North America · P.O. Box 27519 · Philadelphia PA 19118-0519 · USA

Table of contents

Acknowledgements   IX

CHAPTER 1
The language centre concept   1
1. Preamble 1
2. What a language centre is 3
3. Centres chosen for detailed discussion 5

CHAPTER 2
The National Foreign Language Center (NFLC), Washington DC, United States of America   7
1. Address 7
2. The centre 7
3. Background and origin of the centre 8
4. Geographical and administrative locations 22
5. Purpose and mission of the center 25
6. Activities 27
7. Interactions and links 32
8. Staffing 33
9. Facilities 33
10. Budget 34
11. Constraints and opportunities 35
12. Uniqueness and impact of the center 36

CHAPTER 3
**The Centre for Information on Language Teaching
and Research (CILT), London, United Kingdom**   39
1. Address   39
2. The centre   40
3. Background and origin of the centre   40
4. Geographical and administrative locations   49
5. Purpose and mission of the centre   51
6. Activities   52
7. Interactions and links   58
8. Staffing   59
9. Facilities   60
10. Budget   60
11. Constraints and opportunities   61
12. Uniqueness and impact of the centre   61

CHAPTER 4
The European Centre for Modern Languages (ECML), Graz, Austria   63
1. Address   63
2. The centre   63
3. Background and origin of the centre   64
4. Geographical and administrative locations   71
5. Purpose and mission of the centre   73
6. Activities   75
7. Interactions and links   78
8. Staffing   80
9. Facilities   81
10. Budget   81
11. Constraints and opportunities   82
12. Uniqueness and impact of the centre   83

CHAPTER 5
The SEAMEO Regional Language Centre (RELC), Singapore   85
1. Address   85
2. The centre   85
3. Background and origin of the centre   86
4. Geographical and administrative locations   91
5. Purpose and mission of the centre   92
6. Activities   94
7. Interactions and links   101
8. Staffing   103

9. Facilities 104
10. Budget 105
11. Constraints and opportunities 106
12. Uniqueness and impact of the centre 107

Chapter 6
The Centre for Applied Linguistics and Languages (CALL), Griffith University, Brisbane, Queensland, Australia 109
1. Address 109
2. The centre 109
3. Background and origin of the centre 111
4. Geographical and administrative locations 114
5. Purpose and mission of the centre 127
6. Activities 129
7. Interactions and links 140
8. Staffing 142
9. Facilities 143
10. Budget 145
11. Constraints and opportunities 149
12. Uniqueness and impact of the centre 151

Chart One: Centre for applied linguistics and languages (CALL) academic model 157

Chart Two: Centre for applied linguistics and languages (CALL) administration organisational model 157

Chapter 7
A comparative view of five language centres 159
1. Preamble 159
2. Essential nature of each centre 159
3. Backgrounds and origins 159
4. Geographical and administrative locations 161
5. Purpose and mission 162
6. Activities 163
7. Interactions/links 166
8. Staffing 167
9. Facilities 168
10. Budget 169
11. Constraints and opportunities 170
12. Uniqueness and impact of the centres 171

Chapter 8
Issues to consider in establishing and developing a language centre — 173
1. Preamble   173
2. Roles, functions and purposes   173
3. Scope of language centres   181
4. Governance and management   187
5. Interactions and links   215
6. Activities   220
7. Advantages and constraints   229
8. Conclusion   230

References — 233

Index — 239

Acknowledgements

The background research for this paper was largely undertaken while the author was on research and study leave from Griffith University, June 1998 to January 1999, and while an Adjunct Fellow at the National Foreign Language Center, Washington DC from June to September 1998.

The author wishes to express his thanks to both Griffith University and the National Foreign Language Center for the funding and other assistance which made this book possible and to the Directors and staff of each centre discussed for their assistance in providing documentation on their centres and on the contexts in which each centre exists. Particular thanks are due to those Directors who gave freely of their time in talking to the author or in responding to emailed requests for information.

Chapter 1

The language centre concept

1. Preamble

Language centres have made a major contribution to the development of applied linguistics since its emergence as a distinctive field in the mid-1960s. National and international centres, such as those discussed in this volume, have stimulated applied linguistic research and development and, in particular, have played a major part in the development and implementation of international, national, State and institutional language policies and language education. University-based language centres have provided a significant means by which universities have sought to improve the quality of their language teaching, to foster applied linguistics, and to provide language consultancy services to their communities (not least to education and industry). In many universities (especially in Australia), it has been language centres that, as universities were forced by the economic rationalism of governments in the 1990s to generate more of their own capital, have led the way in the commercialisation of universities' intellectual capital. Thus language centres have not only strongly influenced the development of applied linguistics but they have been at the forefront of the changes that universities have encountered in the last decade of the 20th century and that will undoubtedly continue into the 21st. The tension that exists between, on the one hand, the traditional managerial purposes and approaches of established universities and, on the other, the new managerial exigencies of the present era and the problems inherent in managing and working through that tension are an essential part of the history of language centres and discussion arising from that tension will recur throughout this book, especially when university-based centres are discussed.

Language centres take many forms but they are established by and answer to universities, governments, multigovernmental organisations, or their own independent governing boards invariably in the expectation that they will serve some significant purpose and respond to some significant need in the area of applied linguistics and language education as identified by the founding body. For the purposes of this volume, language centres are distinguished from language *teaching* centres even though some language centres may include a language teaching programme. Though language teaching centres were not uncommon earlier, it was in the 1960s when applied linguistics first emerged as a distinctive field and started to grow rapidly that language centres of the sort discussed in this book also appeared and rapidly proliferated around the world. Some centres, like most of those considered in later chapters in this book, have been brilliantly successful; others, like the National Languages and Literacy Institute of Australia (late in its life, known as Language Australia), have failed, sometimes damaging the field in their country in doing so. Others, like the highly successful University of Essex Language Centre, established by the late Peter Strevens, have continued to operate but have changed their original form to become, for example, Departments of Language and Linguistics or Schools of Applied Linguistics and Languages. Many universities and governments continue to contemplate the establishment of language centres and a quick internet search today suggests that there are hundreds, if not thousands, of language centres of one form or another in institutions, in government or private agencies, or standing independently around the world: many of these continue to make impressive contributions to research in linguistics and applied linguistics, to language or language education policy, to the monitoring and implementation of policy, or to the maintenance and development of high quality language education in their institutions, their countries, or internationally.

Yet, despite the important roles that language centres are intended to play, the diverse forms they take, and the distinctive issues involved in their management and administration, extensive searches of the literature of applied linguistics, whether in the traditional databases and abstracting services or over the internet, yield virtually nothing that discusses language centres, their nature, roles and functions, or their management, administration, and funding models. Thus there is little one can read about language centres, the purposes they serve, how they can best be organised, and why some succeed and others fail.

For these reasons, it seemed useful for the present volume to consider what language centres are, what roles and functions they can characteristically serve, and what their distinctive management requirements might be. Chapter 1 briefly considers the concept of a language centre as discussed in this book. The next five chapters provide five contrasting examples of language centres on four different continents:

- The National Foreign Language Center (NFLC), in Washington DC, United States of America
- The Centre for Information on Language Teaching and Research (CILT) in London, Britain
- The European Centre for Modern Languages (ECML) in Graz, Austria
- The Regional Language Centre (RELC) in Singapore, and
- The Centre for Applied Linguistics and Languages (CALL), Griffith University, Brisbane, Australia.

Chapter 7 briefly draws out the similarities and differences between these centres. Growing out of this discussion of five different examples of language centres, with different purposes and different management approaches, the final chapter, Chapter 8, discusses the roles, functions, and management of language centres in general and, either overtly or by implication, seeks to provide guidance on the establishment and management of language centres.

This volume can be seen as following up an earlier study by the same author, a survey of language centres around the world commissioned by the Fédération Internationale des Professeurs de Langues Vivantes (FIPLV) and submitted to that body in 1990 (Ingram 1990). Since that survey was undertaken, other centres have been identified, new centres have been established (e.g., ECML and NFLC), and undoubtedly some of those included at that earlier time have disappeared. In any case, the FIPLV survey was intended to do little more than list whatever centres could be identified and provide a brief description of them. The present volume aims to consider in more depth the nature of language centres and to report in some detail on ones of particular interest either because of the role they fill (e.g., CILT, ECML, RELC and NFLC), because of the contrasting models they all offer, or because of some distinctive management feature (e.g., CALL as a wholly self-funding, commercial but academic university centre whose resources are dependent on projects and students in contrast to the others, which receive the largest part of their funds in core grants from governments or donors). Wherever possible in the course of discussion of particular attributes of language centres, especially in Chapter 8, reference is made to these centres in order to exemplify or clarify particular points that are made about language centres though the main discussion of each centre occurs in its own chapter.

2. What a language centre is

Fundamentally, *language centres* are units formed to gain synergy in the area of language education and applied linguistics from bringing together in appropriate facilities enthusiastic, well-qualified personnel working together in pursuit of the goals set for the centre. Thus language centres coordinate activity and focus resources towards the goals the founding body has set for the centre rather than disperse them through, for example, disparate language departments in a university or universities.

Language centres take many forms but, essentially, they are units with a defined purpose related, differentially, to the development of applied linguistics, the improvement of language education, and the implementation of language policy in the institution, nation or region that they serve. They receive dedicated funding either through their own efforts or through their founding organisation (e.g., a government or a multi-governmental organisation). A language centre is a synergetic organisation that generally concentrates a high degree of expertise in some aspect or aspects of applied linguistics within a single unit, providing mutual stimulus for the enhancement of language education in a particular institution, state, nation, or region. In the best examples, language centres gain synergy by bringing together well-qualified applied linguists and language educators whose enthusiasms, knowledge and ideas feed off and support each other: perhaps the National Foreign Language Center discussed in the next chapter is the best example of a centre specifically designed to capitalise on that synergy, drawing on the best experts from around the globe through their fellowship schemes and meeting arrangements though the other national and international centres discussed also exemplify, in one form or another, this synergetic design.

Apart from a design intended to produce a synergy in applied linguistics (or in that portion of it that is the focus of the centre), the most successful centres seem also to have four common characteristics (while some of those that have failed, e.g., the National Languages and Literacy Institute of Australia, NLLIA, seem to breach one or more of these in some significant way):

– They are clearly focussed, quite specific in their purpose, and limited in scope (even though often quite large institutions).

– National and international centres seek to provide stimulus and advice, they do not try to take over the field, but they stimulate, advise, and provide information, while allowing other players in the field to pursue their own activities independently of the centre itself even though they draw help from the centre.

– Language centres have their own discrete funds, which they themselves exploit and manage and which they either generate themselves or obtain from government or donor sources following reasoned justification.

– Language Centres are autonomous in their decision-making even though they may answer to a governing board of some sort which is sympathetic to and knowledgeable about the nature of the centre's operations and its operational requirements: they are not supervised in their normal operations by other organisations or units (such as a university faculty) whose interests, skills and experience lie elsewhere and which, in the case of some university faculties, may be quite ignorant of or unsympathetic towards the goals and methods of applied linguistics or of commercially-run language centres.

One needs to distinguish language centres with a research and advisory element to their duties and sometimes the teaching of applied linguistics from **language teaching centres** or "language resource centres" (cf. "Centre de Ressources" in *Mélanges Pédagogiques*, No. 21, 1995), which are not the subject of this volume. Some language centres of the sort discussed (e.g., CALL) may include components of language teaching for a variety of possible reasons: revenue-raising, an immediate site for classroom-based research, and the synergy and awareness of practical reality that can be derived from grouping academics and researchers with language teaching practitioners. However, the distinctive feature of language centres as discussed in this book is that they also include a substantial interest in applied linguistics for purposes of research, consultancy or teaching.

There are many examples around the world of highly successful language teaching centres that provide courses for their institution's award programmes or to meet the community's language education needs and their omission from this book is only to limit the scope of the present discussion and in no way reflects on their value or academic worthiness. The Institute of Modern Languages in the University of Queensland is a noteworthy example of one that principally serves the community but is also able to offer language courses to students in award programmes. According to its webpage, the Oxford University Language Centre provides courses in some eight languages, a language library, and a study area consisting of computer-based learning resources and audio/video study rooms, all of which are available to staff and students of the University and, when available and on payment of fees, to members of the wider community (see http://units.ox.ac.uk/departments/langcentre/userguide/introduction.html). The University of Cambridge Language Centre, as noted subsequently, seems to serve a somewhat different role in advising and offering materials for language learning and teaching and provides facilities in which the language courses of other departments can be taught (http://www.langcen.cam.ac.uk).

Nearer to the concept of language centres discussed here are the seven **National Language Resource Centers** in the United States funded under Title VI. These centres do not seem to have the wider language policy and advisory roles of the national centres described in this volume but have been funded under Title VI to undertake "a number of research and action initiatives designed to advance the quality of second language teaching, learning, and assessment" in such areas as second language assessment, the less commonly taught languages, second language learning and technology, and second language learning strategies (cf. the description of the Centre for Advanced Research on Language Acquisition, CARLA, a National Language Resource Center, at the University of Minnesota, webpage at http://carla.acad.umn.edu/NLRC.html).

3. Centres chosen for detailed discussion

This book selects five language centres for detailed discussion. These centres have, in most cases, made and continue to make important contributions to, variously, applied linguistics, language policy, and language education in their areas of responsibility and, in some cases, in the world. They have been chosen because they provide contrasting illustrations in their missions, roles and functions, and, especially, in their management from which to draw out for discussion a number of issues generally applicable to language centres, their establishment and management that are discussed in the final chapter. Some of the centres are funded by government or multi-governments, one is largely donor-funded, and one is wholly self-funding and effectively commercial.

The centres chosen for discussion and the significant, contrasting characteristics that have led to their being chosen for detailed discussion are these:

– The **National Foreign Language Center (NFLC)**, Washington DC, in the United States is a national language centre, funded largely by philanthropic organisations and dedicated to advisory and development activities in the area of language policy in the United States. At the time when this book was going to press, the NFLC was changing somewhat as a result of changes to its funding base but, since those changes were still being implemented, it was more useful to discuss NFLC in the form it had taken since its establishment. The changes that have confronted the NFLC are not, in any case, entirely of its own choosing and its original form provides a more useful and interesting contrast in the context of the discussion in this volume than its future form (however successful that may turn out to be).

– The **Centre for Information on Language Teaching and Research (CILT)**, based in London but with branches in other parts of Britain, is a largely government-funded national centre dedicated to improving the quality of language teaching in Britain principally by providing a complex information service.

– The **European Centre for Modern Languages** (ECML), in Graz, Austria, is an international, regional centre for Europe established and funded by the Council of Europe and dedicated to facilitating the implementation of the Council's language policies. It is significant both because of its distinctive nature and, especially, because of its relationship to the Council of Europe's language activities, activities that have probably had more influence on the development of applied linguistics and second or foreign language education in Europe and globally than anything else in the history of language education.

– The **SEAMEO Regional Language Centre (RELC)**, in Singapore, is an international, regional centre for South East Asia, established and partly funded by the Southeast Asian Ministers of Education Organization (SEAMEO). It is dedicated to supporting the development of high quality language education in South East Asia, principally by offering advanced training to senior teachers and administrators who can have a multiplier effect in their own countries.

– The **Centre for Applied Linguistics and Languages (CALL)**, in Griffith University, Brisbane, Australia, is a wholly self-funding, university-based language centre directed by the present author and dedicated to offering high quality language programmes to Australian and overseas students, providing expert applied linguistic research and consultancy services, and offering a range of non-award and award courses in applied linguistics. Its unique character comes from the diversity (and complementarity) of its responsibilities and the fact that it is required to operate on a commercial and wholly self-funding basis in contrast to the other centres above that are largely government- or donor-funded.

CHAPTER 2

The National Foreign Language Center (NFLC), Washington DC, United States of America

1. Address[1]

   ```
   National Foreign Language Center
   at the University of Maryland,
   1029 Vermont Avenue, NW, Suite 1000,
   Washington, DC, 20005,
   United States of America.[2]
   Telephone:   1-202-637-8881
   Fax:         1-202-637-9244
   Email:       info@nflc.org
   Website:     http://www.nflc.org/
   ```

2. The centre

   The National Foreign Language Center[3] is an outstanding example of an autonomous centre planned to be able to critique language policy and language education and to give dispassionate advice on them with the status of an expert observer. It is able to do so with the objectivity that comes from standing outside the formal education system,

---

1. See the postscript at the end of this chapter concerning the changes that took place in NFLC commencing at the end of 1998 and implemented largely in 2000 at the time when this volume was going to press.

2. From its foundation until mid-2000, the Center's address was:

   National Foreign Language Center,
   The John Hopkins University,
   4th Floor, 1619 Massachusetts Avenue, NW,
   Washington DC, 20036,
   United States of America

3. In preparing this chapter on the NFLC, the author had access, in addition to the documents in the list of References or otherwise identified in the text, to a number of in-house documents from the NFLC that cannot be referenced. In addition, he was able to discuss many of these issues with then Center Director, Dr David Maxwell, the founding Director, Dr Richard Lambert, and with other Center staff, including Dr Dick Brecht, who subsequently became Director. He gratefully acknowledges the assistance given by these people and the documents viewed though any errors of interpretation from them remain entirely his own.

its politics, and its resource battles. It was the creation of Dr Richard Lambert, a sociologist with a lifetime interest in international studies who, until becoming NFLC's founding Director in 1986, was a Professor of International Studies at the University of Pennsylvania, Philadelphia.

In its webpage, the NFLC describes itself as

> …a nonprofit research and policy institute dedicated to the development and implementation of policies and programs that make the language learning system more responsive to the national interest.

An "overview" document from the Center describes it as

> …a research and policy institute focused on the teaching, learning, and maintenance of cross-cultural communication competence — particularly in languages other than English — in the United States. It is the **only** independent think tank committed to identifying national needs for that competence, assessing our capacity to meet those needs, and developing strategies to increase national capacity in this critical area.

3. Background and origin of the centre

The NFLC's concern is to contribute to the improvement of language policy and language education planning in the United States. While it recognises the many values of language education, in its current practice and in the activities that preluded its establishment, the NFLC places particular emphasis on the development of competency in foreign languages for practical purposes and on the development and maintenance of language skills for use in adult life. In recognising the benefits to be gained from a proper national recognition of the value of language skills, the NFLC is concerned at what it regards as the deplorable inadequacy of the language education system in the United States. The state of foreign language education in the United States, its changes over the last decade, and its current progress have been discussed briefly elsewhere by the present writer (see Ingram, forthcoming: Chapter 3). The situation which the NFLC seeks to address is summed up in this reference to a survey of language enrolments by the Modern Language Association taken from the NFLC's *Perspectives* newsletter, significantly under the heading, "A System in Crisis":

> Collectively, these four projects …[provide] a broad and rather unsettling picture of the environment for foreign language teaching and learning in post-secondary education … the major characteristics of what we believe can legitimately be termed a crisis…
>
> …Most disturbing is the fact that the dismally low percentage of undergraduates studying any foreign language at all continues to decline.
> (*NFLC Perspectives*, Winter 1996)

It asserts that there is national need for competency in foreign languages, that the needs are significant and cross all domains of national life (private, business and industry, government and education), that they are not being met under existing policy and practice, and that there is no present indication that they will be met in the future. It was out of this realisation that the NFLC was founded and on which it justifies its existence and bases its on-going activities.

As indicated earlier, the establishment of the NFLC was, to a very large extent, the personal initiative of its founding Director, Dr Richard Lambert, who was not himself an applied linguist but a social scientist, a sociologist with a strong interest in international studies and languages. Undoubtedly this origin has profoundly influenced the nature and functions of the Center, most importantly, making it highly sensitive to the societal and national role of foreign languages and to the importance of making the language education system responsive to societal and national need. Lacking the traditional "baggage" that language teachers carry (including the traditional view of foreign language teaching and learning as "esoteric", a dilettante activity, and one serving largely literary, general educational, and linguistic purposes), Lambert was able to focus on the practical, societal and national need for language skills and to embue the Center itself with this abiding sense of the practical relevance of language skills and the need to ensure that language policy and language education respond to the nation's practical needs.

Though Lambert was writing on related themes before this, perhaps the earliest, decisive steps leading to the foundation of the National Foreign Language Center are seen in Lambert's (1986) book, *Points of Leverage*, whose title itself is significant and reflects the way in which the Center targets its activities: at points in the national system where maximum effect can be had to achieve the greatest change. Though *Points of Leverage* does not recommend the creation of a National Foreign Language Center but rather a National Foundation for Foreign Languages and International Studies, it clearly is the precursor of the initiatives Lambert was later to take, which are reflected in the document referred to subsequently, *The Case for a National Foreign Language Center: An Editorial* (Lambert 1987). This latter document was published as he was about to start work as the NFLC's founding Director and makes the case for the Center in very similar terms to the comment and recommendations in parts of *Points of Leverage*.

In the Preface to *Points of Leverage*, Kenneth Prewitt of the Rockefeller Foundation describes how, in 1984, the Smithsonian Institution hosted a dinner in Washington to discuss what could be done to stabilize Federal support for international studies and foreign language education (cf. Lambert 1986: v). There was strong concern expressed at the deficiencies in language education and the meeting concluded that

> The international challenges facing the society are inadequately and in some instances ineptly serviced by the existing federal arrangements for support of foreign and

international studies. (Lambert 1986: v)

The meeting resolved that the best way forward was to seek the establishment of a National Foundation for Foreign Languages and International Studies modeled on similar national agencies for the Humanities, the Arts, and Science (Lambert 1986: v). To do so, the Association of American Universities was given the task of preparing a legislative proposal for a National Foundation, published in 1986 as *To Strengthen the Nation's Investment in Foreign Languages and International Studies: A Legislative Proposal to Create a National Foundation for Foreign Languages and International Studies*. To go beyond a document proposing the legal form of such a Foundation, the meeting also commissioned Richard D. Lambert to prepare a document that would provide "more extended analysis and justification" for such a Foundation. The result was the publication in 1986 of *Points of Leverage: An Agenda for a National Foundation for International Studies* (New York: Social Science Research Council) whose intent, in Prewitt's words,

> …is no more, but no less, than that of presenting for public discussion and debate the rationale for a National Foundation for Foreign Languages and International Studies. (Prewitt in Lambert 1986: vi)

In *Points of Leverage*, Lambert marshals the usual array of arguments in favour of a strong foreign language learning system, discussing the challenge of internationalisation, the importance of foreign language competency, international expertise in business, the training of academic specialists, international information flows, research, overseas links, and international education (each of which constitutes a chapter in his book). In the course of doing so, he focuses, at one point (in Chapter 2), on the case for a "National Foreign Language Resource Center".

Specifically in relation to the foreign language learning situation in the United States in the mid-1980s (and reflecting the views of the NFLC still in the late 1990s), Lambert says:

> In foreign languages, we spend almost nothing on providing foreign language training for English-speaking adult Americans who may need to use another language in their work. Yet we spend millions to serve the language needs of immigrant populations whose foreign language skills we are busily trying to eradicate. We spend billions of dollars annually to train millions of American students in one or two years of French or German — languages of countries that are no longer our primary trading partners or cultural models — without having any way of knowing what level of competency those students have attained. We are fairly sure, however, that the skills they have attained would be barely enough for survival if they were called upon to use them. Moreover, we have no idea — indeed, no way to measure — what students retain of those competencies as adults, although our suspicion is that it is close to zero. (Lambert 1986: 4)

Foreshadowing the subsequent function of the NFLC, Lambert saw a National

Foundation for International Studies as making the national response to the "increasing internationalization of our society" more effective by

> (1) placing the various developments within some overall framework of national needs; (2) identifying redundancies, misdirections, and important gaps; (3) shifting existing resources and marshaling new ones from the various sectors of our society to better meet those needs; (4) assembling and disseminating data ... essential for national planning; and (5) setting criteria and evaluating the effectiveness of programs drawing upon national resources. (Lambert 1986: 5–6)

He went on to recommend steps by which the proposed Foundation might help to meet the challenges of internationalisation. Some of these edge beyond the function of a foreign language centre to encompass activities more germane to international studies but they are predominantly things that the NFLC now envisages within its mission:

- improving the foreign language competencies of important segments of our population;
- enhancing the capacity of American business to be competitive in an increasingly internationalized economy;
- shoring up and improving our cadres of foreign affairs specialists;
- expanding international communication and the gathering, management, and analysis of information from abroad;
- building durable linkages and opportunities for overseas sojourns for those engaged in international studies; and
- internationalizing the education of substantial portions of the successor generation. (Lambert 1986: 7)

It should be remembered that Lambert was writing a case in support of the establishment of a foundation whose interests would encompass both international studies and foreign languages but, here, since our present interest is to observe the origins, role and functions of the National Foreign Language Center whose interests are strictly within the area of languages and language learning, the focus will be on only that part of Lambert's case principally concerned with foreign languages.

In his chapter on foreign language competency, Lambert deplores the ineffectiveness of the foreign language system in developing people with any practical ability in the languages, the poor quality of what is offered, and the limited relevance of the languages principally available:

> The trouble is that while we invest an immense amount of student and teacher time and huge amounts of money in foreign language teaching, survey after survey documents how inadequate our current foreign language capacity is: the skills it imparts are too low and too scholastic; the languages taught were appropriate for the nineteenth century but not for the twenty-first; the ways of measuring skill acquisition are outmoded; the levels of instruction are totally unarticulated, so that the cumulative aspect of skill acquisition by a student is unattended and accidental; and no one knows

> or seems concerned about how much of early foreign language training survives to be available for adult use.
>
> …a major shift in emphasis, organization, and teaching technology is needed. (Lambert 1986: 9–10)

This is not simply an educational deficiency that he is identifying but these problems have national and international repercussions:

> There is nothing more damaging to the American capacity to cope in a global society than the abysmally low level of foreign language competency of most Americans. (Lambert 1986: 9)

It is commonplace in the United States (as it is in any federal system of government, including Australia in the late 1970s), for advocates of national language policies that touch on education to be told that it cannot be done, that States are autonomous in these matters, that federal or national level initiatives would be intrusive and cause adverse political reactions, and this would limit the contribution that a National Foundation or National Centre could make. While acknowledging that, in a federal system where education is a State responsibility, any Federal initiative (including a National Foundation) can play only a marginal role, Lambert goes on:

> There is, nevertheless, an important collective responsibility at the national level that can assist in making the marginal investment and providing the necessary intellectual catalyst that a major shift in national policy demands. The high degree of dispersion of foreign language instruction … makes it unlikely that such a transformation will well up spontaneously from the thousands of classrooms. There are some things, such as setting national standards, that must be done centrally or they will not be done at all. Thus there must be a national as well as a state effort to strengthen our foreign language teaching and learning system. (Lambert 1986: 11)

Not least, there is need for coordination and for the effectiveness of the initiatives to be judged against the national need. Lambert cites many initiatives being taken at the time he is writing by the Federal Government and other agencies to stimulate foreign language education but he emphasises the need for some central body to coordinate these efforts:

> These many initiatives in the improvement of the national capacity to teach foreign languages are most encouraging. However, right at the beginning of this upsurge of interest and investment, it is extremely important that a central planning, initiating, coordinating, and implementing organization be put in place to assure that the scattered efforts in the area of foreign language education are cumulative, that they address the central agenda issues, and, above all, that they are effective and represent the best use of our national resources. …
>
> …Assuming such a catalytic role in the development of a more effective system of foreign language instruction would be a natural first priority for the proposed National Foundation for International Studies. (Lambert 1986: 12)

Consequently, a national foundation, like the National Foreign Language Center subsequently, would have

> A primary function … to provide central planning, coordination, and the necessary marginal resources to improve the nation's foreign language education system. (Lambert 1986:12)

Lambert goes on to discuss in some detail the agenda for such a National Foundation, focussing, in his words, on "the points of leverage" in order to effect change in the foreign language teaching system. He proposes that the Foundation undertake needs and use surveys especially in key occupations where foreign language use would be most productive, the creation of experimental pilot programmes for adults, the development of a "common metric" (both a scale and its application procedures) for measuring foreign language proficiency, and the conduct of critical research (Lambert 1986:12–22). He proposes the foundation of a National Foreign Language Resource Center whose tasks would be to create, evaluate, and work for the adoption of satisfactory techniques of language instruction and whose functions would be:

(1) carrying out or commissioning the research and materials development required for that transformation [of American language teaching];
(2) implementation of the strategies that emerge from this research, particularly with regard to training;
(3) diffusion and articulation;
(4) evaluation (Lambert 1986:23).

The actual recommendation for the creation of the national foreign language resource centre reads as follows:

> The Foundation should help create and sustain a national foreign language resource center to assist in the upgrading of the national foreign language teaching system by conducting and coordinating the needed research; preparing new teaching materials as needed; training teachers; administering intensive teaching programs; providing instruction in languages not taught elsewhere; articulating the various levels of instruction; diffusing the results of research and experimentation in new teaching technologies; evaluating teaching methodologies and programs; and managing a national proficiency test network to administer the common metric.
> (Lambert 1986:25)

This notion of a national centre includes much of what the NFLC does but it also includes teaching and testing functions that would have enabled it to generate some of its own revenue but would have made it less independent of the system than the NFLC currently is, a feature of its current status that is of considerable importance to its policy advisory role.

Subsequent chapters underline the importance of the role of foreign languages in national and international affairs and argue for things designed to enhance those activities through the work of the Foundation (and, later, the NFLC). Lambert makes a strong argument for improved foreign language skills for business purposes, the development of resources, facilities and techniques suitable for adult learners, languages for business purposes, high level skills, research and development in the maintenance and rejuvenation of language skills, the development of self-access (or autonomous learning) facilities and programmes, the establishment of centres to teach the "less commonly taught" languages of high priority (especially Asian and African languages), and the need to "internationalize" business education (Lambert 1986: Chapter 3).

Other issues raised include the training of academic specialists in "language and area studies" (Chapter 4), the enhancement and management of the flow of information to and from international sources, better and more internationally-oriented library resources, improved translation facilities, and the development of automatic translation facilities (Chapter 5). There is need for more and improved research on international affairs, into particular languages, for the production of teaching materials, and to achieve better and more effective teaching methods (Lambert 1986: Chapter 6, 98–99). Lambert argues that there is need for evaluation of research in order to determine the most profitable agenda to follow and the directions in which the whole field of international studies (including foreign languages) should be going. He argues for a balance between research targeted by the client and basic research identified by researchers, chosen and evaluated by peer review (p. 100), and he asserts that only a national body able to oversight the national need and the research activity can achieve a comprehensive needs-related agenda. Clearly, the form the NFLC and its management have taken has been considerably influenced by such views:

> The Foundation should establish a proactive program of research support to direct research toward topics of great national importance, to fill in gaps in country or language coverage, and to carry out the evaluation and planning activities for the field as a whole. To establish the priorities for and to supervise this proactive program, a distinguished national advisory group should be established, comprising research scholars and representatives of universities, major international business firms, national research organizations and government agencies along lines similar to the National Science Board. Both private and public funds should be provided to support research on the topics selected by the group. …
>
> …Pilot projects and piecemeal solutions will not meet the demands of organized knowledge about other countries that the coming decades will bring. To provide durable, cross-sectional support for research in international studies, an organization for which this is a principal purpose will have to be created. This is a task for the Foundation. (Lambert 1986: 99–100; 106)

Foreshadowing some of the projects that the NFLC was later to take on, Lambert stresses the importance of "overseas linkages", programmes under which Americans travel to other countries and other nationals come to America for study and other experience, and, not least, he provides a strong argument for language study abroad:

> We obviously cannot deal with the increasing internationalization of our society by staying at home....
>
> ...if citizens whose career requires a foreign language skill are to be other than novices, they will benefit by topping off their domestic training with a disciplined course of training overseas. If they are going to keep those skills active or rejuvenate them after a period of disuse, then repeated periods of exposure in the country where they are spoken is absolutely essential. ...an even more urgent case can be made for foreign language teachers who might infect generations of students with their inadequate or decaying competencies. (Lambert 1986: 109, 117–118)

In fact, Lambert sees a particular role for a national foundation in addressing the need for an adequate supply of qualified teachers:

> The Foundation should join with the states through the chief state school officers in supporting and managing a cooperative program to increase the supply of qualified language teachers, and to sustain and upgrade existing foreign language teachers' competencies, through the sharing of successful innovative teaching strategies, in-service training programs, and fellowships for foreign sojourns. (Lambert 1986: 147)

Not all of *Points of Leverage* is directly relevant to the foundation of the NFLC since much of it goes beyond language issues and deals with international studies in general. While there seems to have been considerable interest generated by *Points of Leverage*, it did not achieve its goal of the creation of a National Foundation for International Studies, and, a few years later, Lambert was speaking of it as "ill-fated" (Lambert 1990: 237). However, he had much greater success with the foreign language components of the *Points of Leverage* ideas and, when it was evident that *Points of Leverage* would not be successful in producing a National Foundation for International Studies, a number of philanthropic organisations agreed in 1986 to help Lambert establish the National Foreign Language Center (Lambert, personal communication, 20 August, 1998). This funding was provided by the Exxon Education Foundation, the Ford Foundation, the Andrew W. Mellon Foundation, and the Pew Charitable Trusts (information supplied by Dr David Maxwell, Director of NFLC).[4] With this success just being realised and his role as founding Director about to commence, Lambert argued the case for the NFLC and outlined its role and function in an editorial in *The Modern Language Journal*, in the Spring of 1987.

As in *Points of Leverage*, Lambert asserts in *The Case for a National Foreign Language Center* that the foreign language capacity of Americans is "abysmally low" and "damaging to the American capacity to cope in a global society" (Lambert 1987: 128). He also states that the language teaching system is inefficient, ineffective

---

4. In early 1999, Dr Maxwell resigned from NFLC to accept an appointment as President of Drake University, Iowa. He was replaced by Dr Richard Brecht, who had been a senior researcher and Deputy Director in NFLC for much of its existence.

and cannot "solve the current national problem" even though he acknowledges that there have been many individual initiatives by authorities at different levels (Lambert 1987:129). What is needed, he says

> …is not just a tinkering with this or that specific aspect of language instruction as it is now carried out, but an examination of the system as a whole … a measurement of its performance against the needs of the society of the future. …The various proposals for the expansion of American international competencies in general and for the creation of a centralized funding structure to further that goal must have an important foreign language component. …it is essential that a well-thought-out plan for making our foreign language teaching system better serve those needs be made a conspicuous part of those proposals, and that the necessary marshalling of the field to address those needs be undertaken. (Lambert 1987:129)

Lambert asserts that there are three aspects of American foreign language teaching that make it difficult to change: the fact that it is only loosely tied to the goal of producing "an adult population with significant and durable foreign language competencies", the "extreme disaggregation" of the system, and

> …the surprisingly weak tradition of empiricism in the search for what works and what does not work … [instead] wildly exaggerated claims for one or another way to teach a foreign language. In place of theory linked firmly to applied study, we have staunchly asserted opinions on how students learn. In place of carefully formulated relationships among practice, theory, research and curriculum and materials development, we have teachers, theorists, researchers, and pedagogues each going their separate way. And none of them is relating to the social scientists where some of the expertise that needs to be brought to bear on the problem resides. (Lambert 1987:129)

Clearly, these views of American foreign language teaching have profoundly influenced the form and function of the National Foreign Language Center. In arguing for the creation of the Center, Lambert identifies its task as:

> …to create, evaluate, and work for the adoption of satisfactory techniques of language instruction capable of carrying a wide variety of learners to a high enough level of competency to permit genuine use. (Lambert 1987:130)

Though he acknowledges that many individuals and organisations have similar aspirations, he sees the NFLC as a new organisation able to provide

> …some central space where scattered efforts can be coordinated, made cumulative, and brought to bear on a common agenda. In this central space the efforts of the language community can be interwoven with those of professionals in other academic fields, and with the needs of the eventual users — corporate, government, individual — who will employ those with foreign language skills. (Lambert 1987:130)]

An important aspect of the function of the NFLC was seen as providing a place where persons interested in foreign language instruction "can work for substantial periods of time on their own research alongside others with similar interests" (Lambert 1987:130). This aspect of the Center's functions has led, especially, to its distinctive staffing structure in which a relatively small number of permanent, full-time academic or research staff is supplemented by staff employed fractionally while holding positions in other institutions, staff employed for specific projects, and, most notably, to the Center's extensive fellowship schemes. Some of these are at the pre- and post-doctoral levels but they also target senior national and international figures who receive fellowships (funded by the Andrew Mellon Foundation) to enable them to spend months at a time writing and researching at the NFLC. In addition, the Center has established an Adjunct Fellow scheme whereby selected former Fellows are invited to return for a month a year to pursue their own research and writing. While at the Center, the Fellows also interact with Center staff, discuss projects that are proceeding, participate in colloquia and "brown bag lunches", and generally contribute to the life of the Center. In this sense, the role of the Fellows and of the other staff of the Center is to create a substantial and quite unique "foreign language think-tank" (Lambert 1987:130–131).

As he had discussed in *Points of Leverage*, Lambert's intention was that the Center would not only coordinate activities going on elsewhere but would also determine its own research agenda within the context of national need and selected to exert maximum leverage. Thus the Center would

> serve to identify and address important unmet needs. …its special contribution resides in its guiding principles and in the selection of research and development tasks that have a high priority from a national perspective, have high leverage on the overall language teaching system, and are relatively unattended elsewhere. (Lambert 1987:131)

Activities undertaken by the Center were to have three guiding principles:

- they should be "applied"… directly related to the improvement of the foreign language competency of Americans, particularly adult Americans, and to lifting a more substantial number of them to a genuinely high level of skill;
- they should reflect an empirical orientation, constantly measuring practice against outcomes;
- they should bridge the various segments of the language teaching community and link them to social scientists and those in public policy and administration whose participation is essential to the upgrading of our national pool of foreign language competencies. (Lambert 1987:131)

The initial tasks he set for the Center were these:

- to develop a comprehensive national policy on foreign language teaching
- to determine research priorities tied to national objectives
- to foster the development of innovative instructional methodologies aimed at increasing the effectiveness of teachers and language learners …
- to initiate a limited number of key high leverage projects to inform the policy

process and serve as prototypes for more general developments in the field.

The first of these is of particular interest, first, because of the scepticism in the United States (referred to earlier) over the practicality and even desirability of having a national policy because of the inherent conflict it is believed to pose with a federal system in which education is a State and local (not a Federal) responsibility. On the other hand, in the present writer's experience, there remains strong interest in the Center in the possibility of a national policy, there is recognition of its desirability if only the scepticism referred to above could be overcome, and there is some envy of countries such as Australia that have been able to achieve successive national policies, in Australia's case, despite a similar federal system of government.

The fourth task with its emphasis on a "limited" number of projects has also, of necessity, been eroded somewhat in the years since the NFLC commenced operations as projects have come to be seen as important funding sources: nevertheless, it must be emphasised that, over the years, thanks to the nature of the Center's base funding from major donor organisations, discretely funded projects have not had the salience that they have in other language centres (such as CALL or, in the United States, the Center for Applied Linguistics) where they are the lifeblood of the centre and must be sought in order that the centre survive. The NFLC submission writing seems to be more specifically targeted at projects that contribute directly to the Center's mission and the national need and, most significantly, rather than being part of the blanket submission writing that other self-funding centres have to pursue in order to win enough for survival, the submissions are targeted at projects that contribute to the Center's agenda and enjoy a higher chance of success in terms of being funded. This is important for several reasons:

- Blanket submission writing is time-consuming, costly and dispiriting.
- The endless pursuit of projects, its corollary submission writing, and the minimal funding levels that competition for projects creates undermine the capacity of any centre to be innovative or to engage in important activities that, either totally or in the early stages, are not cost-effective.
- Equally, competition for projects, though superficially in the taxpayers' or donor's interest, means that the minimum funding levels achieved for projects is rarely capable of building adequate centre infrastructure or of supporting activities, even further submission writing, beyond the scope of the immediate project.
- Reliance on the good offices of governments, institutions or other agencies to fund projects could be seen as undermining the independence and objectivity of a Center that aspires to be able to provide high-quality, objective policy advice, standing off from the system that it is partly established to critique and advise.

Lambert goes on to indicate that the NFLC will engage in research, materials development, training, diffusion, articulation, and evaluation and that it will serve the needs of teachers and learners at all levels of education and the needs of users of language skills in business, government, education, research and public affairs (Lambert 1987:131). Only some of this work is to be carried out at the Center itself, his intention being that much would occur at other "participating" centres on the campuses of other institutions, be undertaken by national "membership organisations", or be carried out by individuals, in other words by a mixture of the Center and others "all of them dedicated to the same core national agenda" (Lambert 1987:131–132).

Clearly, this is an ambitious attempt at coordination and cooperative activity requiring strong involvement from other organisations and individuals but it is important that, in *Points of Leverage*, Lambert (1986:113–114) had ruled out the temptation of an organisation that espouses such a function becoming a "czar" aiming to control the national agenda and dictating to all in the field, a fatally serious flaw always at risk of creating profound antagonisms and a nightmare of bureaucracy, "accountability" and redtape. It was this seductive but damaging trap into which, it seemed to the present writer, the National Languages and Literacy Institute of Australia (later, significantly, re-named "Language Australia") fell but which the NFLC has so far avoided.

Lambert goes on to indicate the initial projects that the Center will undertake. It is of particular interest, for the reasons indicated above relating to Americans' suspicion of national-level language policies, that the first project that Lambert proposes is to "develop a comprehensive national policy on foreign languages" (Lambert 1987:132). This is to be done by getting together a high-level task force to marshal public opinion, gather alternative suggestions for the design of a policy, gather information on other models that exist, and develop information on the cost-effectiveness of alternative arrangements. In doing so, Lambert says, special attention is to be paid to ways to improve the effectiveness of classroom teaching, other learning approaches, and, in particular, the use of alternative technologies. The recommendations that the task force makes were to be used to guide the Center's and nation's long-term agenda (Lambert 1987:132). It seems that the forces against the notion of a national language policy have, so far, prevailed since the list of projects undertaken by the NFLC that appears on its webpage makes no mention of such a project though the Center has clearly maintained its interest in it as evidenced in, for example, the final conference on language policy-making that Lambert chaired at the NFLC prior to his retirement in September 1993 (see Lambert 1994, 1994a).

Lambert acknowledges that many people are working to try to improve the effectiveness of language teaching but proposes that the NFLC give high priority to ways of maximizing classroom teaching effectiveness, ways of integrating formal and informal learning, overseas and domestic learning experiences, teacher-delivered and machine-delivered instruction, and various other approaches to language learning. He makes particular reference to the need to improve the current system for the production of foreign language teaching materials, developing prototypical formats, and focussing especially (though not exclusively) on "languages and learners that would otherwise not be covered", starting with Chinese and possibly Japanese (Lambert 1987:133). It is worth observing that these languages, amongst the lesser taught languages in the United States, are widely taught in Australia where considerable resources have been put into the development of teaching materials. There would be advantage to the NFLC and to American language teaching if it were to draw on such materials or, at least, seek dialogue with the authors — the structure and philosophy exist in the NFLC for such dialogue though it had not occurred at the time of writing.

Lambert also wants the Center to explore the use of "expert systems in language learning", with particular reference to computers and their capabilities as supports for the teachers and learners.

In order to evaluate and diffuse the new procedures and materials, Lambert proposes that some experimental classrooms be established. This leads him to dwell on the need for "comparison, observation and evaluation" (Lambert 1987:134) and the need, therefore, for "the development of objective, efficient measures of the overall level of the language competency of individuals" both to measure and certify their language skills and to evaluate the language programmes (Lambert 1987:134). He refers to the need for "a common metric", the need for standardised tests (not just standardised testers) by which to match learners to the common metric, and the need for means by which to measure finer gradations of skills than methods current at the time would allow.

Lambert lays considerable emphasis on the need to develop techniques that will enable learners to reach higher proficiency levels. He refers to State Department concerns about the cost to the United States of the low level of competency of Foreign Service staff and the contrast between their proficiency and that of diplomats from other countries. He elaborates to say that the focus should be on ways of taking learners' proficiencies from about 2+ to 3 or 4 on the ILR scale. He relates this to the need to give attention to the development of adult competencies with the ultimate test of the success of the Center, "the final payoff", being improved foreign language proficiency in the adult population (Lambert 1987:136). As background to this, he proposes two initial surveys for the Center: one of "desirable and actual foreign language use", in which he distinguishes between actual employment demand for foreign language skills, and a more informed notion of national need (Lambert 1987:136). Secondly, he recommends a survey of existing facilities for the teaching of languages to adults leading to recommendations for better serving this need. He calls for better understanding of adult maintenance of language skills, "the loss or retention of language skills once acquired", and so recommends that the Center undertake research into language attrition (Lambert 1987:136–137).

Finally, Lambert attaches great importance to the Center's seeking to improve communication amongst all interest groups within foreign language education, to assist them to share their insights and perspectives, and to disseminate widely through the system whatever is known about improving teaching and learning strategies. A part of this leads him to call for the Center to be involved in the training of teachers of foreign languages and the "teachers of teachers" (Lambert 1987:137–138). It is not wholly clear how the Center is to be involved in teacher training but Lambert does make specific reference to several activities: the use of language teachers-in-training as interns in the experimental schools and classrooms that he also advocates, the inclusion of established professionals amongst the visiting fellows at the Center, and the inclusion of "representatives of the language teaching professionals" on the advisory and governing bodies of the Center (Lambert 1987:138). A core function of the Center, Lambert says, will be to establish close links between developments in foreign language pedagogy in the United States and abroad by including "a representative of one of the centers concerned with the management of foreign language instruction in Europe" on the Center's advisory body (Lambert 1987:138). It is relevant to note that, at the time when this book was being written, the Center's Research Director was an internationally eminent Israeli academic, Dr Elana Shohamy, who shared her time between Tel-Aviv University and the NFLC and that the list of the Center's Adjunct Fellows included applied linguists from several European countries and Australia.

The organization and governance of the Center seem to closely match what Lambert recommended in this initial article. The Center was to be located (and remained until 2000) in the Johns Hopkins University in Washington DC, within the School of Advanced International Studies, and, geographically, in the SAIS Building at 1619 Massachusetts Avenue, NW, Washington DC, 20036. Its location in Washington DC, the national capital, was intended to facilitate its national role and its influence on the political and bureaucratic decision-makers. The administrative arrangements were designed to give the Center the advantage of a presence in a major research university but with enough autonomy to serve a national rather than a local agenda (Lambert 1987:138). These administrative arrangements included:

- full autonomy in staffing and budget
- retention of all interest and overhead accruing to the Center
- university charges limited to rent, a 6% management fee and any other direct costs the Center generates
- no charge for funds disbursed to other locations
- staff appointments incorporated within the academic structure of the School, and
- allocation of an entire floor of the SAIS building at 1619 Massachusetts Avenue to the Center (a building in which all of the language-related activities of the School were housed). This space is sufficient to cater for the Center's accommodation needs together with space for visiting fellows. (cf. Lambert 1987:138–139)

This location was selected to best enable the Center to carry out its national role, to enable the Center to integrate its work with that of the other Washington-based language activities including the Foreign Service Institute, the Center for Applied

Linguistics, the Linguistics Society of America, Georgetown University, the Joint National Committee on Languages, and the proposed National Foundation for International Studies, and to facilitate it in carrying out its national "leverage" and coordination role. (Though in the year 2000, largely for financial reasons, the Center moved from its original location, it remains within Washington DC, not very far from its original Massachusetts Avenue site.)

A distinctive and crucial concept within the Center has been the use of visiting fellows of various sorts, including at least one from the secondary school level, pre- and immediate post-doctoral students, senior scholars, and foreign visitors (Lambert 1987:140). Lambert sees this element of the NFLC design as important in making it a "foreign language think-tank" and he describes this distinctive, almost defining, feature of the Center thus:

> In addition to the core staff, if sufficient funds are available the Center proposes to host five or six visiting language professionals and social scientists on a rotating basis. Visitors will be selected for their distinction in their field and will carry out their own research or writing on a topic related to foreign language teaching. However, while visitors will work on their own research projects, they will also supplement the core staff to create a critical mass at the Center, and by their presence will guarantee fresh interdisciplinary and interspecialty collaboration on issues relevant to the national agenda. Preference will be given to those whose interests lie in one or another of the items on the national agenda, and they will be expected to help the Center flesh out its own agenda and to formulate RFPs for the work to be done elsewhere. …
> (Lambert 1987:140)

Lambert proposed that the Center be governed by an Advisory Council consisting of about twelve individuals drawn from foreign language professionals, persons influential in the formation of public policy with respect to foreign languages, and representatives of business corporations and other enterprises whose employees use foreign language skills (Lambert 1987:140).

4. Geographical and administrative locations

In describing the origin of the National Foreign Language Center and the considerations that went into its creation, reference was made above to its **geographical location** on the 4th Floor of the building of the School of Advanced International Studies in the Johns Hopkins University, at 1619 Massachusetts Avenue, NW, Washington DC, to the reasons for this choice, and to the **administrative location** as a wholly autonomus centre nominally within the Johns Hopkins University. These locations were not accidental but, as is evident from the discussion above, were carefully selected to support the role and function of the Center. Though, as noted above, financial exigencies led, in the year 2000, to the Center's changing its affiliation to the University of Maryland and re-locating to other premises, the general principles discussed here remain relevant.

The **governance** of the Center has been determined in response to its national and expert role and the importance it attaches (as did Lambert as its creator) to its autonomy, to its independence from the language education system, and to its role in identifying national need for foreign language skills and in setting the national agenda in this field. Reference has been made above to these issues in the papers that led to the establishment of the Center.

The senior body oversighting the Center is its National Advisory Board which, in Maxwell's words,

> …consists of nationally and internationally recognised leaders in the foreign language field, education, government, and the private sector. In addition to their governance and oversight responsibilities, these distinguished board members are valuable links between the NFLC and their respective areas of professional activity.

Lambert had justified this element of the governance thus:

> …To establish the priorities for and to supervise this proactive program, a distinguished national advisory group should be established, comprising research scholars and representatives of universities, major international business firms, national research organizations and government agencies … (Lambert 1986: 99–100)

Inspection of the list of persons that form the NFLC National Advisory Board (available on the NFLC's webpage at <http://www.nflc.org/about/board.htm>) shows that it consists of eminent persons from American politics, industry, academia (both within applied linguistics and from other fields), and the relevant national professional associations (in the person of the Executive Director of the Joint National Council for Languages). The choice of the Chair at the time of writing, Senator Paul Simon (a former businessman, long-time Senator, and quite prolific writer and speaker on language issues), illustrates the considerations and the aspirations of the NFLC:

> …former Senator Paul Simon (D-IL) has been appointed Chairman of the Board….
>
> The NFLC is honored that Senator Simon has decided to assume this leadership position. Director David Maxwell said, "The Senator's public policy expertise and legislative experience will give the issue of foreign language competency the national visibility it deserves. We anticipate that with Senator Simon's guidance the NFLC Advisory Board itself will become a major voice in public policy discourse on matters related to national needs and capacity for language competence. We expect as well that this discourse will further focus the NFLC's efforts to affect and support systemic change on a national scale." (*NFLC Perspectives*, Fall 1997)

Within the Center itself, the Director is assisted by two Deputy Directors (one of whom is a fractional appointment shared with the University of Maryland), a Research Director (also a fractional appointment, as referred to earlier), an Associate Director for Administration, a Budget Officer, three Personal or Administrative Assistants, and some research assistants. There is a minor supplementation of this staff as a result of the Center's being located within the University which provides some additional financial management and telecommunications facilities (though the Center pays the costs of the latter). In addition, as already discussed, there are a number of Fellows of different categories, including Adjunct Fellows. The latter are mainly senior scholars from around the world, who come to the Center at intervals to research and write but who are also called upon from time to time to comment on Center documents or to provide advice, which, coming from eminent international experts with no obvious "axes to grind" in the American system, adds to the Center's claims of expertise, independence and objectivity.

This administrative structure would seem to be well designed to minimise costs, attract an exceptional range of expertise, create a vital and stimulating environment, and support the Center's claim to be an expert and independent advisory, research and development institution in the area of language policy and language education planning. The structure is also flexible and adjustments have been made as different projects and activities have been taken on. In particular, the substantial changes in the Center that occurred in 2000 and the new activities that occurred at that time have led to further adjustments to its administrative and staffing arrangements.

The concept of **autonomy** for the Center has been an important determinant of the funding sought and its administrative location. As reiterated throughout this chapter, the NFLC was conceived by Lambert as an independent, autonomous institution, able to stand outside the formal education system, not rely on funding sourced through it, and able, as an objective and expert observer, to observe, critique, and advise. For this reason, the Center's funding is sought mainly through philanthropic organisations that do not have "axes to grind" in education or specifically in language policy, and funds sought and accepted are accepted only unconditionally so as not to intrude on the independence of the Center's decision-making and advice (cf. NFLC Director's personal comments, 21 July, 1998). It does not seek to generate its revenue through, for example, the conduct of language courses or the offering of fee-based teacher education or other programmes (which would put it in competition with the system it is seeking to critique and advise dispassionately), it is located within a university that does not have language or applied linguistic programmes that could be seen to be favoured by advice given by the Center, and, though it is within a major university, it is independent of it in its management, decision-making and activities. The Director, in an in-house document, observed:

> The Center enjoys mutually beneficial relationships with a number of national organizations and associations; however, the NFLC's fundamental independence from the interests of any specific constituency is essential to an objective perspective on the issues.

Though, as noted earlier, the Center also seeks to augment its income through projects and grants, it does so only

- where its independence is not put at risk,
- where the project or grant relates to something central to the Center's mission and goals,
- where the activity provides a useful field-testing opportunity for ideas the NFLC wishes to test, and/or
- where the project or activity provides a critical point of leverage in furtherance of the Center's mission. (From personal discussion with the Director, 21 July, 1998)

5. Purpose and mission of the center

Mission: The mission of the National Foreign Language Center, as stated in its webpage, is to improve United States capacity for cross-cultural communications, particularly in languages other than English. In doing so, it seeks to view the totality of United States need and capacity, observing all of the sectors and their interactions, whether academic, private, in the various language communities, governmental, business and industry, or US international and overseas programmes, organisations and institutions.

In carrying out this mission, the National Foreign Language Center seeks to stand outside the education system, to be independent and able to observe, critique and advise objectively, divorced of vested interest. It does not seek to take over educational or other activity but to be a research, development and advisory unit in the areas of language policy and language education planning. In seeking to be able to advise on and provide a level of coordination of the disparate elements of the language and language education system in the United States, it is an important issue of principle that the NFLC remain small and distanced from the system itself. Lambert's words in writing of the National Foundation he recommended in *Points of Leverage* and in discussing the need for coordination of "overseas linkages" are very relevant to the NFLC and to this issue. He stresses the need for a balance between "productive diversity", on the one hand, and centralised policy-making and coordination, on the other. He says:

> We are not suggesting that in the area of overseas linkages, any more than in the support of research…, our system of productive pluralism should give way to a single czar in charge of all exchanges, nor that our exchange policy should be bent to a single purpose. It would be useful, however, if the Foundation were to take a more than occasional look at what the full range of transnational exchange and training programs is with respect to a particular country or set of countries, private as well as public. (Lambert 1986; 113)

This "balancing act" is of great importance. Other national centres have failed to achieve the appropriate balance: in the Australian experience, the National Languages and Literacy Institute of Australia (significantly re-named late in its existence, "Language Australia") tried to become the "czar", seemed to aspire to control all language education in Australia, and thereby created profound antagonisms, a maelstrom of redtape and bureaucratic "busy-ness", and made Australian language education, especially language research, highly vulnerable to the whims of its own hierarchy and its very existence vulnerable to the whims of the government of the day. In such circumstances and with declining government research allocations, the NLLIA's demise was inevitable. Unlike the Australian experience, there is strong justification for a relatively small, independent centre to provide advice to governments and others independently of the projects and programmes themselves, to monitor for inappropriate gaps and overlaps, to stimulate and act where national need is not being met, and, rather than seek to become the "czar" of language policy, to encourage "productive diversity". Lambert sums up:

> At the minimum we must create a grid of purposes, clients, countries, and programs so that the government's various programs can get into an overall national strategy …The difficult task is to develop a coordinating and facilitating strategy that retains the best of the energy and inventiveness of the individual initiatives but allows the nation constantly to take the overview … (Lambert 1986:114)

Goals: The NFLC's goals are stated in different ways in different places but the webpage provides a process summary:

- Making language and culture issues an integral and intelligent part of public policy discourse in the United States
- Developing methods to measure national needs and demands for language competence
- Promoting systemic reform to more effectively meet national needs
- Improving access to language learning opportunities in the education system
- Supporting basic research on effective language teaching and learning strategies, and bridging the gap between research and the classroom
- Developing strategies to maintain and enhance first language competence within linguistic heritage communities
- Providing information to facilitate a more sophisticated understanding of language-related issues
- Offering expertise and guidance to educational and other institutions on program design and implementation, materials development and assessment of programs and practices.

Functions/Strategic Approach: The NFLC's central and ultimately most important strategy in seeking to identify and respond to national needs for foreign language skills and the focus of much of its activity is to seek to influence the decision-makers, whether they be the politicians, administrators or leaders of industry or other sectors of American life. To do so, the Center engages in strategic research, needs identification, policy development, or other activities that identify and respond to national need or encourages others to do so. It states its overall strategic approach as an expert and independent research and policy institution is to

- undertake research to improve the quality of language teaching and learning, ensuring that that research, put to the improvement of language teaching and learning, draws on the rigour available from the paradigms of social science research
- develop policies in relation to cross-cultural communications and foreign language learning in particular with the aim of strengthening the national capacity, recognising the importance of articulation of policies and practices across the various educational levels and domains, and drawing on language policy and policy implementation experiences worldwide to inform the activity in the United States
- conduct conferences, meetings and colloquia on language issues
- stimulate public policy discourse on language issues
- encourage the formation of national and international organizations with interests relevant to the Center's mission and goals
- cooperate with other individuals, organizations and institutions that have the potential to stimulate systemic change at the national level, and
- disseminate information on language issues through publications, websites, conferences etc. (cf. NFLC webpage)

6. Activities

Many of the activities of the National Foreign Language Center have been referred to in passing during the discussion thus far. Fundamentally, the Center engages in activities that enable it to identify the national need for foreign language skills, develop policies, conduct research, and undertake development activities in response to that need.

Language policy is seen as the fundamental activity of the Center. As was noted earlier, language policy-making was identified by Lambert as the most basic task for the Center and, even though it seems to have been proven fruitless to pursue a formal national language policy because of the vicissitudes of the American federal system, provision of policy advice while operating within some systematic notion of a policy framework is an important determining feature of NFLC activity. In particular, the Center recognises the danger of dysfunctions across and within the various levels and domains of the education and language-use systems in the United States and it realises that productive solutions derive from research-informed and systematic policy-making at all levels across all domains (local, State and Federal political levels, education, industry, communities and so on). This is especially important in determining the Center's activities since it asserts that the fundamental weakness in the American response to language needs and language education is systemic, that there is much to be learned from the policy experience of other nations, and that the Center's activities should focus around the identification of language needs and the articulation of responsive policies. The Center, as an independent but research-based and informed observer, can help to inform, develop and coordinate policies that are compatible across the systems and domains within and across which language policies and language education operate.

In seeking to identify and respond to national need, the Center sees a major role for itself in exerting **leverage** at strategic points. As we have seen, the notion of leverage was a fundamental concept in the mind of the founding Director of the Center even before the Center commenced operations and it has strongly influenced the Center's activities throughout its existence: no institution, certainly not a centre of some dozen permanent staff, can aspire, on its own, to change a system as large as that of education in the United States but, by specifically targeting its activities, maintaining its distance from the system itself so as to be seen as independent, and by drawing on expertise that goes way beyond that of its own staff, the Center is able to exert influence greatly beyond that implied by its size and staffing structures. Though a national policy on languages is considered not to be feasible, the Center exerts leverage through its conversations and representations with decision-makers, by providing briefings on critical issues relevant to language needs or to foreign language education, by lending expertise to the operation of Federal activities such as the allocation and evaluation of scholarships and study abroad programmes, by providing assistance in developing national standards for private providers of language instruction, and by providing seminars, colloquia and publications on important issues.

This notion of "leverage" has strongly influenced the projects that the Center has chosen to undertake and the staffing arrangements in which a small number of on-going Center staff are complemented by Fellows, including an impressive array of senior scholars of international standing from around the world who, at relatively low cost, spend time at the Center contributing to its research profile, enhancing its reputation (and hence its capacity to exert leverage), and providing advice in support of Center activities.

Staff of the Center not only provide policy advice to government, academic institutions and industry but they serve as members of relevant boards, serve on committees of relevant professional associations, and thus contribute to an array of research, policy development and its implementation that extends considerably beyond the Center itself and its immediate activities. One such example has been the role of the Center in establishing and administratively supporting the National Council of Organizations of Less Commonly Taught Languages and the Association of Public and Proprietary Language Schools, both relevant to areas of national need which, in the Center's judgement, were not being met. Through this intervention, the Center was able to assist in encouraging the teaching of such languages of obvious critical international importance to the United States for reasons of trade and international politics as Japanese, Chinese, and Russian.

Germane to language policy advice and to the basis on which leverage may be exerted is the notion of the Center as a **think-tank** on foreign language education and language policy, a notion that we have already seen greatly influenced Lambert in developing the underlying concept of the Center. The structure that has been adopted, its attempts to maintain a flow of international expertise through the Center, its use of colloquia, meetings, and "brown bag lunches", all contribute to the think-tank atmosphere and activity of the Center. Being located in Washington DC with the opportunity to invite government personnel and decision-makers to participate in these activities, the Center is able to extend its think-tank role and its leverage beyond its own walls. In brief, the think-tank focuses around the identification of national needs, assessing the national capacity to meet those needs, and identifying or developing strategies by which to meet the needs.

An important feature of the think-tank, as has been indicated, is the array of **Fellowships** that the Center offers and that enable it to attract in scholars from around the world as well as from all over the United States. The Center Director has stated in relation to the Fellowship scheme:

> The IAS/Mellon fellows Program has served consistently as an extremely productive, ongoing connection between the NFLC and researchers, language professionals, and policy makers in the US and abroad. In addition to pursuing their own research projects within the framework of the Center's agenda, Fellows continue to be a generous source of expertise, experience, and diverse points of view that has a powerful impact on the development of the Center's national and international activities. At the same time, it is clear that residence at the NFLC has had an equally important impact on the Fellows themselves; returning to their institutions and organizations, they continue their research with new knowledge, expertise, and perspective.

Much of the funding for the fellowships has come from the Andrew Mellon Foundation and is directed to the Institute of Advanced Studies, the element of NFLC responsible for the Fellows. In the call for applications on the NFLC webpage, the fellowship programme is described as providing

> …support to scholars for empirical research projects that have potential for direct impact on the teaching and learning of languages other than English in the U.S. …Projects may focus on a variety of educational settings, including classrooms and other attentive learning environments, immersion programs, heritage communities, study abroad, technological interaction, self-instruction, etc.

Fellowships are awarded at the pre-doctoral and post-doctoral levels, principally for research done at the NFLC but, in some instances, for a collaborative project, part of which is conducted there and part by a team at the Fellow's home institution.

The **colloquia, conferences, brown bag lunches, forums and seminars** that the Center mounts provide an important addition to the "think-tank" role of the Center. In addition to raising issues, stimulating discussions, and fostering the exchange of ideas, these events, which usually involve an impressive array of experts from around the nation and around the world, help to give the Center credibility, raise its profile as an expert Center, and highlight its status as an expert Center. They also serve to draw people into the Center from the national capital and its environs and so help to inculcate the notion of the Center as precisely a centre where expertise resides that can be mobilised in response to language issues in the nation.

The Center's project on heritage languages (in progress at the time this book was being written) demonstrates the sweep of activities that the Center undertakes: a series of meetings are being held, a national conference is being sponsored, a webpage has been created with contributions, comments and discussion being invited, a discussion paper has been prepared and circulated, and eventually policy proposals and other action will be forthcoming.

Research has been referred to continually as a key element of the NFLC's activities. It is directed, especially, at gaining a thorough understanding of the nation's language needs and appropriate responses to them and aims to substitute rigorous research methods for anecdotal discussion as the basis on which language education moves forward. The Fellowship scheme enables the Center to extend the range of research it undertakes.

The Center also has an **information diffusion** role which is carried out through some of the activities above, including the Fellowship scheme, the colloquia and other meetings, its publications, its website with its information on publications available, Center activities, and discussion papers, and the Center's availability for consultation and advisory services.

In particular, the **publications** are a crucial element of the information diffusion. Many of the Center's projects lead to publications, as do many of the colloquia and conferences. In addition to the papers that are made available through the website, the Center produces:

- *NFLC Occasional Papers*
- *NFLC Working Papers*
- *NFLC Policy Issues*, a "white paper" series, and
- *NFLC Perspectives*, a biannual newsletter

In addition, many of the projects and colloquia lead to their own publications as a report, book or submission while many of the staff and Fellows produce journal articles and more substantial publications emanating from the work they have done at the NFLC and acknowledging its contribution. The webpage lists a dozen or more books that are currently available, some published by the NFLC itself, some from other publishers acknowledging the NFLC source.

The list of the Center's **projects** is long and impressive, provides some of the resources on which the Center operates but, most importantly, provides a major part of the base on which the NFLC operates as it seeks to identify national foreign language needs and to respond to that need. A comprehensive list of the Center's projects since it commenced operations in 1986–87 is shown on the webpage and here reference will be made only to some examples indicative of how the Center operates while some others have been referred to in passing above.

One of the Center's largest projects is a five year review of the critical HEA Title VI (in progress at the time this book was being prepared). This project, funded at over $US1.4 million, aims to develop an evaluation data-gathering instrument, it will evaluate the usefulness of this device for the allocation of Federal resources to language education in higher education, and the project will attempt to give more rigorous and informed information on the national language needs (not least as the basis against which the success of Title VI must be judged).

The project on heritage languages was referred to above. As in many multicultural nations, the issue of the heritage languages is not only politically sensitive but is fraught with serious policy difficulties relevant not only to the maintenance of those languages, the society's recognition of their value, and their contribution to economic and societal development but also with profound impact on language education within the formal school and higher education system: serious issues include, *inter alia*, those of teacher supply, teacher credentials, continuity of learning, and the impact of background speaker enrolments on enrolments by English-background learners. In a climate where, in addition, doubt is being raised concerning bilingual education programmes which, in turn, seems to be raising questions about the value and viability of the languages themselves, this issue of heritage languages is one that is politically sensitive, it responds to individuals' needs and interests, and it requires careful, informed handling by an objective and well-informed set of experts. The NFLC, drawing on experience from around the world, is well placed to provide appropriate advice.

Another on-going initiative is that of fostering the development of Japanese language teaching, the language of a major trade and political partner of the United States, a heritage language of a sizeable ethnic community in the United States, but a language that, in the views of the NFLC, is very much under-represented in the language education system, disproportionately so in the light of the importance of the country to the United States. In April 1997, the NFLC convened a "Japanese Language Summit" at which there were representatives of key interest groups from the professions, industry, organisations with interest in Japanese language and culture, and the United States and Japanese governments. The purpose of the meeting was to explore the situation affecting the teaching and learning of Japanese, to explore options for the future, and to move towards an effective strategy for increasing the teaching and learning of Japanese in the American education system.

As already noted, in selecting projects, the Center is careful to choose only those that are relevant to its mission and goals. It seeks to avoid a situation where it is only funded as a research centre, where it becomes reliant on projects for its financial survival, and where, consequently, its opportunity to operate as a think-tank would be seriously eroded.

7. Interactions and links

Because of its role in identifying national need and developing policies and strategies that respond to that need, the NFLC places considerable store on the links it has with all sectors (academic, private, government, industry, the heritage communities, and overseas programmes, organizations and institutions) and on its ability to draw on expertise from around the nation and the world. While doing so, it has already been noted that the Center seeks to remain independent in order to be able, objectively, to identify and respond to need without accusations of self- or vested interest or lack of objectivity. The Director has stated:

> A variety of NFLC activities provide essential connections between the Center's research and the external world of policy formulation and diversified practice. These efforts enable the NFLC to disseminate the results of its research and policy studies; to connect to the broad range of constituencies whose needs, interests, and support are vital to the Center's mission; and thereby to make concrete contributions on a national scale to the understanding of a broad range of language-related issues, and to systemic improvement in foreign language teaching, learning, and maintenance.

To achieve its results, it is essential for the NFLC to achieve and maintain a high profile with the field but, in particular, with the decision-makers. Reference has already been made to its use of colloquia, lunches, forums, conferences, publications, lobbying and advice for this purpose while the association of the Center with eminent persons in the field through its fellowship schemes helps to give the status, credibility and visibility that it requires locally in Washington, nationally and internationally.

The NFLC actively seeks liaison with the relevant professional associations. On the one hand, this is partly achieved through its Fellowships which have included persons extensively involved with professional associations both in the United States and internationally. In addition, as noted above, the Executive Director of the Joint National Council for Languages is a member of the Advisory Board. The Center has also sought to take a leading role in establishing and facilitating the operations of certain professional associations, especially where, as with the "less commonly taught" languages, there was need to foster their learning in order to respond to a national need that was in danger of neglect. In this context, the NFLC has created CouncilNet, a web-based system promoting communication and information-sharing amongst the associations representing the less commonly taught languages, the National Council of Organizations of Less Commonly Taught Languages itself, and the governmental, private, heritage, and overseas sectors of the language community. Successful attempts have also been made or are being made to bring together private and proprietary language schools and to establish standards for their operation, to bring together organisations concerned with interpreting and translation and to develop quality standards for their operations, and to bring together and collaborate with foreign language departments in American universities. (cf. NFLC webpage: http://www.councilnet.org)

8. Staffing

As already noted, for a centre that aspires to change language policy and language education in a system as large as the United States, the National Foreign Language Center operates with considerable economy so far as staffing is concerned (see Section IV above). This minimal staffing is supplemented by temporary project staff, the cooperation of (sometimes quite numerous) outside persons on particular projects (e.g., the review of Title VI referred to above), and the Fellows (though, in the case of the senior Fellows at least, their role is mainly to do their own research and to make incidental contributions to any discussions going on during their time in the Center). Though the Center is responsible for its own staffing costs, its association with Johns Hopkins University enables it to take advantage of some of the ancillary staffing services required (including liability coverage) and the Center staff are staff of the University which accepts liability even though the staff are not wholly bound by the University's staffing regulations in the way that the University's own staff are bound. Though NFLC staff are regarded as staff of the University, they do not carry obligations for committee membership and other administrative duties beyond those of the Center itself. This contrasts with, for example, the Centre for Applied Linguistics and Languages where all staff salaries and supplementary benefits are paid for by the Centre, where staff are staff of Griffith University, where all obligations pertaining to University staff are held to apply to Centre staff, but where the cost of such obligations (e.g., performance review systems, committee responsibilities, and so on) have to be borne by the Centre.

9. Facilities

As noted above, from its foundation to the the time of writing, NFLC has been located on one floor of the Massachusetts Avenue building of Johns Hopkins University occupied by the School of Advanced International Studies (SAIS). The facilities consist of a reception area, staff offices, a wing of offices for the Institute of Advanced Studies (the Fellows), a meeting room, storage area and lunchroom. Computer facilities are provided for all staff with ready access to the internet and email through the Center's own server. Ready access is available to library facilities in the Johns Hopkins University and in other universities in Washington, especially Georgetown University and the Library of Congress. No language laboratory, teaching space or similar facilities are located within the Center though there is ready access to meeting rooms and conference rooms in the SAIS and other buildings of the University. To the present writer's observations, the facilities are comfortable though, if the Center were to have several projects requiring additional space operating at the same time, it might have some accommodation difficulties. There is no sign to an outside observer, however, that the facilities, supplemented as they are by facilities readily accessible in the University and elsewhere in Washington, are anything but adequate for the Center's purposes.

10. Budget

As already noted, the Center relies heavily for its finances on donors that provide its unconditional base (or core) funding, an arrangement that is important, in its view, for it to be able to maintain its claim of complete independence and objectivity in the advice it provides. Additional funding is obtained from project work, chosen, as already indicated, on condition that it does not infringe on the Center's claims of independence and on condition that the projects further the mission and goals of the Center. Documentation available to the writer suggested that the Center's budget has fluctuated over the last five years between about $US1.5 and 2 million annually. It received almost $2 million over a fifteen year period to fund its Andrew Mellon Foundation Fellowship scheme, an amount it was able to supplement through investment on the principle to create its Adjunct Fellowship scheme. The fact that, although its funds are held and accounted for within the University's financial system, it is able to draw on the interest on its invested funds, is of considerable benefit, in contrast, for example, to CALL, whose budget and cashflow are somewhat larger, which often holds more funds in advance payments at any one time, but which receives no benefit from the interest on its invested funds, all of which goes to the host University. The Center pays rent to the University and also pays a 6% levy on its income to cover the costs of services and utilities. In addition, like other institutions receiving government funds, it is able to charge indirect costs (essentially undistributed administrative support costs) to projects at the rate of 20%, a figure which, in the present writer's experience in his own centre, would probably cover costs but leave little if any margin towards other real costs (such as submission writing, senior administrative salaries, or utilities).

The budget appears to fluctuate depending on the Center's success in soliciting funds from donors and on the number and magnitude of the projects that it takes on. The budget graphs indicate that some of the donations seem to be stable over a period of years though the Center is constrained to put in submissions at intervals and to undergo reviews at the request of donors. Project funding depends on what is identified, what government or donors can be persuaded to support, and the nature of the projects themselves. Though programmes that the Center itself controlled and marketed (e.g., courses sold to students) might give the Center more stability in funding, give it some financial independence as a business, and allow it more control over its own destiny, it would, as already noted, be at the cost of its perceived independence and objectivity in providing advice and consequently it has eschewed this option.

Donors that have provided funds over recent years and in amounts that range from half to two million dollars (US), include the Pew Charitable Trusts, the Ford Foundation, the Exxon Education Foundation, and the Andrew W. Mellon Foundation. A list of projects undertaken is available on the webpage and funding for these has come from a great variety of organisations including the Andrew W. Mellon Foundation, the Center for Global Partnership, the Charles E. Culpeper Foundation, the College Board, the Freeman Foundation, the Geraldine R. Dodge Foundation, the Ford Foundation, the Henry Luce Foundation, the National Endowment for the Humanities, the National Security Agency, the United States Department of Education, and the United States-Japan Foundation.

11. Constraints and opportunities

The National Foreign Language Center is serving a distinctive and important role in the context of the state of language policy and foreign language education in the United States. Though it seems to have made substantial achievements, it is also clear that there remains a great deal yet to be done to ensure that the United States has a language policy situation and a foreign language teaching and learning system that can be assumed to meet the nation's needs. Foreign language enrolments remain slow and are not increasing sufficiently (if at all) to meet those needs. Furthermore, the global role of the United States and the leadership that it is expected to assume especially since the decline of the Communist world mean that it has continually to confront new language requirements. The rapid pace of technological change with dramatically easier transport and daily communications that are now global, continual demands arising from the need to compete economically on a global scale, a continually high (and, in recent years, increasing) rate of migration, an increasingly diverse population, and substantial domestic tensions over language and language education issues, all of these factors are increasing the need for language policy issues to be confronted and leadership provided on a national scale. The National Foreign Language Center, as it itself asserts, is the only institution in the United States that is able to address these issues independently, nationally and with the exceptionally high level of national and international expertise that it has at its command. Provided that the available donors can continue to be convinced to support this institution, its role for the foreseeable future is obvious and necessary.

12. Uniqueness and impact of the center

The uniqueness of the Center is already evident from the discussion above. That uniqueness rests in its independence, its exceptional funding base that makes that independence possible, its perception of languages and language learning as serving highly practical ends intimately related to national social, economic, political, and security needs, and in the unique structure it has been able to adopt with the cooperation of its financial donors that enables it to retain a small staffing quota but to supplement that quota with many of the world's leading figures in the field of applied linguistics and language policy. It is the only national and independent think-tank committed to identifying national language needs and to devising strategies to meet them. It combines with that its research, its language policy focus, its design to enable it to focus nationally rather than locally, its multi-sector interests, and its commitment to the view of language as serving practical needs in the nation's interests. Though it has existed for a little over a decade (a short time to achieve national status and effect major systemic change), the Center can point to significant achievements. Documentation from the Center used in presenting its case for on-going funding identifies some examples of these achievements:

- It impacts on Federal legislation, as demonstrated, for example, in its major project to review Title VI and provide a reporting system for institutions funded under this Act.
- It has brought together national organisations with interests in language education for more effective collaborative work and to set quality standards.
- It is called upon by government and private agencies to assist in their language-related activities (e.g., in the design of selection criteria for the awarding of government-funded scholarships).
- Its Fellowship programme has, to the mutual advantage of the Center and the Fellows, brought international discussion to bear on United States language policy and has served as a catalyst for informed language policy debate.
- The Center in all its activities has emphasised the practical nature of the contribution languages and language education can make to the national welfare and thus has extended the language debate beyond academia to all sectors of American life: education, government, industry, and society in general.

In summary, it is because of these unique features that the National Foreign Language Center in its original form has been included in this study:
- its independence,
- its use of donors to provide core funding for the Center while ensuring that independence,
- its skilful and academically admirable use of international resources to supplement its small staff, to give the Center a high and respected profile, and to marshal international skills to enhance the Center's name and further its national language policy goals, and
- its creation, using both national and international resources, of a lively national think-tank in the area of language and language education policy and implementation.

Postscript: In late 1998, the Ford Foundation, which had been providing core funding to NFLC, changed its funding arrangements. Though it indicated that the overall level of its contributions would not be significantly different, it changed the basis from core to project funding. This clearly has profound implications (as discussed above and in Chapters 6 and 8) for the way in which NFLC can function, not least for its leverage and think-tank roles and the amount of staff time and effort that has to be re-directed towards submission writing. This decision has also forced NFLC to re-consider its Adjunct Fellowship programme, to change its location and affiliation from the Johns Hopkins University to the University of Maryland and to premises in Vermont Avenue (hence still in Washington DC). Amongst the reasons for the change of affiliation from the Johns Hopkins University to the University of Maryland were lower costs and increased support from the University of Maryland.

At the time when this book went to press, the new arrangements were still being introduced and settling in and their full effects on the Center's operations were not clear. The greatest dangers in the new arrangements are that the Center may lose some of its independence and Center staff may be obliged to spend more of their time and the Center's resources in meeting University requirements and in submission writing to win projects to fund the Center. For these reasons and for the purposes of this book, it seemed most useful to present the original form of the Center which most effectively enabled it to pursue its independent think-tank role. That initial form was, in the views of the present writer, imaginative and quite distinct from the structures and functions commonly found, including in the other centres reviewed in this volume.

Lest it might seem that the new form that the NFLC has been obliged to develop for itself is inferior to the original form (it is clearly different from it), it should be emphasised that, at the time that this volume went to press, the NFLC Director, Dr Richard Brecht, expressed considerable satisfaction with the form that he and his colleagues had developed for the Center, he was pleased with the support for the NFLC that the University of Maryland was demonstrating, and he was looking forward to a successful future. Indeed, regular inspection of the NFLC website reveals that the Center has been actively creating new positions and appointing staff to them, it has taken many new initiatives related to its mission, and it has commenced many new projects in the course of the two years since its funding arrangements forced it to review its affiliations, location, and roles. The future remains highly optimistic for the NFLC and there is every reason to believe that, rather than reduce the NFLC's effectiveness, the challenge of re-forming seems to have brought a renewed vigour. In the words of the Director, Dr Richard Brecht, in a memorandum to the Fellows in September 2000:

> The University of Maryland affiliation and the staff additions have given us new standing, a stronger national presence, and a major infusion of energy and ambition. (Brecht 2000:2)

CHAPTER 3

The Centre for Information on Language Teaching and Research (CILT), London, United Kingdom

1. Address

>   Centre for Information on Language Teaching
>   and Research,
>   20 Bedfordbury,
>   London, WC2N 4LB,
>   England.
>
>   **Telephones:** 44-0171-379-5101 (Administration, Conferences, Publications)
>   44-0171-379-5110 (Resources library & Information Services)
>   **Fax:** 44-0171-379-5082
>   **Email:** library@cilt.org.uk
>   [first name.last name]@cilt.org.uk
>   confs.direct@cilt.org.uk
>   **Website:** http://www.cilt.org.uk
>
>   There are branches of CILT in Scotland and Northern Ireland with the following addresses:
>
>   **Scottish CILT:**
>   Pathfoot Building,
>   University of Stirling,
>   Stirling,
>   Scotland, FK9 4LA.
>
>   **Telephone:** 44-01786-467-631
>   **Fax:** 44-01786-467-632
>   **Email:** lg1@stir.ac.uk
>   **Website:** http://www/stir.ac.uk/scilt/
>
>   **Northern Ireland CILT:**
>   8 College Green,
>   Belfast,
>   Northern Ireland, BT7 1LN.
>
>   **Telephone:** 44-01232-326-476
>   **Fax:** 44-01232-326-571
>   **Email:** nicilt@qub.ac.uk
>   **Website:** Information on NICILT is available at http://www.cilt.org.uk/www.comenius/ninews.htm

2. **The centre**

The Centre for Information on Language Teaching and Research (CILT) is primarily a clearinghouse and information centre on foreign language teaching and some other foreign language-related matters such as the use of language skills by industry. Though some members of the CILT staff may have an interest in language policy and be called on to give advice in relation to language policy and language education planning (cf. Michael Hammond, CILT Library, personal communication, 17/6/1997), it is not primarily a language policy centre (in contrast to NFLC, for instance). Though it stimulates research and conducts some research activities (especially reviews of the state of research or of aspects of language education), its primary purpose is not to engage in research: where research is carried out in its name, it seems to be done by commission to other persons or organisations. Its primary role seems to be to provide information, to act as a stimulus, to be available as a manager of policy- and planning-related projects, to provide a location for activities relevant to foreign language needs and foreign language education, and, sometimes, to coordinate. On the back cover of its *1998 Languages Yearbook*, it describes its role and function in these terms:

> CILT provides a complete range of services for language professionals in every stage and sector of education. …Our Information Centre and Teaching Resources Library are open to the public, and a wide range of training events is held on site.
>
> CILT also houses the Languages Lead Body, NatBLIS — the National Business Language Information Service — and the secretariat of the University Council for Modern Languages.
>
> We aim to be of practical assistance to all language teaching professionals through our regional network of Comenius Centres, and through collaboration with our national partners.

A similar statement appears on the cover of the *1999* and *2000 Languages Yearbooks* except for some minor re-wording including replacing reference to the Languages Lead Body and NatBLIS with reference to the Languages National Training Organisation.

CILT's services are available to teachers of all types and at all levels: classroom teachers, language advisers, school administrators, teacher educators, industry language trainers, researchers, academics, librarians, and, indeed, anyone involved with language education or the use of language in industry.

3. **Background and origin of the centre**

The **language context in Britain**, in which CILT operates and to which it responds, is very different from that of the NFLC in the United States or of CALL in Australia, despite the fact that all three centres serve English-dominated societies. The differences arise principally from the proximity of Europe, the influence of the Council of Europe and the European Community on language education policies and practices in Britain, and, consequently, the readier access CILT seems to have had to government funding. There remains considerable concern at the state of language education in British schools (though, overall, language learning seems to be on the increase) but perusal of the CILT webpages and the documentation available about it and its activities suggest that there is a very lively, diverse, and vigorous interest in addressing foreign language needs in Britain and in developing the language education system in order to meet those needs.

Undoubtedly also, the small geographic area of Britain, its efficient network of public and private transport, and hence the rapidity and ease of communications and travel from all parts of the country have meant that any centre established in London has a substantial mass of professionals to serve within easy reach of it — in contrast to the United States, Australia or South East Asia, for example, where the geographic expanse any centre must serve is many times that of Britain, where resources for any comparable operation would have to be spread out over a much larger area, and where there are, therefore, considerable implications for travel and communications costs and the availability of skilled staff. Thus, CILT is able, both from its London office, its Scottish and Northern Ireland offices, and the Comenius Centres (essentially its branches established around the country) to serve critical masses of language-interested professionals. Despite these advantages, one has to admire the vigour, professionalism and initiative with which CILT pursues its tasks and the obvious success and favourable profile it enjoys both in Britain and internationally.

Nevertheless, and despite the stimuli referred to earlier from the Council of Europe and the European Community, the language context in which CILT exists has not been easy, it suffers from similar English-monophobia as other English speaking countries and, over the years, this context has led to frequent threats to the Centre's funding base and its very existence. The language context seems to be quite ambivalent with, on the one hand, increased overall interest in language learning (especially for vocational purposes), considerable vigour evident in the innovations that are occurring in policy and its implementation, and strong encouragement from the nation's European context to stimulate language education. On the other hand, Britain suffers the same disadvantage as other English speaking countries which depend excessively and myopically on English. Much of the documentation from CILT emphasises the importance of developing language skills in Britain and deplores the unsatisfactory state of language education. The Chair of the CILT Governors recently summed up the British situation thus:

> The improvement of competence in modern foreign languages is the prime objective … Another objective is to ensure that measures to promote competence in modern foreign languages will feature strongly in successor programmes.
>
> The UK gains advantage and suffers disadvantage from the current place of English as the main language of international communication. We hardly ever lack partners in bilateral or multilateral programmes of co-operation. On the other hand, we are less and less obliged to seek that cultural understanding that can only come from learning another's language. Apart from impoverishing our own experience, this makes us less effective communicators. Employers can now find mastery of English amongst many non-native English speakers who possess other linguistic and cultural skills, in addition. It is not hard to work out who are the winners, and who the losers, in this employment market.
>
> There can hardly, therefore, be a more crucial or challenging task than training those who will teach our young people to communicate effectively and, as an essential prerequisite, to respect the linguistic and cultural diversity of others. A key contribution to our national well-being is at stake. (Jones 1998:3)

Similar views were expressed by Davis in the context of further education in Britain, in observing that the task of further education is to prepare young people for the workplace, a global workplace where, today, practical foreign language skills must be considered vocationally desirable (cf. Davis 1998:2). The community concern at the lack of skills was reflected in an editorial in *The Guardian* newspaper following the delivery by the British Prime Minister, Tony Blair, of a speech in French to the French National Assembly when it commented:

> It was, rightly, a good news story even though it would have been much better for Britain if speaking publicly in a foreign language wasn't so rare that it was regarded as a news item in the first place. (See *CILT News*, Vol. 18, Spring 1998:1)

Public attitudes in Britain were shown in a National Opinion Poll survey reported in the December 1998 edition of *Language World*, the newsletter of the Association for Language Learning. The NOP survey found "an astonishing 81%" of people felt that more needed to be done to promote the learning of modern foreign languages, 86% thought that some knowledge of foreign languages was useful, and only 14% believed that there was no need to learn a modern foreign language.

Despite such growing realisation and the pressures from Europe, Britain seems to have been reluctant to systematically formalise national language or language education policies beyond that contained within school curricula. The Association for Language Learning has called for systematic language policy development while documentation from CILT refers to the Nuffield Languages Inquiry being commenced in 1998 with the aim of scrutinising Britain's capacity in languages and assessing its language needs over the next twenty years. Because of a perceived lack of "overall vision or framework" in the present situation of language education, the Inquiry was given the task of looking especially at questions of strategy and coherence (cf. *Comenius News*, Issue 12, Summer 1998: 1). Before its most recent entry into government, the British Labour Party issued a policy statement in which it noted that other European countries require their children to learn one or two foreign languages, that Britain had fallen short on this, and that, when it was in government, it would encourage the development of children's language skills by teaching languages in the Primary School (Satchwell 1998: 2–3). An article in CILT's *Further Education Bulletin*, No. 3, Spring 1998 lists a number of the deficiencies in the British language teaching system as a result of the lack of a national policy, attributes to that lack the continual decline in language learning, and points to the lack of coherence between sectors. The author says:

> Currently the lack of a national policy adversely affects both providers and learners, and is instrumental in the continuing decline in FL learning…
>
> …suffice it to say at this stage that not only is there little coherence, consistency and continuity between these sectors, the picture post-16 becomes even more confused. This state of affairs is overwhelmingly due to the myriad of courses and accreditation schemes currently in use, the various initiatives undertaken by regional bodies, or the go-it-alone approach by consortia or even individual providers, leading to the wheel being re-invented many times over, without this curriculum area coming any closer to a national policy on FL teaching and learning. (Huyghe 1998: 5)

There has also been considerable awareness of the need for language skills in industry with a number of policy elements emerging in response and a number of projects in implementation. CILT has been involved in some of these and reference will be made to them subsequently. Amongst the initiatives undertaken are the National Languages for Export Campaign, the establishment of the Languages Lead Body, and its subsequent replacement, in April 1998, with the Languages National Training Organisation (LNTO) (cf. *CILT Direct 1998 Languages Yearbook*: 51–52 and *CILT Direct 1999 Languages Yearbook*: 37–38; see also *Language World*, December 1998: 2). The Chair of Governors of CILT, in the *1999 Languages Yearbook*, cites a *Daily Telegraph* article which refers to the fact that British graduates are being beaten for employment in the City and in commerce by "continental competitors" simply because the British applicants lack foreign language skills (*CILT Direct 1999 Languages Yearbook*: 1). At the launch of the Nuffield Languages Inquiry on 13 July, 1998, the co-chair, Trevor McDonald, noted that British industry is often forced to recruit multilingual executives from other countries because there are insufficient available in Britain (*Language World*, September 1998: 1). A report by Her Majesty's Inspectorate on the quality of language education in Scotland, reported by the Association of Language Learning in its December 1998 newsletter, was highly critical of the quality of language education noting a "marked decline" in quality of language courses in Secondary Schools from 1994 to 1998 and pervasive weaknesses at the Primary level. The Minister for Education expressed great concern at the effects on the Scottish economy and stated:

> Scotland's ability to compete on the world stage is being damaged by shortcomings in the teaching of modern languages. Our young people must be equipped with the necessary skills to allow them to seize the opportunities which exist for those with sound foreign language abilities. (*Language World*, December 1998:2)

As the preceding quotes indicate, there seems to be widespread concern in Britain over the state of foreign language education. Though there is evidence of a growing awareness of the need for foreign language skills if Britain is to compete in Europe, there is concern that foreign language enrolments are declining and that the quality of output is not always high enough or relevant enough to the needs of industry (cf. Davis 1998:2). The webpage of the Scottish branch of CILT refers, in the context of two research projects, to a decline in student enrolments in the upper Secondary School and to statements by the Scottish Examination Board identifying "a substantial decline in the numbers taking Modern Languages in the past twenty years" (see Scottish webpage at http://www.stir.ac.uk/scilt/RESEARCH.htm). CILT provides tables showing the number of examination entries at GCSE, GCE 'A' level and GCE 'AS' level, in all of which there is a decline in 1997 with the language worst affected being French and with the decline at 'A' and 'AS' levels being most severe and more or less continual over the preceding five years (*CILT Direct 1998 Languages Yearbook*: 35–39). CILT's 1999 Yearbook shows that A-Level entries in the three main foreign languages (French, German and Spanish) rose by 53.9% from 1988 (total 30,739) to 1992 (47,319) but dropped steadily away by 16.6% from 1992 to 1998 (39,463) with falls also occurring in the other languages (*CILT Direct 1999 Languages Yearbook*: 42–43). At GCSE level, examination entries in recent years show a fluctuating pattern rising from 518,379 in 1994 in all languages to 575,771 in 1996, and dropping unevenly to 566,013 in 1998 (*CILT Direct 1999 Languages Yearbook*: 40–41). The British Council's *Global English Newsletter*, Issue 4, 1998 also refers to "falling numbers of people learning foreign languages in the UK". The launch of the Nuffield Languages Inquiry in July 1998 was told that fewer students are learning two foreign languages than in the early 1990s despite a commitment made in the European Union context that all young people should do so and, in fact, seven out of eight students abandon language learning at age 16 (cf. *CILT Direct 1999 Languages Yearbook*: 1): later, the 30% who go on to Higher Education "cram into remedial or *ab initio* classes" in order to be able to complete their studies abroad (*Language World*, September 1998). There is also concern at a decline in teacher recruitment for modern languages with serious implications for the quality of the teaching that will occur (cf. Lid King, Director of CILT in *CILT Direct 1998 Languages Yearbook*: 3).

Despite these negative aspects of language education in Britain, there are also positive signs. CILT refers to its involvement in the Fund for the Development of Teaching and Learning, under which some £4.3 million was to be allocated to teacher development projects in 1997, half of them in language teacher education. CILT is also supporting a new scheme of more than fifty language colleges, a significant development which includes the introduction of "less widely-taught languages" such as Japanese, Chinese, Arabic, Russian, modern Greek, and various community languages. There has also been considerable growth in and support for the teaching of languages in Primary Schools with a governmental initiative managed and coordinated by CILT to promote the development and quality of language teaching in Primary schools (see *CILT Direct 2000 Languages Yearbook*: 55; *CILT Direct 1998 Languages Yearbook*: 47); the professional association of language teachers (the Association for Language Learning) and the Labour Party, which forms the present British government, have both expressed support for languages in the Primary School in their respective policy statements (see *The CILT Primary Languages Bulletin*, Issue No. 3, Spring 1998: 1–4; *CILT Information Sheet*, No. 55, February 1998: 1). In addition, the National Curriculum has, since the early 1990s, required that all students study a foreign language throughout Secondary schooling in "Key Stages 3 and 4" (*CILT Information Sheet*, December 1998, No. 76: 1). There are also concerted attempts to improve the level of educational attainment, including in foreign languages, with the establishment of the Qualifications and Curriculum Authority and the introduction of statutory attainment assessments (see *The CILT Community Languages Bulletin*, No. 2, Spring 1998: 6–7). Furthermore, in contrast to the decline in the secondary school sector, it seems that, overall, there has been a considerable increase in the activity of language learning in Britain in recent years with a great deal of this increase occurring in the adult and further education sector where languages are seen (and treated) as vocationally relevant (see CILT's *Further Education Bulletin*, No. 3, Spring 1998: 2–5).

Most encouragingly, throughout the time this book was being researched and written (1998 to 2000), a national inquiry into the British languages situation was being undertaken by the Nuffield Foundation with the final report due in April 2000 (*CILT Direct 2000 Languages Yearbook*: 68). The Nuffield Languages Inquiry was established to explore the UK's capacity in languages, estimate British languages needs over the next two decades, assess whether current provisions provide an adequate basis for the future, and assess whether *the teaching of languages in the UK is effective, timely and imaginatively harnessed to society's wishes* (Nuffield Languages Inquiry undated, c. 1998: 2). The Inquiry aimed to consider the role of English, whether it is sufficient, and the cultural attitudes and practical consequences of the view that "English is enough". The Inquiry seems to be cognisant of the fact that, despite the considerable developments that have occurred in Britain in recognising the need for language skills, the system still lacks a coherent and systematic national policy on languages that responds to the diverse needs across the whole society. The Inquiry states in its explanatory document:

> What is needed is a coherent national view of the future, in which strategic thinking will seek to build on our successes while addressing the chronic problems. Such a task cannot be undertaken by a single sector, but needs to be a partnership between the many interests and stakeholders involved.
> (Nuffield Languages Inquiry undated, c. 1998: 3)

Noting the impact of technology, increasing globalisation, the "merging of cultures", and the key role of communication, the Inquiry poses these questions for consideration:

> 1. What capability in languages will this country need in the next twenty years if it is to fulfil its economic, strategic, social and cultural responsibilities and aims, and the aspirations of its citizens?
> 2. To what extent do present policies and arrangements meet these needs?
> 3. What strategic planning and initiatives will be required in the light of the present position? (Nuffield Languages Inquiry undated, c. 1998:4)

It is this diverse and changing context that the Centre for Information on Language Teaching and Research serves. It is a context that is very different from that which existed when, according to the CILT webpage, CILT was established in 1966 as

> ...an independent charitable trust supported by central government grants, with the aim of collecting and disseminating information on all aspects of modern languages and the teaching of modern languages.

The **history of CILT** is outlined in contributions to Hawkins's (1996) overview of language teaching in Britain in the thirty years from 1966 to 1996, in particular in a tabular "calendar of events" compiled by Gill Tench (1996) and in John Trim's "view from the bridge" as a former CILT Director (Trim 1996). The latter two documents provide quite a detailed history of CILT, only the most salient points of which will be briefly reported here.

The stimulus for the establishment and growth of CILT has come from the context of British language teaching referred to above with its fluctuating but, overall, declining enrolments on the one hand and, on the other, the increasing pressures brought to bear by European language and language education policies and the growing demands from industry for better language skills. In the early 1960s, there were a number of inquiries into the state of language education, several of which called for the establishment of a national languages institute or a centre for information on language teaching (cf. Tench 1996:353–355). In October 1964, a Committee on Research and Development in Modern Languages was established by the Secretaries of State for Education and Science and for Scotland with its terms of reference being to examine needs, review what was happening elsewhere, and provide advice on modern languages and their teaching (Trim 1996:321). This Committee recommended the establishment of CILT, which was finally announced on 27 July, 1966 and officially opened on 29 September, 1966 with George Perren as its foundation Director (Tench 1996:356). Its very specific, and somewhat limited, remit was

> to collect, coordinate and disseminate information about all aspects of modern language teaching and learning for the benefit of teachers and others professionally concerned in Great Britain. (cited in Trim 1996:322)

Tench quotes CILT's "Declaration of Trust" from 25 August, 1966, which set as the objective for CILT:

> ... the promotion of education by means of the collection of information on all aspects of modern languages and the teaching of modern languages and the making available of such information to such persons or bodies of persons as may be concerned with the educational interests of the people of the United Kingdom. (cited in Tench 1996: 355–356)

It is significant that research and development were not a part of CILT's terms of reference and, especially during Perren's tenure from 1966 to 1978, its primary role was seen as the gathering and distribution of information. For this reason, CILT developed its language teaching library, its registers of research in progress, and its many publications, including *Language Teaching Abstracts*, which later became *Language Teaching*, and the numerous books and lesser publications giving practical advice to language teachers. These activities have continued as major foci even though the scope of CILT's activities has diversified over subsequent years.

From early in its history, CILT was closely involved with the Council of Europe's modern languages projects and, in the Council's seminal Resolution (69)2 in 1969, "each Government member state" was invited to found or identify a national centre. According to Trim, this recommendation was closely based on the CILT model but the resolution also made reference to research and enabled CILT to argue successfully for increased funding to expand its role in the collection and distribution of research information. It was this expanded initiative which led to the extension of CILT's title from the "Centre for Information on Language Teaching" to the "Centre for Information on Language Teaching and Research", though the original acronym of "CILT" was retained (cf. Trim 1996: 323). Later, in 1976, the European Economic Community invited CILT to develop plans for a network of information centres on modern language teaching (Tench 1996: 361).

When Trim became Director in 1978 and Alan Moys Deputy Director, the Centre's role expanded beyond that of information gathering and dissemination through publications to

> ...go out actively into the field and give support and encouragement to a hard-pressed profession, to bring it out of isolation and fragmentation and reverse the reputation modern languages seemed to have acquired for being difficult, formal, boring and irrelevant to the real needs of young people and society more generally.
> (Trim 1996: 325)

This initiative entailed much closer contact with language teachers and their professional organisations, the organisation of conferences, and, not least, encouragement for the adoption of a communicative approach to language teaching that emphasised the practical relevance of language skills, as was being fostered under the Council of Europe modern languages projects in which Trim also played a leading role (Trim

1996:325–326). Some of the most successful efforts were directed towards promoting "activity-based learning", removing the "boring" image from modern language learning, and fostering interest and enthusiasm amongst learners. This led to the promotion of the successful Festival of Languages and Young Linguists Competition (Trim 1996:327). Steps were also taken through conferences and other activities (including the development of a common library resource between CILT and the English Language Division of the British Council) to try to bridge the gap between the teaching of English and modern languages. However, funding difficulties, including the need for both organisations to find new premises following sharp rental increases and other expenditure cuts, meant that the efforts being made towards cross-disciplinary co-operation had to be abandoned (Trim 1996:326–327).

Trim's appointment as CILT Director in 1978 also gave stimulus to CILT's emerging international profile since he was already involved with the Council of Europe modern languages projects and had been Director of two major Council projects since 1971 (Tench 1996:362).

Despite the success of efforts made by CILT through the 1970s and 1980s to help teachers recover "their self-confidence and sense of purposive direction", there remained much apathy in the community, efforts to create an awareness in the community at large and in industry in particular of the value and importance of language skills had little response, and CILT was subject to an extended review over four years, during which its budget was reduced and it was not permitted to plan beyond the current year (Trim 1996:328–329). However, at the end of the four years, largely as a result, it seems, of the strong support that CILT received from its clients especially in the language teaching profession, the value of the Centre's "continued and effective operation" was recognised, the Centre was re-organised with a new Board of Governors and new financial arrangements, and its agenda was set to focus on the teaching of languages in schools, to provide information services to further and higher education, to foster communication among the different sectors, and, most significantly perhaps, to both support and seek support from industry and commerce (cf. Trim 1996:329 quoting the then Secretary of State for Education). This mandate seems to have continued to represent the efforts of CILT as it has extended the services it provides to the language teaching profession and as it has, increasingly into and through the 1990s, extended its involvement with industry. From the mid-1980s, its history shows a growing focus on vocational languages and career opportunities, in 1989 it was asked to provide a base for the Language Export network of centres providing services to business, and in the 1990s it helped to stimulate the formation of and subsequently housed such industry-related services as the Languages Lead Body, the National Business Languages Information Service (NatBLIS), and the Languages National Training Organisation (see Tench 1996:367–376; *CILT Direct 1999 Languages Yearbook*: 2, 9, 37–38 and *CILT Direct 2000 Languages Yearbook*: 42). Throughout this period, its list of activities show frequent reference to the notion of the national capability in languages, commencing with a national conference on the theme in 1990 and being reflected in its three year development plan for 1992–1995 under the theme "Promoting a national capability in languages: an agenda for progress".

Through the 1990s, CILT also seems to have adopted a policy of localisation in order to make its services more readily available to teachers throughout the United Kingdom. In 1991, Scottish CILT was opened at the University of Stirling, Northern Ireland CILT commenced in 1995 with the assistance of Queen's University of Belfast, the National Comenius Centre of Wales was opened in 1995 in Cardiff and Bangor, and from 1992 its growing network of Comenius Centres was commenced with new centres being opened every few years (Tench 1996: 372–376).

Increasingly also, CILT has become involved in international activities. As we have seen already, almost from its commencement, CILT was involved in various international projects, generally in response to the Council of Europe or the European Economic Community, this involvement accelerated when Trim became Director, and it has continued to grow through the 1990s (Trim 1996; Tench 1996). The Chair of Governors of CILT, in his letter in the *CILT Direct 2000 Languages Yearbook*, lists some of the recent international activities as the provision of courses for British teachers of French, German and Spanish languages in the home countries of these languages, the Graduate Teacher Programme under which qualified native speaking teachers are recruited to teach in British schools, and expanding involvement with Council of Europe and European Union languages projects, including piloting the Council of Europe's European Language Portfolio, Lingu@netEuropa (a web-based virtual languages centre), the European Award for Languages, and administration of the European Union's Socrates programme (see *CILT Direct 2000 Languages Yearbook*: 7).

4. Geographical and administrative locations

The **geographical location** of the CILT headquarters is in Covent Garden, London, though its activities extend throughout Britain through the conferences and other events it organises but, more importantly, through its network of Comenius Centres and its major branches in Scotland and Northern Ireland (Stirling and Belfast, respectively).

The Comenius Centres were established in 1992 in collaboration with more than a dozen "national partners" including government agencies, foreign cultural organisations (such as the Goethe Institute, the Institut Français, and the Istituto Italiano), the Institute of Linguists, and various educational organisations. The Comenius Centres (more than a dozen at the time of writing (*CILT Direct 2000 Languages Yearbook*: 26–32)) facilitate access to CILT's services across Britain, bring other organisations (e.g., universities) into the network as host sites, and provide a means for the other national partners to provide some of their services regionally. In return for directing some of their services through CILT, its branches and Centres, the national partners receive substantial publicity for their activities through CILT, its webpage, and its publications. The current locations of Comenius Centres include Birmingham, Bristol, Manchester, Cambridge, Loughborough, Sunderland, Lancaster, Oxford, Southampton and Basingstoke, Leeds, Swindon, Exeter and Pool, Worthing, York, and Cardiff and Bangor (see also *CILT Direct 1998 Languages Yearbook*, pp. 14–30, for more information on CILT's partners; also *CILT Direct 2000 Languages Yearbook*: 26–32). In the information bulletin *Comenius News*, Issue 11, Spring 1998, the following comment was made on the Comenius Centres:

> According to a recent survey of CILT users, setting up the Comenius network is possibly the most important initiative that the CILT has ever undertaken. Teachers have high expectations of the support that the Comenius Centres can offer, and there is demand for even greater regionalisation. The Comenius network is a three-way partnership between the regional centres, CILT and the other national agencies which provide support for language teaching. Working together in a network which allows us to exchange information and expertise enables us to achieve more together than any of us can in isolation. (*Comenius News*, Issue 11, Spring 1998:1)

Scottish CILT was established in 1991 in partnership with, and on the campus of, the University of Stirling and with the financial support of the Scottish Office of Education Department. It has a resources centre, acts as the Scottish access point for CILT's services, and provides a programme of courses and conferences. Northern Ireland CILT was established in 1995 in conjunction with the Queen's University of Belfast and with supportive funding from the Department of Education for Northern Ireland. It offers a resources centre, a variety of courses, seminars and conferences, and local access to CILT's services. (see *CILT Direct 1998 Languages Yearbook*: 8–11; CILT webpages)

In all, as the *CILT Direct 1998 Languages Yearbook* suggests, CILT is in the process of major change in its operations as it devolves its network of support throughout Britain in order

> …to develop a comprehensive and locally sensitive network of support — CILT UK. (*CILT Direct 1998 Languages Yearbook*: 7)

In terms of its **administrative location**, CILT is an autonomous centre but, since most of its funding comes in the form of a grant from the British government, it is answerable to the government through the relevant Departments (see below). In addition, as we have noted, CILT is creating links with many other organisations in order to extend its services around Britain and in stimulating developmental activity in foreign language education in Britain. In doing so, there is no indication in the documentation available that CILT is attempting to take over those organisations or to do other than cooperate and stimulate activity. The partner organisations remain independent but direct some of their activities through the CILT networks.

Some of CILT's funding comes from course fees or other fees and subscriptions attached to publications or other services and it anticipates that, by the Year 2001, it will be 50% self-funding but the majority of its funding comes from the British Government through the Department of Education and Employment (and the Scottish Office and the Department of Education for Northern Ireland for Scottish CILT and Northern Ireland CILT respectively) (see *CILT Direct 1998 Languages Yearbook*: 1, 7, 9, 11 and Webpage http://stir.ac.uk/scilt/). Undoubtedly, also, the network of partners that cooperate with CILT especially in the Comenius Centres effectively provide financial support for activities in which they are involved. There is also both overt and "hidden" funding from the host institutions such as the University of Stirling, Queen's University of Belfast, or the institutions that host the Comenius Centres (see, for example, the comment from the Scottish Director in the *Scottish CILT Newsletter*, December 1997: 1 concerning the lack of funding for academic and professional staff). In Wales, support is provided through the National Comenius Centre for Wales at three sites in Cardiff and Bangor (see *CILT Direct 1998 Languages Yearbook*: 12–13).

CILT's **governance** is under the direction of a Board of Governors appointed by the Secretary of State for Education and Employment (see the CILT webpage at http://www.cilt.org.uk/www/about.htm). CILT seems, however, to act independently with no indication in the documentation viewed that it is constrained to act in support of government policy.

5. Purpose and mission of the centre

The **objectives** of CILT are:

- To promote a greater national capability in languages;
- To support the work of all those concerned with language teaching and learning (see CILT webpage http://www.cilt.org.uk/www/about.htm).

Its objectives for 1996–97 as stated in *CILT Direct 1998 Languages Yearbook* were to expand its operations, specifically its training programmes, its information services, CILT Direct (see below), its resources library, and to continue to give support to languages in business and strengthen the Comenius network and CILT branches. The corporate plan for the period 1998 to 2001 identifies four strategic priorities:

- Extending language competence
- Improving the quality of language teaching and learning
- Integrating technology with teaching and learning
- The promotion of foreign languages (see *CILT Direct 1998 Languages Yearbook*: 5–6).

CILT's objectives, as outlined above, are very general and non-specific, almost "motherhood" statements, but they are elaborated in the CILT Corporate Plan for the

1998–2001 period in which the Centre's **strategic approach** becomes evident. The objectives are to be realised through a range of activities and services (discussed in more detail below), which the 1998 Languages Yearbook specifies under four headings. *Information services and resources* are seen as central to CILT's mission and encompass both hardcopy and electronic materials for distribution, the resources libraries, an enquiry service, research reviews and evaluation. Considerable emphasis is laid on communications technology to facilitate the dissemination of information, making particular use of Lingu@NET (see below) for conferencing and discussion and to extend this service internationally in collaboration with other European centres. *Publications* are seen as an essential and expanding part of CILT's activities. *Professional development and training* continues to grow in significance in CILT's activities. In addition, *developmental projects, working parties and funded projects* are used to focus on specific needs such as teacher education, research and community languages (see *CILT Direct 1998 Languages Yearbook*: 6–7).

6. Activities

Many of CILT's activities have been referred to in the preceding discussion. Unlike NFLC, it does not have a major **language policy** advisory role and does not identify the sort of leverage role that NFLC has as a major part of its mission. Partly this is because of the different language contexts in which the two centres operate, as well as the different purposes for which they were created. To the extent that the concept of **leverage** is relevant to CILT, it is in exerting that leverage on the language teaching system in order to improve the quality and coverage of language education, to make it more responsive to the needs of the community, and to assist industry to identify its needs and have them met. Individual staffmembers may, of course, in their personal capacities, provide policy advice or exert some leverage. To the extent that CILT has a **think-tank** role, it is through its developmental and funded projects, the advice of the Advisory Committees on various projects, and through its range of conferences and meetings where the "think-tank" activity is rather to have teachers think about their approach to language education than to arrive at national language policy-making initiatives. CILT is essentially a service provider, a clearinghouse and information centre on language education. These services are numerous and varied and provide invaluable assistance to the whole field of language education in Britain and, indeed, internationally.

CILT's **services** include conferences and training programmes on areas relevant to language education and languages in industry, it produces a wide range of publications providing information and support for language teachers and academics at all stages of their professional development, a resources library, information services, a collection of teaching resources and examination materials in the languages that are taught in Britain, and materials and information services of assistance to researchers (including abstracting journals, texts on methodology, a register of current research, and official publications). Its webpage offers an increasing range of information of use to the Centre's clientele. CILT also encourages visits to its premises by individuals, groups and institutions, offering assistance, offering meeting places, and offering its facilities for use (see CILT webpage).

One particular service that comes to the fore regularly as one seeks information about CILT is *CILT Direct*. CILT Direct is a scheme providing a direct link between CILT and individuals and institutions with an interest in language education. It is subscription-based, the subscribers receiving a number of bulletins and services at no cost and a reduced fee on other things. This service is also available to subscribers beyond Britain. In particular, there is a general information bulletin, *CILT Direct Information Bulletin*, which gives a range of information on pertinent topics, the *Comenius News* carries news from the Comenius Centres and the national partners, and there is a range of more specialised publications on such areas as Special Education, language teacher education, Primary School language teaching, community languages, languages in Further Education, business languages, and adult education. The *CILT Direct Yearbook* appears annually and is a particularly valuable information source. It gives a useful and comprehensive overview of the state of language education in Britain and the CILT services available, it contains information on CILT's strategic plan, the CILT national network and how to access it, conference reports, and "reviews" of critical issues (e.g., reports on major examinations, developments in the various levels of education, languages in industry, technology and research). It also provides other general information such as contact addresses of useful bookshops, a list of acronyms, and a diary of events mainly offered by CILT and its partners for persons involved or interested in languages and language education.

CILT has played a significant role in the important developments in Britain in the area of *languages in industry*. While the impetus for developments in this area have come from many directions, from the Council of Europe, the European Union, the British government, and eminent academics and language educators (including, *inter alia*, John Trim, Stephen Hagen, Anne Stevens, and Nigel Reeves), CILT has served as a venue for many of the discussions and is providing on-going support. Two areas of CILT activities of particular importance in this regard have been with NatBLIS (the National Business Language Information Service) and the Languages Lead Body, which have become absorbed into the CILT-based Languages National Training Organisation (see *CILT Direct 1999 Languages Yearbook*: 37–38 and *CILT Direct 2000 Languages Yearbook*: 42).

NatBLIS is a free information service to business, available nationwide. It provides information using its database of professional language teachers, cultural consultants, interpreters and translators, and it advises on the appropriateness of the providers according to the nature of the business and the service required. Information concerning NatBLIS is available in the *CILT Direct 1998 Languages Yearbook* (pp. 51- 52) and from the CILT webpage at http://www.cilt.org.uk/www/business/business.htm. NatBLIS cooperates with the Department of Transport and Industry on the National Languages for Export Campaign, which it clearly supports through the NatBLIS services. The aim of the campaign is to promote the importance of language skills and cultural understanding to industry while, at the same time, benefiting language professionals through sensitising their market to the value of the services they provide. The aims of the campaign are:

- To help exporting companies recognise their language and cultural needs and develop appropriate strategies to meet them
- To enable companies to make more informed choices on language and cultural needs by providing access to new sources of information
- To establish local business networks to run the campaign locally to meet local business needs
- To give ownership of the languages and culture issue to the local business world and embed it within the work of business agencies. (See CILT webpage at http://www.cilt.org.uk/www/business/business.htm)

It is important to note in this approach that, though the campaign, the language experts, and, not least, CILT are available to provide expert input, the emphasis is on industry advising and assisting industry, on localisation of the advice, and on having industry build in language considerations as a normal part of their total management and activity. The devolution of CILT's services around Britain is obviously an important element in the whole strategy that facilitates this process.

The other element of CILT's portfolio of particular relevance to industry is the work of the Languages Lead Body that has been funded by the Department of Education and Employment and housed in CILT virtually since its inception. The Languages Lead Body has developed the *National Language Standards* that are applied to the use of languages in the workplace; there are also *National Language Standards* for Translation and Interpreting. The *National Language Standards* provide a way of specifying and assessing language skills, a way of specifying the foreign language needs of industry, a useful framework in the preparation of language programmes for industry, and a means for setting goals and evaluating outcomes of language courses. The Languages Lead Body also provides advice and training on the use of the Standards for teachers, industry and workers.

The services provided under NatBLIS and the Languages Lead Body have continued but the organisations have been incorporated into the Languages National Training Organisation (LNTO), which continues to be based in CILT and is part of the new employer-led National Training Organisations launched by the British Government in May 1998. The aims of the LNTO are:

- standards development ...
- raise awareness among employers of the importance of language skills ...
- provide information and support to the UK companies on language and cultural issues and raise standards of language training for industry
- work with national and international agencies to promote the language competence and strengthen the cultural understanding of the UK workforce
- ensure the continued development and implementation of a national language standards framework which supports language training in the workplace, and the teaching and learning of vocational languages in the education system. (see CILT webpage at http://www.cilt.org.uk/www/business/natpres.htm; see also *CILT Direct 1998 Languages Yearbook*: 52, *CILT Direct 1999 Languages Yearbook*: 37–38, and *CILT Direct 2000 Languages Yearbook*: 42)

Perhaps the most important element of CILT's services is the *clearinghouse and information services* that it provides. Frequent reference has already been made to these numerous and diverse services. One already referred to is the Resources Library which contains a wide range of foreign language teaching materials (textbooks, supplementary materials, software, and audiovisual and multimedia aids) which are available for viewing as well as textbooks and other materials on both the languages taught in Britain and methodology (encompassing the broad spectrum of applied linguistic research and writing). Its examinations collection covers the examinations, syllabuses, examiners' reports and other materials from the various examining boards around Britain. It maintains a research register and holds journals and other publications useful for researchers, produces information sheets on many aspects of language teaching and research, and it provides an individualised information service responding to queries by telephone, letter, or in person on any issues relevant to foreign language education, language policy, examinations, technology and languages. It also produces newsletters, brochures, its Yearbook, and its diverse webpage with links to other organisations.

As noted earlier, CILT has a wide range of *publications*, which serve as an important element of the information service. Some have been referred to in passing earlier and in discussing CILT Direct. The list includes newsletters, brochures, books, and information sheets or bulletins while the publication perhaps best known internationally but scarcely mentioned in the webpages is *Language Teaching*, each issue of which provides a review article on some aspect of language education or applied linguistic research and numerous categorised abstracts of articles in journals published worldwide (though with a very heavy preference towards Europe). *CILT Links* is a bulletin designed especially for language teacher educators and there are other bulletins for other areas of education including primary language teaching, community languages, special education, adult education, and further education. *Comenius News* provides information on the work of the Comenius Centres and CILT's national partners. The many *CILT Information Sheets* are designed to provide quick and concise reference information (books, resources, and organisations and addresses for further assistance) on a wide range of topics relevant to language teaching including some languages (especially community languages), associations and organisations, methodology and materials, technology, the various levels of education, business and vocational languages, language careers and teaching, research, statistics, and Europe. The *FDTL News* gives bi-annual information on the progress of the ten projects funded under the "Fund for the Development of Teaching and Learning", projects that include, for example, independent learning, use of the web, study abroad, and assessment. The CILT publication list includes many books giving practical assistance to teachers with advice on methodology, curriculum, materials and research. These books include the Pathfinder series and, for teachers of young children, the Young Pathfinder series. CILT also provides teaching materials such as *On est fou du foot*, a video and workbook providing authentic materials for listening practice in French at key Stages 3 and 4.

CILT and its branches and Comenius Centres offer many *courses, conferences, meetings and seminars* throughout Britain for language teachers, policy-makers and others interested in foreign language education or languages in industry. These are advertised on the various webpages (e.g., http://www.cilt.org.uk/www/confs/confs.htm) and in virtually every issue of CILT's information bulletins; they cover a wide array of issues of practical interest to language teachers, to policy-makers, and to language professionals in industry and cover all of the areas of CILT's interests (including all levels of language education and industry). A major activity in this area is the CILT national conference which, for example in 1998, focussed on adult education under the title of "Languages for Life: The Adult Education Languages Show" and included both regular conference presentations and an exhibition of teaching materials and other services from commercial and other providers (see CILT's information bulletin, *Netword: Languages for Adult Learners*, Issue No. 23, Spring 1998: 5). The range of conferences, seminars and meetings offered around Britain and abroad by CILT, its branches, or the Comenius Centres is very great, very diverse, and focusses on CILT's mission of giving practical assistance for the betterment of foreign language education. The calendars of events for each year in the various *Yearbooks* list literally scores, sometimes hundreds, of events in Britain and overseas that are offered by either CILT or its partners (e.g., *CILT Direct 1998 Languages Yearbook*: 68–84, *CILT Direct 1999 Languages Yearbook*: 70–72, *CILT Direct 2000 Languages Yearbook*: 74–76).

CILT engages in developmental **projects** and hosts expert advisory groups, in its words on the webpage,

> …as a way of maximising our collective understanding and developing new thinking. (http://www.cilt.org.uk/www/about.htm)

The number and range of projects, funded by itself or with national and international partners, is too great to be fully described here but a cross-section gives a picture of the diversity offered and the wide-ranging support and development that CILT projects provide. Amongst the projects listed in its various publicity material are projects in support of industry, specific assistance to teachers of adults in the form of a network of self-help groups for tutors and an information bulletin, *Netword,* support for community languages (including an advisory group), an action research project in Wales on the development of speaking skills, and a collaborative research project (in which CILT's role is as an information disseminator) entitled "Leverage" on the use of multimedia broadband technology in supporting language learning. With financial support from the Department of Further Education, CILT, together with the National Council for Educational Technology, has established Lingu@NET, a virtual language centre on the world wide web providing on-line information and resources for language teachers, learners and researchers. Related to this is the Lingu@NET Forum, an email discussion group for anyone involved in language teaching or research. The Spring 1998 issue of *Comenius News* announced that the British Government had used Lingu@NET as a model for its National Grid for Learning, a Virtual Teachers' Centre which will, in future, include Lingu@NET. This has, evidently, served as a model for another web-based virtual languages centre funded by the European Union, Lingu@net Europa (*CILT Direct 2000 Languages Yearbook*: 7).

A project of major significance on which CILT is acting as the information centre is the ten foreign languages projects funded under the rubric of the Fund for the Development of Teaching and Learning. Half of the projects funded were in the area of modern languages and were awarded on the basis of the previous year's "quality assessments". Some of these have been mentioned above in referring to the *FDTL News*, which CILT uses to disseminate news on the projects. The projects cover five broad areas : residence abroad, independent learning, staff development, assessment, and transferable skills (see *CILT Direct 1998 Languages Yearbook*: 53). In addition to the newsletter, CILT provides a website for the project, a staffed information unit, brochures, materials and conferences.

Under the Department of Further Education and Employment, some 50 specialist **Language Colleges** have been established since 1995. To be accredited as Language Colleges, schools have to provide high quality programmes seeking high proficiency levels, maintain language offerings beyond age 16 and offer a third language, offer a broad range of languages, equip students for use of the language in vocational contexts, and develop the teaching staff's ability. They are also expected to make links with their community, especially feeder Primary schools. CILT provides support to these institutions:

> CILT is providing a programme of support for the Colleges as they develop their provision, and is working to ensure that as many other schools as possible benefit from the experience of these "flagship" schools. (*CILT Direct 1998 Languages Yearbook*: 42)

Another project of considerable interest has been the *CILT Special Needs Project*, in which CILT provides assistance to language teachers working with children with "special needs". This project has taken the form of developmental work with people involved in the field, information dissemination especially through a dedicated information bulletin, and conferences at which the project findings were presented and discussed. This support is for a project of particular interest since it is providing assistance to teachers of children who are commonly excluded from language classes elsewhere because language learning is considered either too difficult or to be taking time from other "more basic" subjects on which these children need to spend time.

CILT also provides support in the area of technology, reference to which has already been made several times. This support has taken the form of conferences, seminars and workshops, participation in the Leverage, Lingu@NET, and Lingu@NET Forum projects referred to above, provision of materials and resources (including on-line), and information dissemination.

Finally, CILT sometimes offers projects directly to students in support of their teachers. Reference was made earlier to the start of this activity during John Trim's tenure as Director with the Festival of Languages and the Young Linguists Competition. Similarly, in 1998, it offered a language competition, "Allons en France 98", in which students contributed an audiocassette and written material on an imaginary visit to a town in France at the time of the Soccer World Cup played in France in 1998.

It is evident from many of the activities and projects discussed above that, though CILT is not primarily a **research** organisation, it undertakes activities that may involve research, it acts as a stimulus to research, it sponsors conferences on research, and it provides supportive information, networks and facilities that assist researchers. It also disseminates information on research, including the regular review of research already referred to several times. Its on-line version of the research register lists, for 1993–95, almost 200 projects, the researchers involved, their affiliations, a project description, and a bibliography. CILT's support for research commenced, its webpage indicates, with a research forum in 1996 (see http://www.cilt.org.uk/www/research/research.htm and *CILT Direct 1998 Languages Yearbook*: 58–59) and now extends throughout Britain through CILT's branches and Comenius Centres though other forms of research support (including research registers and its abstracting service) have existed for much longer than this. In these activities, CILT is assisted by the CILT Advisory Group on Research which meets three times a year to discuss their research and provide guidance to CILT on its research activities.

7. Interactions and links

It is evident from the discussion thus far that many, if not most, of CILT's activities are carried out in collaboration with other organisations with an interest in foreign language education. Much of its system and procedures are set up specifically to involve other organisations, as we noted, for instance, with the Comenius Centres, which are established in conjunction with CILT's national partners, whose activities are publicized through CILT's newsletters and information bulletins. CILT's branches and centres have been established together with and often located in other institutions around Britain. Its webpage, for instance, is hosted by Middlesex University and its Scottish branch by the University of Stirling. The *Yearbooks* list the national partners (by 2000, some sixteen British and European organisations) and provide information on their activities and their contact details (*CILT Direct 1998 Languages Yearbook*: 23–30; *CILT Direct 2000 Languages Yearbook*: 33–42). In addition, there are a number of networks in areas such as Primary language teaching, teacher education, or adult language teaching that link together large numbers of teachers and researchers with CILT. The various advisory groups referred to above also have the effect of extending CILT's involvement widely into the language and applied linguistics community and, increasingly, into industry. It is also evident that CILT is used as a coordinator but especially as an information disseminator for many government-funded projects in the foreign languages area. Clearly, CILT's strategy of deliberately extending its activities out through many other organisations and deliberately using both British and foreign partners to support CILT's activities has been invaluable in terms of increasing the services available to support language teaching, in bringing an enormous range of expertise to bear on CILT's policies and practices, and, not least, in increasing the security of a Centre that is still largely government-funded and therefore vulnerable to the changing whims of the politicians and successive governments. This strategy, together with the high quality of the work it carries out and the information it provides, has succeeded in giving CILT a high profile both nationally and internationally. The fact that it has done this as an equal and cooperative partner rather than as an empire-builder has undoubtedly contributed to the high regard in which it is clearly held by the clientele it serves.

8. Staffing

We have noted that CILT is managed by a Board of Governors. There is a Director and some 30 staff. In addition, there are other persons in the various branches and Centres, many of whom are not paid by CILT but by their own institutions. As we have also noted, CILT has succeeded in establishing a rich set of networks and has established working procedures that involve many other partner organisations and individuals who are working, if not for CILT, at least in cooperation with it and supplementing its staff. Thus it has succeeded in establishing a very cost-effective (and politically astute) mode of operating with a minimum of staff and a maximum of input, sense of ownership, and commitment from many other people and organisations.

9. **Facilities**

   We have noted that CILT's head office is in Covent Garden in London where it accommodates its 30 staff, meeting rooms, Resources Library, and other facilities. In addition, its branches and Comenius Centres are located in considerably more than a dozen different cities and their universities around Britain. This devolved pattern of a relatively restricted operation in the main base (London) and many branches and related centres around Britain clearly has been highly effective in giving the intended clients access to CILT's services, in getting them involved in CILT's activities, and in giving the profession a strong sense of ownership of the Centre. Again, this is not only valuable in terms of reaching the clients but it is politically astute for an organisation that is heavily dependent on government funding, is therefore always at the mercy of political whims, and needs to find ways of generating resources to give it greater security and independence without increasing the cost of its services to the clients.

10. **Budget**

   No information was available on the actual size of the CILT budget. It was commented above that most of the funding comes from the British Government through the Department of Education and Employment and CILT hopes, by the year 2001, to generate about half of its own resources. Though CILT has been in existence for more than three decades, its existence has not always been assured, and there have been occasions when funding has been threatened to be cut off (as during the extended review in the early 1980s, referred to earlier, when funds were reduced). It would seem probable that some of the strategies CILT has adopted have been influenced by the realisation that sole dependence on government funding makes any organisation vulnerable and that, to provide greater security, it is desirable to tap into other funding sources and create networks of involvement and support in the community and amongst the clients that are served. Whatever the motivation, this is clearly what CILT has been doing and with good effect. It is also clear that the approach of establishing and maintaining a relatively small enterprise which, through minimal cost strategies, extends its influence and attracts involvement from a wide range of people and institutions across the nation, is a far more effective, cost-effective and diplomatic way of operating (and is much more secure) than is the approach that was adopted in Australia for the same purpose of security by its national centre: there, the National Languages and Literacy Institute of Australia seemed to want to take over the entire field, created as many enemies as it did friends in the process, and eventually had most or all of its funding taken away by government action.

11. Constraints and opportunities

Few constraints and many and diverse opportunities confront the Centre for Information on Language Teaching and Research. Finance always imposes constraints on such an organisation but, as already noted, it has adopted a mode of operating that is highly cost effective. The Centre is clearly serving much needed purposes; seen from outside, it is effective and cost-effective; it enjoys an enviable reputation both nationally and internationally and has many useful and respected initiatives to its credit; if it were to close (as had been threatened in the past), it would leave an enormous hole in the language teaching field in Britain and be almost equally missed world-wide; if it were to close, it would seem, to an outsider, to be more likely for political reasons, a purely political or budgetary decision to reduce expenditure, than for any professional or academic reason. On the other hand, there are very strong pressures on Britain to improve the quality and extent of language learning, to make it more relevant to the needs of the country (especially to the needs of business and industry), and to seek to ensure that language education in Britain is no less efficient, effective and universal as it is in Britain's partner countries in Europe. There are also strong moves emerging in Britain in recent years urging the development and adoption of a national policy on languages or language education and, if this formalisation and more thorough articulation of language or language education policy should occur, it is probable that CILT could find a role for itself in the on-going monitoring and development of the policy and its implementation. In such circumstances (whether or not a national policy is adopted) and granted the outstanding success of the Centre's endeavours, one has to consider that, barring unpredictable political whims, the future of CILT is secure.

12. Uniqueness and impact of the centre

CILT is a unique centre. Its distinctive features are found in the strong national and, increasingly, local roles that it fulfils, in the on-going government support it has received (despite a few hiccups) for more than three decades, in the excellence and magnitude of the information services that it provides, and, not least, from the managerial point of view, in the quite brilliant design that is evolving. Through that design, it has come, from a relatively small base, to extend its services across the country, it has involved many people in the Centre's activities at quite low cost to them or to CILT, and it has been able to have professionals across the nation identify with it in ways that increase dramatically both the Centre's operations and its own security while, at the same time, giving the language practitioners a strong sense of support being available from both their own national and their local centre of expertise.

It is for these reasons that CILT has been included in this study. It is very different in funding, activities, and management approach from all of the other centres that are considered, and it is highly effective in its prime roles of information gathering and dissemination, as a clearinghouse, and as a centre charged with stimulating and facilitating research, development, and high quality practice in the field of foreign language education.

Clearly CILT is highly effective in fulfilling its mission and seeking its goals. Its impact on language education, not only in Britain but around the world, is very considerable. Its effectiveness and impact are well summed up by this statement from the Chairman of the Board of Governors reporting on relationships with the main funding body, the Department of Education and Employment, and on the outcomes of the reviews that it had undergone:

> CILT takes seriously its accountability to its clients. An important element of this is contained in CILT's relationship with its major funding Department, the Department of Education and Employment. Under the Department's procedures, CILT is regularly reviewed from the policy and financial management points of view. Both types of review occurred in 1997 and I am glad to report that CILT has emerged positively from each. In the words of the Policy Review: "CILT fulfils its remit to be a source of expertise on language teaching very effectively. It meets real Government need at low cost. It should continue to be sponsored by the Government." (*CILT Direct 1998 Languages Yearbook*: 1)

In addition and probably more importantly, it is clear that the clientele that CILT serves has responded appreciatively to it, as was confirmed in an external review that CILT itself commissioned in 1997:

> As we announced in the last Yearbook CILT itself commissioned an external review (Benchmark Survey) during 1997. …The survey confirms that we are fulfilling real needs and that our activities are highly regarded. This is of course extremely pleasing. (*CILT Direct 1998 Languages Yearbook*: 7)

CHAPTER 4

The European Centre for Modern Languages (ECML), Graz, Austria

1. Address

>   European Centre for Modern Languages,
>   Mozarthof,
>   Schubertstrasse 29,
>   A-8010 Graz,
>   Austria.
>   **Telephone:**   43-(0) 316 323554
>   **Fax:**   44-(0) 316 322157
>   **Email:**   ecml@via.at
>   **Website:**   http://culture.coe.fr/ecml
>   http://www.ecml.at
>   http://culture.coe.fr/ecml/eng/
>   gralist.html
>   or   http://culture.coe.fr/ecml/index_e.htm

2. The centre

The European Centre for Modern Languages (ECML) is an instrument of the Council of Europe, established under a statute of the Council of Europe, with its prime function the implementation of the language policy decisions of the Modern Languages Projects[1] of the Council based in Strasbourg. In its webpage, it describes itself as

> A non-residential institution whose aim is to promote the learning and teaching of modern languages in a multilingual Europe. (http://culture.coe.fr/ecml/eng/egraorg.html)

In other documentation, the ECML describes itself as

> A forum in which educational policy makers can meet up with specialists in language teaching methodology to discuss and seek solutions to the specific tasks and challenges that face them in the coming years and which will play a decisive role in the

---

1. The various documents reviewed in writing this chapter use both the singular and plural forms, "Project" and "Projects", apparently interchangeably.

process of European integration. (From papers supplied by the Director of ECML to the present writer)

The *1998 Programme of Activities* elaborates in saying that the European Centre for Modern Languages offers

> ...a platform and a meeting place for officials responsible for language policy matters, specialists in didactics, teacher trainers, curriculum developers, textbook authors and other multipliers in the area of Modern Languages. The Centre undertakes to promote the dissemination of good practice in language teaching and learning and to contribute to the reinforcement of linguistic diversity in a multilingual, multicultural, democratic and tolerant Europe. (ECML 1997:7; cf. ECML c.1996:6)

3. Background and origin of the centre

As the above quote indicates, the European Centre for Modern Languages was established by the countries of the Council of Europe to serve the needs of the multilingual and multicultural context of Europe and to assist with the implementation of policies developed by the Council through the Modern Languages Projects oversighted by the Council for Cultural Cooperation (CDCC) of the Council of Europe. Thus, the ECML is an instrument of both Councils assisting in the implementation of their policies and goals.

The European language context within which the ECML exists and which it serves is summed up by Trim in these words:

> The communications revolution is transforming European society, inevitably and inexorably breaking down the economic, social and cultural barriers of the past. The fundamental task of the European organisations is to manage this process, optimising its benefits and averting the twin dangers of hegemony and xenophobic backlash.
>
> Language barriers, which block the very process of communication, are perhaps the most resistant to change and the most formidably challenging to individuals. The promotion of language learning for participatory democratic citizenship in a fully interactive, yet multilingual and multicultural European society is thus necessarily a permanent concern of both the European Union and the Council of Europe. (Trim 1995:9)

An important aspect of this context which the ECML is to serve was referred to repeatedly in the ECML's First Annual Colloquy which has served, at least in part, to set the Centre's subsequent agenda. Reference was made to the inadequacy of both the quality and the supply of language teachers. Both Bim and Little identified this as a critical problem and proposed that the Centre should assist in this area, especially by identifying and disseminating good practice in language teaching and learning, designing language teacher training courses, and encouraging effective visits to the target countries (cf. Bim 1995, Little 1995).

The **Council of Europe (COE)** is said to be the oldest European political institution, the first international organisation to be established in Europe after World War II. It is described and its history outlined in its webpage at http://www.coe.fr/eng/present/about.htm. It was founded on 5 May, 1949 to seek greater unity between the European democracies, to strengthen democracy, to protect human rights and the rule of law, to safeguard and realise the ideals of their common heritage, to facilitate their economic and social progress, to harmonise the policies of the member states especially in such fields as education and culture in pursuit of their common goals, and, of particular relevance to language learning, to foster social cohesion (cf. Trim 1997: Preface; Council of Europe webpage at http://www.coe.fr/eng/present/about.htm and the ECML webpage at http://culture.coe.fr/ecml/eng/egraorg.html). Its activities impact on many aspects of the daily lives of Europeans and focus on a number of critical social issues, including, of particular relevance to language learning,

- education, where a vital aim is to transmit democratic values and prepare each generation for life in a multilingual and multicultural Europe;
- culture and heritage, where the aim is to develop a European cultural identity and protect Europe's heritage; and
- to combat racism, xenophobia, anti-Semitism and intolerance with the aim of making young people the advocates of an open and tolerant society (cf. the Council of Europe webpage http://www.coe.fr/eng/present/about.htm).

These aspirations are pursued, not by mandate, but by discussion and common agreement; on occasions, decisions are taken and action proceeds even where all countries are not in accord or do not agree to participate though it remains open to non-participating countries to join at later dates: the ECML, as we shall observe later, is one such instance.

Starting with just 10 countries on 5 May 1949, the member states of the COE now number forty: Albania, Andorra, Austria, Belgium, Bulgaria, Croatia, Cyprus, the Czech Republic, Denmark, Estonia, Finland, France, Germany, Greece, Hungary, Iceland, Ireland, Italy, Latvia, Liechtenstein, Lithuania, Luxembourg, Malta, Moldova, Netherlands, Norway, Poland, Portugal, Romania, Russia, San Marino, Slovakia, Slovenia, Spain, Sweden, Switzerland, "the former Yugoslav Republic of Macedonia" *(sic)*, Turkey, Ukraine and the United Kingdom (Trim 1997: Preface; Council of Europe webpage at http://www.coe.fr/eng/std/states.htm). Former Communist or totalitarian countries have become members of the Council when they have embraced democracy and, in some cases when dictatorships have usurped power (Greece was an example), countries have had their membership cancelled until democracy was restored.

Education and culture and, in particular, language policy and language education, are important concerns of the Council and, specifically, of its **Council for Cultural Cooperation (CDCC)**. As early as 1954, each government that was a member of the

Council of Europe agreed in the European Cultural Convention (which forms the basis of inter-governmental cooperation in the fields of education, culture, European heritage, sport and youth activities) to

> a. encourage the study by its own nationals of the languages, history and civilisation of the other Contracting Parties and grant facilities to those Parties to promote such studies in its territory, and
>
> b. endeavour to promote the study of its language or languages, history and civilisation in the territory of the other Contracting Parties and grant facilities to the nationals of those Parties to pursue such studies in its territory. ...(European Cultural Convention, ETS No. 18, Article 2)

In April 1961, Resolution No. 6 of the Second Conference of European Ministers of Education, stated:

> The Ministers of Education express the conviction that greater importance than ever before must be attributed to increasing the knowledge of modern languages. The Ministers are well aware how indispensable this knowledge is, both for the individual and for Europe as a whole, and how much international cooperation and the safeguarding and development of our common heritage depend on it.... The Ministers confirm their intention to assist each other in the task of improving and expanding the teaching of languages. This will, of necessity, affect the teaching methods as well as school curricula and the training of teachers. (cf. Trim 1997:5)

The CDCC's role is described in the Preface to the Council's report, *Language Learning for European Citizenship* (Trim 1997) in these terms:

> Work in the field of **education and culture** is conducted under the aegis of the **Council for Cultural Cooperation** (CDCC), which brings together the forty-four states which have acceded to the **European Cultural Convention**:[2] the forty member states of the Council of Europe, the Holy See, Belarus, Monaco, and Bosnia and Herzegovina. The main purpose of its activities is to develop a type of education in Europe which meets the needs of present-day society, and to draw the peoples of Europe closer together by fostering the awareness of a sense of common European identity.
>
> In the field of **modern language learning** the CDCC's action aims to assist member states in taking effective measures which will enable all citizens to learn to use languages for the purposes of mutual understanding, personal mobility and access to information in a multilingual and multicultural Europe. Its objectives are to help implement reforms in progress and to encourage innovation in language teaching and teacher training.

---

2. From its founding in 1961, the Council for Cultural Cooperation (CDCC) has allowed non-member countries of the Council of Europe (COE) to join and to participate in projects. Thus, Finland was a member of the CDCC for 28 years before joining the COE in 1989 and the note above indicates four signatories to the Cultural Convention that are not COE members. [see http://www.coe.fr/eng/present/history.htm]

The CDCC pursues these aims by promoting language learning centred on the needs and motivations of learners and by preparing teachers and teacher trainers to play their role, taking into account, among other things, the rapid changes in our European society. (Trim 1997: Preface)

The basic aims of language teaching in the context of the educational and political aims of the Council of Europe were defined in 1971 by an expert group working on the development of a European unit-credit system for adult language learning in these terms:

- to facilitate the free movement of people, information and ideas in Europe with access for all and to encourage closer co-operation by providing the linguistic means of direct interpersonal communication, both face-to-face and at a distance;
- to build up mutual understanding and acceptance of cultural and linguistic diversity in a multilingual and multicultural Europe, with respect for individual, local, regional and national identities, developing a common European intercultural identity by unforced mutual influence;
- to promote the personal development of the individual, with growing self-awareness, self-confidence and independence of thought and action combined with social responsibility as an active agent in a participatory, pluralist democratic society and a well-informed, positive attitude towards other people and their cultures, free from prejudice, intolerance and xenophobia;
- to make the process of language teaching and learning itself more democratic by providing the conceptual tools for the planning, construction, conduct and evaluation of courses closely geared to the needs, motivations and characteristics of learners enabling them so far as possible to steer and control their own progress towards autonomy in language learning and use;
- to provide a framework for close and effective international co-operation in the organisation of language learning. (Trim 1997: 5)

In 1972, the language education policies of the Council of Europe were further defined by the Committee of Ministers in the seminal Recommendation No. R (82) 18 which states, in part:

The Committee of Ministers ...

Considering that the aim of the Council of Europe is to achieve greater unity between its members and that this aim can be pursued in particular by the adoption of common action in the cultural field; ...

Considering that the rich heritage of diverse languages and cultures in Europe is a valuable common resource to be protected and developed, and that a major educational effort is needed to convert that diversity from a barrier to communication into a source of mutual enrichment and understanding;

Considering that it is only through a better knowledge of European modern languages that it will be possible to facilitate communication and interaction among Europeans of different mother tongues in order to promote European mobility, mutual understanding and co-operation, and overcome prejudice and discrimination; ...

> Recommends the governments of member states … to implement by all available means and within the limits of available resources, the measures set out in the appendix to the present recommendation… (Recommendation No. R(82) 18 of the Council of Europe Committee of Ministers)

The appendix to this Recommendation spells out in some detail the "measures to be implemented concerning the learning and teaching of modern languages". These proposals fall under six headings: general measures, language learning in schools, language learning by migrants and their families, initial and further teacher training, and international cooperation. In summary, they emphasise the practical skills that should be developed for purposes of social interaction, business, the exchange of ideas and information, and to achieve international understanding. Teaching should respond to the needs and motivations of the learners, provide explicit goals and objectives, and be evaluated relevantly. All children were to learn at least one other European language and be able to use the language effectively for communication with speakers of that language. Migrant families were to be given the opportunity to acquire the language of their host community so as to enable them to participate in the life of that community. Teachers were to be given the opportunity to develop appropriate skills and to spend time regularly in the country where the target language is spoken. Finally, all countries were encouraged to cooperate for the improvement of language teaching and of the materials available for the teaching and learning of their languages.

Since its establishment, the CDCC has undertaken a series of "modern languages projects" through which its goals for modern language education were, largely, to be realised and which, in the words of John Trim, the eminent British applied linguist who led many of the projects, were designed

> …to support the efforts of member governments to achieve the necessarily long-term aim of converting the study of modern languages from being the exclusive concern of a restricted social, cultural and professional élite to the necessary basis for large-scale international communication affecting whole populations. (Trim 1997:5)

The "modern languages projects" are realised in and give coherence to a wide range of research, development, and training activities. A project is defined in the CDCC webpage as

> …a medium term plan with target groups, themes, objectives and working methods. (see http://culture.coe.fr/lang/eng/eedu2.2.html)

Up to 1997, there had been five broad projects:

> Earlier projects first established patterns of international cooperation (1962–1971), then developed basic educational and linguistic principles (1971–1976), piloted these in many contexts (1977–1981), and supported their application to the reform of language teaching in many member countries (1982–1987). The current project: "Language learning for European citizenship" will conclude in 1997. (see http://culture.coe.fr/lang/eng/eedu2.2.html)

The CDCC webpage indicates that workshops deal with the four sectors from pre-primary and primary education, to upper secondary general education, to vocationally-oriented language learning, and advanced adult education. A number of themes recur through the projects relevant to their sectors: specification of objectives, using information technology, bilingual education, educational links, visits and exchanges, learning to learn and learner autonomy, evaluation, and teacher education (pre-service and in-service) (see http://culture.coe.fr/lang/eng/eedu2.2.html).

The principles that have evolved through the Modern Languages Projects and that have guided the work of the Council on languages are spelled out in the Council of Europe's webpage. These principles emphasise that languages and language skills are the right of all citizens and are not restricted to a social or intellectual elite. Every child should learn another language at least from age 11 to the end of compulsory schooling. Language study should not be just formal study of grammar and literature but aim at developing those skills and attitudes needed for practical communication in everyday life. Language learning should not be limited to the school years but should continue throughout life to meet changing needs, demands and opportunities. Though parents' wishes and society's needs must be considered, the learners' own needs, interests and other characteristics should influence what is taught, the methods used, the objectives set, and the tasks and content of the assessment used.

There is strong evidence that the efforts of the Council of Europe and its organisations in the area of modern language education since 1961 have been successful. Trim, in an opinion expressed to the tenth meeting of the Bureau of the Governing Board of ECML, summarised what has taken place:

> The Council of Europe has been actively engaged continuously since 1961 in the promotion of foreign language learning in member states. Its success is convincingly demonstrated by the evidence presented by EURIDICE to the Second Annual Colloquy of ECML. At least one ML is now taught to 90% of young people in EU countries and over 70% of young people (15–25) claim to be able to converse in at least one language other than their mother — in both cases by far most commonly English, followed at some distance by French, then German. Motivation is high. Only in UK and Ireland would less than 80% of young people like to learn a further ML. Language competence and communication skills are the two specialised qualities "most useful in finding a good job". However, "language difficulties" are cited as by far the main obstacle to work and study abroad, which are seen as the principal benefit of European citizenship. Young people show low levels of cross-cultural antipathy, and are not in fear of losing cultural diversity. We may say that the primary objective of CE policy as set out in Recommendation R(82)18 of the Committee of Ministers is close to full achievement in the long-standing member states, but that much still remains to be done before European linguistic competence is everywhere adequate to meet the communicative needs of the new Europe as it is rapidly emerging. (Trim in ECML 1998:9)

It is within this framework and in pursuit of the aims implicit in the principles of the COE's modern languages projects that the **European Centre for Modern Languages (ECML)** exists and serves the Councils and the participants in the various education systems. The Centre sees improved communication and better mutual understanding between all the peoples of Europe as a pre-requisite to better European integration and, the Centre asserts, it "fully partakes" in such aims (http://culture.coe.fr/ecml/eng/egraorg.html; see also ECML c.1996:6 and Council of Europe and Modern Languages 1998:4). It sees itself as promoting the aims of the Councils by seeking more efficient, effective and relevant language learning responding to the practical needs of all Europeans and contributing

> ...to a more active and responsible European citizenship, which would be truly multilingual and sensitive to the cultural diversity within Europe through a more efficient and holistic approach to language education and training. (See ECML webpage at http://culture.coe.fr/ecml/eng/egraorg.html; cf. ECML c.1996:7).

Thus, though the Centre is located in Austria, it has a pan-European role but, according to its webpage, in its initial phase (1995 to 1997 and, subsequently, 1998), it was to give particular attention to the critical needs of the newly independent states of Central and Eastern Europe. In its pan-European role, ECML differs from the NFLC and CILT (which are national bodies) and CALL (which is a university centre) and, in this regard, resembles the other centre in this study, the Regional Language Centre in Singapore which also serves the needs of a regional grouping, the countries of South East Asia, while, likewise, attracting interest from language academics throughout Asia and beyond.

The history of the ECML is outlined in its webpage (see http://www.coe.fr/ecml/eng/egraorg.html). It commenced operations in 1995 for an initial period to 1997, which was subsequently extended to 1998, and, following a review of its operations, it was confirmed on 2 July 1998 by Resolution (98) 11 of the Council of Ministers as a permanent part of the Council of Europe (see http://www.coe.fr/ecml/eng/egraorg.html; also Claude Kieffer, Executive Director of ECML, personal communication, 23 September, 1998). Various discussions had taken place through the 1960s and 1970s with a view to establishing some sort of permanent unit but funding was not made available at that time. The need became more acute in the 1990s with the admittance to the COE of members from the newly independent States of the former Soviet bloc and the Centre was eventually established in 1994 under a Council of Europe "Enlarged Partial Agreement" on the initiative of Austria and the Netherlands with support from France. A "partial agreement" is one to which not all members have agreed, only interested member States participate and pay the costs, while the term "enlarged" signifies that other States can join at any time (cf. Council of Europe and Modern Languages 1998:3).

Initially, there were eight founding countries of the ECML: Austria, France, Greece, Liechtenstein, Malta, the Netherlands, Slovenia, and Switzerland (*Resolution (94) 10 on an enlarged Partial Agreement establishing the European Centre for Modern Languages*, 8 April, 1994; see http://culture.coe.fr/Infocentre/txt/eng/egraref.html) but subsequently another sixteen countries (at 1 January, 1998) have lent their support to the Centre in joining the agreement: Andorra, Bulgaria, Croatia, Cyprus, the Czech Republic, Estonia, Finland, the Former Yugoslav Republic of Macedonia, Hungary, Iceland, Latvia, Luxembourg, Norway, Poland, Romania, and Slovakia (cf. Council of Europe and Modern Languages 1998: 3). According to the ECML webpage, the Russian Federation and Lithuania have signified their intention to become members of the Enlarged partial Agreement (http://culture.coe.fr/ecml/members/msl.htm). The Committee of Ministers of the signatories to the Enlarged Partial Agreement can invite non-member states to join the Agreement (see http://culture.coe.fr/Infocentre/txt/eng/egraref.html). In fact, in addition to the 24 member States, there are another ten non-contributing partner States from the newly independent countries of the former Soviet bloc (Albania, Armenia, Azerbaijan, Belarus, Bosnia and Herzegovina, Georgia, Lithuania, Moldova, the Russian Federation, and Ukraine) (cf. Council of Europe and Modern Languages 1998: 4).

4. Geographical and administrative locations

The **geographical location** of the European Centre for Modern Languages is in Graz in the province of Styria in Austria though it also mounts workshops and other activities in suitable locations elsewhere in Europe. Its webpage describes its location as in an historic building in the university quarter of the city. Its location is established under the founding Resolution (94) 10 and is significant because of the centrality of the location in Europe and the considerable financial and other support given to the Centre by the Austrian government, the province of Styria, and the city of Graz. The city and its significance as the location of this Europe-focussed Centre are described in ECML documentation in these terms:

> With its 250,000 inhabitants, Graz is Austria's second largest city. Due to its location in the south-east of the country, it is ideally suited to take on a role which it has played increasingly in recent years: Graz as a crossroads and pivot of cultural and economic exchange at all levels.
>
> Graz constantly seeks to strengthen its position as an intercultural forum ...
>
> A city with a long academic tradition, Graz is home to three universities, with more than 43,000 students. As a result Graz can boast an excellent and extensive infrastructure of conference facilities ...

The Province of Styria has, throughout its history, acted as a bridge; in recent years this region has intensified this bridging function and today Styria is a forum for important economic and artistic events ...(http://culture.coe.fr/ecml/graz/graz.htm).

The **administrative location** of the ECML is as a permanent institution of the Council of Europe, this status having been confirmed by Resolution (98) 11 adopted on 2 July, 1998. The **governance** of the ECML rests under the Council of Europe in the Governing Board, which consists of one representative from each member country of the Enlarged Partial Agreement (Resolution 94 (10), Article 3). Under this Resolution, the role of the Governing Board is to

- adopt the programme of activities of the centre in accordance with the budgetary resources available;
- monitor the implementation of the programme of activities and the management of the funds of the centre;
- forward to the Committee of Ministers a report on its activities, containing also an outline of its future activities. (see Resolution(94) 10, Article 4; http://culture.coe.fr/Infocentre/txt/eng/egraref.html)

The Governing Board also elects a Bureau of five members (including a Chair and two Vice-Chairs). While the Board is required to meet at least once a year, the Bureau meets twice a year and is responsible for:

- preparation and implementation of the Centre's programme of activities
- preparation of the annual report
- recommendations for the themes and speakers for the annual colloquy, and
- preparation of the agenda and documentation for the annual meeting of the Governing Board (cf. the ECML webpage on the structure of the Centre at http://culture.coe.fr/ecml/eng/egrastr.html).

The implementation of the programme of activities is the responsibility of the Centre and its staff but the Centre is also supported in this by the Association of the European Centre for Modern Languages, an association of the Austrian supporters of the Centre, viz., the Austrian government (specifically the Federal Ministry of Science, Transport and the Arts and the Federal Ministry of Education and Cultural Affairs), the Province of Styria, and the city of Graz, each of which provides representatives for the executive committee and the General Assembly of the Association. This Association provides the premises for the Centre, it meets the administrative and running costs, and it coordinates the contributions from the four Austrian funding bodies (see documentation from the Centre and http://culture.coe.fr/ecml/eng/egrastr.html).

Though no **constitution** as such seems to be available for the Centre, something equivalent is set out in the founding Resolution (94) 10, which has been referred to several times already and which specifies the administrative structure within which the Centre operates with a Governing Board, a Bureau, and the Centre structure itself, the functions of these bodies, and the sorts of activities in which the Centre will engage.

In contrast to a university-based centre such as the Centre for Applied Linguistics and Languages, ECML stands alone and has considerable **autonomy**. However, that autonomy is limited by the fact that it is created under the CDCC and the Council of Europe, with the specific purpose of implementing the policies and programmes of those Councils. It is thus very specifically an instrument of those Councils both from the point of view of how it has been established and the funding it receives and it is bound by the clauses in the founding Resolution and by the decisions of the Governing Board and Bureau, which are established to be representative of the participating countries that have signed the Enlarged Partial Agreement under which the Centre was founded and operates. In reality, since the Centre serves these organisations, it can hardly be considered autonomous and probably has less autonomy than a university-based centre in a system where the academic autonomy of universities is jealously guarded. On the other hand, in all organisations, funding inevitably imposes its own limitations and opportunities and impacts on the autonomy of organisations; a centre that serves the whole of Europe through the COE and CDCC, a centre that is backed by the resources of Europe and these Councils, is likely to have fewer financial restrictions on its operations than centres which depend heavily on the money they can solicit from donors (such as NFLC) or raise through competitive student fees and competitive project contracts (as is the case for CALL).

5. Purpose and mission of the centre

The **mission** of the Centre was set out in Article 1 of the Appendix to the founding Resolution:

> The Centre shall:
> – provide training for teacher trainers, authors of textbooks and experts in the area of the development of curricula, educational standards and methods of evaluation;
> – bring together researchers and educational policy makers from all over Europe;
> – facilitate exchanges of information on innovation and research in the field of the learning and teaching of modern languages;
> – set up a documentation centre providing specialists and multipliers with a wide range of teaching aids and with the results of research. (Resolution (94) 10, Appendix, Article 1; also Trim 1997:42; http://culture.coe.fr/ecml/motto/motto.htm)

The Centre's **goals** exist within the context of the goals of the Council of Europe, in particular to seek greater unity amongst the European members, to realise European ideals and principles, and to facilitate economic and social progress, and to do so through discussion and agreement on common action. The ECML's more specific aim is to promote the teaching and learning of languages within the multilingual and multicultural European context, to disseminate good language teaching and learning practice, and

> to contribute to the respect and reinforcement of linguistic diversity in a multilingual, multicultural, democratic and tolerant Europe. (cf. http://culture.coe.fr/ecml/eng/egraorg.html).

In other documentation, the Centre indicates its aims as

> To promote multilingualism throughout Europe … a commitment to improve understanding among Europeans themselves. …
>
> In all its activities prominence is given to promoting multilingualism in a multicultural, democratic and tolerant Europe. Issues relating to foreign languages are discussed, due consideration being given to both linguistic and methodological diversity. Among the most important aims of the European Centre for Modern Languages are:
>
> – Addressing the needs of Central and Eastern European states
> – Dissemination of findings from research into language learning and teaching
> – Diversification, multilingualism
> – Promoting less widely taught languages. (From an ECML information brochure)

Following the First Annual Colloquy in December 1995 when the role and function of the Centre were extensively discussed, the Centre seems to have resolved to pursue more limited objectives around the following themes:

> – autonomous learning and training in the field of modern languages;
> – implementation of information and communication technologies, and the themes "learning to learn" and lifelong education;
> – interculturality and authenticity;
> – aspects of language policy in Europe;
> – teacher training and development and curriculum reform;
> – dissemination of good practices in workshop management and delivery, dissemination of results and management of effective networking and follow-up activities. (http://culture.coe.fr/ecml/eng/egraorg.html; cf. also Council of Europe and Modern Languages 1998: 7; http://culture.coe.fr/ecml/motto/motto.htm)

In Resolution (98) 11, which established ECML on a permanent basis, the strategic role of the Centre was defined as

> – the implementation of language policies;
> – the promotion of innovative approaches to the learning and teaching of modern languages,

and the strategic objectives as

> – to focus on the practice of the learning and teaching of modern languages;
> – to promote dialogue and exchange among the various actors in the field;

- to train multipliers;
- to support programme-related networks and research projects. (Council of Europe and Modern Languages 1998:5)

The basic **functions and strategic approach** of the Centre rests in the conduct of workshops on topics relevant to its mission and goals. As noted earlier, the Centre is seen as a "platform and meeting place" for persons involved in language policy and its implementation, including teacher education, methodology, and textbook writing. In its *1998 Programme of Activities* (ECML 1997), the Centre lists its main functions as:

- promotion of dialogue and exchanges (linking theory and practice)
- training of multipliers (practical aspects of policy implementation and innovation; special assistance to countries with urgent needs)
- action research projects in priority areas (linking up with previous work carried out by the ECML and the CDCC)
- networking and follow-up activities in order to facilitate the dissemination of good practice
- information (documentation centre; database on WWW; availability of downloadable workshop reports; signposting to other European information providers). (ECML 1997:10)

Elsewhere, the ECML describes its approach thus:

> At the heart of the Centre's work is a broad-based exchange of information and cooperation which are reflected in its main spheres of activity: the organisation of conferences, workshops and follow-up activities, the distribution of project-based publications and the financing of research projects. A documentation and resource centre is housed in the Centre. (Taken from an ECML information and conference folder)

Other documentation states that the workshops and colloquy are used to promote exchanges between researchers and practitioners in the various fields (teacher education, programme administrators, decision-makers, and "multipliers" who are likely to further disseminate the work by means such as publications or workshops). The Centre also seeks to focus on research in specific contexts relevant to the needs of Europe, but especially Central and Eastern Europe to whose special needs the Centre seeks to respond especially through workshops and other "decentralised events" in those countries. The Centre participates in European projects and the studies it commissions are published by the Council of Europe. (cf. leaflet CC-ED/GRAZ (98) 7 rev1; ECML 1997:7–8)

6. Activities

The principal activities of the Centre are realised, as has been noted already, through workshops. These activities, which bring together persons involved in language policy and its implementation from across Europe, cover all areas and levels of education and seek to strengthen the linguistic and cultural diversity of Europe and of Europeans, to enhance the vital principles of tolerance and democracy, and to promote "European integration" (cf. http://culture.coe.fr/ecml/motto/motto.htm). The focus of the Centre's activities is that determined in the First Annual Colloquy and identified above under the heading of "Goals". The discussion of the Centre's "Mission" also quoted Article 1 of the Appendix to the founding Resolution in which a range of activities were listed including training teacher educators, facilitating relevant information exchange, and establishing a documentation centre.

The **Programme of Activities** for each of the years since the Centre commenced operations lists the many activities that the Centre has conducted (ECML 1997, 1997a, and webpage http://culture.coe.fr/ecml/eng/egraact.98.html[3]). These cover such diverse areas as, *inter alia*, Primary School foreign language education, piloting the Common European Framework, use of the internet, continuing education for teachers through exchange classes and residence abroad, syllabus development, language teaching and peace, quality assurance, introduction to language policy, computers in foreign language education, the professionalisation of language teacher associations, multimedia, autonomous learning, bilingual schools, and learning objectives and the testing of competences. These are realised, almost without exception, through workshops with an occasional conference and colloquy.

ECML is not so much concerned with the development of **language policy**, as with facilitating its implementation. Claude Kieffer, the ECML Executive Director, stated in a personal communication:

> The brochure explains our role with regards to language policy development; the ECML actually focuses on implementation of such policies, not development which is the focus of the Strasbourg-based Modern Language Projects. (Kieffer 1998, personal communication)

The Centre's principal influence on language policy would seem to be through a general educative process as a result of the workshops and conferences attended by personnel of all levels though "aspects of language policy in Europe" is listed as one of the Centre's concerns following the 1995 First Annual Colloquy (ECML 1997:8). A few projects have focussed directly on language policy, e.g., there was Workshop 12/97, "Introduction to Language Policy: Methods of analysis and Evaluation Fields of Intervention", held in Graz in June 1997 (see Truchot: 1997), while the *1998 Programme of Activities* indicates a continuation of this project through an annotated, language policy bibliography (ECML 1997:7).

Since the Centre is concerned with facilitating the implementation of language

---

3. For the programme for previous years, substitute 95, 96 and 97 for 98 in this address.

policy rather than with its development, it does not have the sort of proactive **leverage** role of the NFLC, for example, though clearly its indirect influence is potentially considerable. Again this comes through the educative effect of its workshops and conferences and through selectively funded research projects though the Centre also has been given a more direct role in the newly independent countries whose needs it was partly founded to assist.

The **services** the Centre provides are principally in the form of workshops and conferences though it also provides a venue and administrative assistance for events offered by other organisations. It also funds research (mainly, it seems, under commission to others) and produces a variety of workshop reports and other publications.

The Centre aims to establish itself as a major *clearinghouse and documentation centre* for European language teaching and to use both its publications and its webpage to make available and to disseminate the information gathered. Apart from its publications (see below), this area seemed, at the time when this book was being researched, to be still under development and the Centre describes its activities in these terms:

> [The ECML] disseminates relevant information and documentation on a wide scale throughout Europe; an ECML WWWsite will soon ... be operational (availability of downloadable information, signposting towards other relevant information providers in Europe). (ECML 1997:8)

The ECML *publications* appear under the name of the Council of Europe as well as that of the Centre and consist largely of reports of conferences, workshops and commissioned research projects. At the time this book was being written, more than 30 such publications were available in either or both English and French. A sample of topics includes the production of modern language textbooks, computers in the foreign language classroom, child development and early foreign language learning, language and cultural awareness, methodology in bilingual Secondary School classes, introduction to language policy, and a reflective model of language teacher education (see flyer CC-ED/GRAZ (98) 10 rev3).

The ECML's major activity, as already noted, is in the area of the organisation of *workshops, conferences, colloquia and other meetings*. Examples of these have been listed above in referring to general activities. The Centre describes these events thus:

> The ECML workshops and annual colloquy should further exchanges between researchers and practitioners, teacher trainers, programme administrators, decision-makers, and multipliers likely to coordinate activities or follow-up projects and to disseminate the results either directly or via the Centre (follow-up or application workshops, publication of reports and networking newsletters, dissemination of information via Internet, as well as the setting up of networks of contacts and action on a thematic basis). (ECML c.1996:7)

The ECML finances some *research* activities relevant to its programme of activities. In one of its documents, the Centre describes its research interests in these terms:

> The Centre will endeavour to position itself in the area of research applied to specific contexts, especially in Central and Eastern Europe; it will commission studies which will be published by the Council of Europe; and, as far as possible, it will take part in European projects. (ECML c.1996:7)

Its 1998 programme lists several research and action research projects that the Centre has commissioned including one on the "theory, experiences and good practice" relevant to the simultaneous learning of several languages, an annotated bibliography on language policy, one on intercultural competences in modern languages in the context of teacher education programmes, and one on the introduction of innovation in modern language teaching and learning (ECML 1997:7–8).

7. Interactions and links

The Centre's basic link is, of course, with its parent organisations, the Council for Cultural Cooperation (CDCC) and the Council of Europe (COE), whose policies it implements. It also has a special relationship with Austrian organisations, in whose country it is located, especially the Association of the European Centre for Modern Languages (referred to above as the association of the Austrian governmental organisations that support the Centre), various language and culture centres across Austria, and the KulturKontakt organisation.

The Centre has a specific aim of establishing links with other organisations and its activities seem to be specifically designed to further that aim and to take full advantage of it. Thus, the ECML quote above in relation to *workshops, conferences, colloquia and other meetings* emphasises that participants in these events are expected to disseminate any information received as widely as possible. Elsewhere, the Centre speaks of its efforts to interact widely across Europe and create links with relevant organisations:

> The dissemination of ideas and good practices relating to foreign languages is given particular emphasis. Participating countries therefore commit themselves to facilitating dissemination of the results of workshops. In addition, the European Centre for Modern Languages itself lends its support to enhancing contact and cooperation among participants and promotes the establishment of national networks. Improvements to national and international networking models is an ongoing topic of discussion. (http://culture.coe.fr/ecml/strukt/as1.htm)

The final stimulus for the creation of the Centre was, as we have seen, the desire of the Council of Europe to provide additional assistance to the newly independent countries of the former Soviet bloc and so the Centre was specifically charged to liaise with those countries and respond to their needs. Thus, the initial task that many centres face of achieving a profile was less onerous for ECML than for more independent centres since it is specifically an instrument of the Council of Europe, the Council for Cultural

Cooperation, and the signatories to the Enlarged Partial Agreement, it serves their needs, and it is one focal point for them in seeking to have their language education needs met. Centre documentation indicates that it

> ...lends its support to enhancing contact and cooperation among participants and promotes the establishment of national networks.

It also links up with other international activities in the area of modern languages, in particular with the European Commission and the various cultural and linguistic institutes such as the British Council, the Institut Français, and the Goethe Institut. Special efforts are being made to build a "substantive cooperative" link with the European Commission (not least to harmonise the policies and practices of the Commission and the Council) (see ECML webpage at http://culture.coe.fr/ecml/eng/egraorg.html; ECML 1997:7; and flyer CC-ED/GRAZ (98) 7 rev1). One example of the cooperation cited in these references was the joint organisation by ECML and the European Commission of the Centre's Second Annual Colloquy in 1996.

The Centre's 1998 brochure lists a variety of international organisations with which it is developing partnerships or with which it is undertaking projects of international relevance (Council of Europe and Modern Languages 1998:9). The first on the list is the European Commission (Directorate-General XXII, Education, Training and Youth) with which it cites the joint organisation of colloquies and special activities in the area of language teaching in vocational training. Other organisations identified include:

- UNESCO's Linguapax, the World Bank and the European Training Foundation (languages and world peace; and participation in the Tempus projects in Central and Eastern Europe);
- non-governmental organisations such as the Fédération Internationale des Professeurs de Langues Vivantes (FIPLV), the Open Society Foundation (Soros Foundation), and KulturKontakt, Austria;
- the language and culture institutes referred to above including the British Council, the Goethe Institut, the Institut Français, the Alliance Française, and the Austrian language and cultural centres; and
- CILT (with which it is setting up a "virtual resource") (cf. Council of Europe and Modern Languages 1998:9; cf. ECML 1997:7)

ECML has a special relationship with the Modern Languages Project of the Council of Europe, based in Strasbourg, France. The two organisations are independent, each serves the Council of Europe and the Council for Cultural Cooperation, but the Modern Languages Project serves, essentially, a policy role whereas the ECML serves an implementational role (cf. Claude Kieffer, Executive Director of ECML, personal communication, 23 September, 1998; ECML 1997:7; Trim 1997:42; Council of Europe and Modern Languages 1998:7–8). The Centre's 1998 brochure is, in fact, a double brochure, shared with the Modern Languages Project, with information on the ECML in one half while the other half is about Modern Languages. The brochure identifies the differing key functions of ECML and of Modern Languages:

ECML:
- promotion of dialogue and exchange (linking theory with practice);
- training of multipliers; practical aspects of policy implementation and innovation; special assistance to countries with urgent needs;
- research projects on priority themes (in conjunction with activities and seminars organised by the ECML or CDCC);
- networking and follow-up activities: to promote the dissemination of good practices;
- information function: documentation centre, Internet site; workshop reports signposting information providers in Europe;

The CDCC Modern Languages Project (Strasbourg):
- planning and enhancing learning, teaching and assessment: development and maintenance of conceptual planning tools and initiatives to promote increased and diversified language learning …
- consensus building and language policy instruments: recommendations and guidelines; expertise and policy analysis concerning educational and linguistic legislation;
- awareness raising: practical measures to raise awareness of the importance of learning languages …
- promotion of innovation: exploratory studies to develop and stimulate discussion on new concepts in the field, and illustrations of good practice. (Council of Europe and Modern Languages 1998:8).

Rather than by a formal definition of the separate roles and functions for ECML and the Modern Languages Project, the same document indicates that the distribution of these functions will be achieved by cooperation between the two bodies to achieve "the highest possible level of synergy" (Council of Europe and Modern Languages 1998:8).

8. Staffing

As noted earlier, the Centre is administered by a Governing Board, which elects a Bureau to oversight the day-to-day operations, which are carried out by the Centre Secretariat with the support of the Austrian Association. According to the 1998 brochure, the Secretariat now consists of six "professionals" (Council of Europe and Modern Languages 1998:6; cf. http://culture.coe.fr/ecml/eng/egraorg.html and http://culture.coe.fr/ecml/strukt/test.html, where the total staffing is shown as seven, including, in the latter case, a General Manager for the Austrian Association). The staffing structure shown in the webpage consists of an Executive Director, two Deputy Executive Directors, a Director of Studies, a documentalist/administrative assistant, and two secretaries (http://culture.coe.fr/ecml/eng/egrastr.html). In addition, the Director of the Centre is empowered under the founding Resolution (94) 10 (Article 7) to call on other institutions and experts in the teaching of modern languages to assist it in its activities (see http://culture.coe.fr/Infocentre/txt/eng/egraref.html). According to the same Resolution, the Secretariat (presumably the professional staff) are provided by the Council of Europe. As was noted earlier, the Austrian authorities provide the administrative support, such staff not being staff of the Council of Europe.

9. Facilities

It was noted earlier that the Centre is located in an historic building in the university quarter of Graz, a short distance from the city centre. It consists of five offices, a main meeting room (with simultaneous translation facilities), and two seminar rooms (see http://culture.coe.fr/ecml/eng/egrastr.html). Under Resolution (94) 10 founding the Centre and in Article 6, the Republic of Austria is committed to providing the facilities and a local secretariat at its own cost. It was noted earlier in the discussion of the Centre's administrative location that the Austrian authorities formed an Association to take responsibility for these matters and to coordinate the contributions from the Austrian partners. In addition to its principal seat in Graz, Austria, the Centre is able to offer events elsewhere in Europe if it is most convenient to do so.

10. Budget

Under the founding Resolution (94) 10, the ECML is funded by the participants in the Enlarged Partial Agreement (see Article 5), the budget and the scale of contributions are approved by representatives on the Committee of Ministers of the participating States and, if agreed by the others, of the participating non-member States. The Centre is also entitled, under the Resolution (Article 5) to accept "voluntary and other contributions" (which may be tied to special projects) and, as noted above, under Article 6 the Austrian authorities provide the facilities, the local secretariat, and the local secretariat's running costs (amounting to approximately 50% of the Centre's annual costs) (see Resolution (94) 10, http://culture.coe.fr/Infocentre/txt/eng/egraref.html, Articles 5 and 6, and http://culture.coe.fr/ecml/eng/egrastr.html). According to Centre documentation, the Austrian funds are provided through the Association of the European Centre for Modern Languages by the Austrian authorities, viz., the Federal Ministry of Science, Transport and the Arts, the Federal Ministry of Education and Cultural Affairs, the Province of Styria, and the City of Graz (see also ECML c.1996:5).

The budget is in two parts: a general budget, covering the necessary running of the Centre, and a Special Programme Account, financed from voluntary contributions by the participating States (see http://culture.coe.fr/ecml/eng/egrastr.html).

11. Constraints and opportunities

The European Centre for Modern Languages serves a very specific set of purposes: to assist in the implementation of the language policies of the Council of Europe and the Council for Cultural Cooperation and, as an initial high priority, to assist the newly independent countries of Central and Eastern Europe to respond to their language and language education needs. The Centre's role is distinctly European, meeting the needs of Europe as a whole but especially of the countries of greatest immediate need and to do so within the budget approved by the partners to the Enlarged Partial Agreement. It is, perhaps, because of this European focus that the Centre is not yet well known beyond Europe: the present writer came across it almost by chance while researching for this book, found no one in the United States or Australia who was significantly aware of the Centre or its function, and found no informative reference to it beyond Council of Europe documents.

Clearly there are constraints on the operations of the Centre by virtue of the reasons for its creation and the role and functions it serves but the opportunities are also immense. The "new Europe" has shown itself highly responsive to language and culture issues and needs, it recognises the distinctive needs of the newly independent countries and is willing to support those countries in responding to their needs, it has already produced much highly creative, innovative, theoretically solid, and globally influential work in the area of applied linguistics (Council of Europe and Modern Languages 1998:9), and, as it grows from this foundation, it is reasonable to see a strong future for the Centre. The work of the Modern Languages Projects of the Council of Europe has, overall, been, unquestionably, the most exciting and influential development in the history of language education and applied linguistics worldwide; the fact that the Centre is to work in a complementary fashion to the Project and support the COE in its language policy development and implementation assures the Centre of a highly significant place in European education and virtually assures it of a significant place in the evolution of language education. Thus, though the constraints are clearly defined by the nature of the Centre's role, functions and funding, they are hardly limiting within the European context and the opportunities for the Centre to be involved in creative and influential activity are immense. Undoubtedly the lack of knowledge of the Centre beyond Europe will rapidly disappear as its activities and publications multiply and as it is seen more and more to be involved in the implementation and dissemination of the on-going and seminal activities of the Council of Europe's language and language education projects.

12. Uniqueness and impact of the centre

The European Centre for Modern Languages was initially established for a period of three years (1995 to 1997), which was later extended to four (to 1998), at the end of which and following a review, it was granted permanent status (see Section III above). Unfortunately, the review report was confidential and not available to the present writer but, granted that the Centre was subsequently accorded permanent status, the report was, presumably, favourable. This assessment is further supported by the fact that, from an initial eight partners to the Enlarged Partial Agreement, there are now 24 plus another ten non-contributing members (see Section III). Certainly the range and variety of the Centre's activities suggest that it is energetic, meeting needs, and receiving a favourable response from the potential clients. One has to conclude that the Centre is performing well and having a favourable impact in the area covered by its terms of reference.

The international status, role and function of the Centre while being located in and partly funded by Austria make it distinctive, as does its specific role of responding to the urgent language needs of the newly independent countries of Eastern and Central Europe. Also striking is the vision of the Austrian authorities at all levels from city government, to provincial and national government in half-funding and strongly supporting such a Centre to serve pan-European language needs. The high degree of international cooperation to create and provide on-going support for the Centre is one of the features that makes ECML (together with RELC in Singapore) distinctive. Its charge of implementing the pan-European policies of the Council of Europe, the Council for Cultural Cooperation and the Modern Languages Project means that it is responding simultaneously to the needs of many countries, surely a highly complex task in itself, and also gives it, almost automatically, a major status in the field of language education and applied linguistics, derived, whatever its own efforts, from the enormous respect in which the work of these bodies is held worldwide in applied linguistics. The inclusion of the ECML in this study is justified by the Centre's status, by the complex nature of the international needs to which it is charged with responding, and by the uniquely international structure of its original creation and its on-going management.

The 1998 ECML brochure sums up the Centre's effectiveness and future role with these words:

> The European Centre for Modern Languages has already proved itself capable of working effectively with other institutions aiming to promote modern languages and plurilingualism in Europe.
>
> In the future, the ECML will increasingly adapt its focus to the changing requirements of its member states. It will continue to develop partnerships with the CDCC's

Modern Languages Project and other institutions and bodies throughout Europe within the framework of a medium-term programme of activities (3 years).

Through the promotion of innovative language teaching and training, the ECML will further work towards a European citizenship which is more active, more responsible, truly multilingual and sensitive to Europe's cultural diversity. (Council of Europe and Modern Languages 1998:10)

Chapter 5

The SEAMEO Regional Language Centre (RELC), Singapore

1. Address

>   30 Orange Grove Road,
>   Singapore, 258352,
>   Republic of Singapore
>
>   **Telephone:**   65-737-9044
>   **Fax:**   65-734-2753
>   **Email:**   srelc@singnet.com.sg
>   **Website:**   http://www.relc.org.sg/

2. The centre

The Regional Language Centre is a centre of the Southeast[1] Asian Ministers of Education Organization (SEAMEO). It is located in Singapore but supported by all the full and associate members of SEAMEO and serves the whole of South East Asia: it is very much a regional centre. The importance of RELC in the Asian-Pacific area and the respect it enjoys worldwide justify its inclusion in this volume. Its reputation extends worldwide and its activities (especially the annual RELC Seminar) attract applied linguists and other language educationalists from around the Pacific and, indeed, the world.

Unlike the previous language centres discussed in the United States, Britain, and Austria, RELC is, firstly, a teaching centre for applied linguistics even though it is also a centre from which consultancy expertise may be sought and where research into language teaching methods, though not a prime focus of RELC's own activities, is encouraged by various means. Its activities focus on language teaching and learning and, in particular, the provision of programmes designed to upgrade the skills of "language specialists and educators" in South East Asia (cf. http://www.seameo.org/Centers/RELC.htm). The RELC webpage describes the Centre thus:

---

1. Within the region, the conventional spelling is Southeast. In this book, the traditional two-word spelling is used except where citations or regional names have used the one-word format.

> [RELC] provides SEAMEO member countries with expertise, training facilities and training programmes for upgrading the skills of language specialists and educators. It assists member countries and associate member countries to cooperate in programmes, projects and activities in the interest of the improvement of language education in the region. (http://www.relc.org.sg/relc.htm)

In preparing this chapter, the present writer had access to the RELC five-year plans spanning 1972 to 2001 (RELC 1972, 1977, 1982, 1987, 1992, and 1997) and drew substantially on information from the RELC and SEAMEO webpages. In addition, he was able to draw on his own personal knowledge of RELC from numerous visits there since the late 1970s. The current Director and other present and former staff of RELC also gave generously of their advice while this chapter was being researched and written.

3. Background and origin of the centre

The Regional Language Centre was established to assist the countries of **South East Asia** meet the language education needs of what, culturally, linguistically and racially, is undoubtedly one of the most diverse regions in the world. It is a region whose economy grew dramatically in the second half of the twentieth century (despite the distressing economic downturn of the late 1990s) with the corollary of increasing demands for skills in English and other languages for economic purposes, to facilitate communication in vocational contexts, and for purposes of inter-cultural understanding and communication. It is a region that, geographically, is at the transport crossroads between Europe-Southern Asia, on the one side, and the dynamic East Asia-Pacific region across to the Americas, on the other. It has ready access to all the major markets of the world, not least to those of China and Japan, which are expected to dominate the global economy in the twenty-first century, and it has ready access, not only to the considerable natural resources of South East Asia but also to those of Australia to the south east and to the oil and other resources of the near-western "Arabic" lands.

Throughout the documentation available on RELC, the Centre's **regional role** is emphasised and is reflected in its title of "SEAMEO Regional Language Centre". Though it is centrally located in Singapore, a compact country which is highly developed and more than capable of managing its own development and implementing its own language policy, RELC is outward-focussed, serving and responding to the needs of the South East Asian region, especially the member countries. This regional focus is also seen as an integral part of and corollary to the globalisation which strongly influenced world language policies in the last decade of the twentieth century and will inevitably become increasingly important in the twenty-first century. This regional context, which so profoundly influences the character of RELC and the manner in which it fulfils its role, was summed up in the 1997–2001 blueprint:

> Southeast Asia is now a part of the world where rapid economic growth and closer regional cooperation make greater demands on education systems for human resource development. Greater regionalism has fostered closer regional cooperation for development in education, trade and international relations. The learning of languages other than one's mother tongue or national language has taken on greater significance for countries that seek to globalize their economy. As the language centre of the region SEAMEO RELC has taken note of the scenario for its work in language and language teaching and has developed strategic plans for providing educational services to the region. Within the context of greater regionalism and globalization RELC has a unique role to play.
>
> To foster international understanding and cooperation SEAMEO RELC aims to help the region in communicating across cultures and languages. (RELC 1997:3)

Significantly, the theme that RELC has adopted for its five-year plan for the 1997–2001 period bridging into the new millennium is "Language Education for Regionalism" (RELC 1997:3 and 14).

This region is marked, not only by a rapidly growing population, enormous economic growth and strategic potential, but by its **linguistic, cultural and political diversity**. Adding to its indigenous diversity and the mobility of the people (and their languages and cultures) within the region, the area was colonised over recent centuries and, until the middle of the twentieth century, by the British, French, Dutch, Portuguese, Americans and Japanese while, over the centuries, the Chinese and Indian peoples also migrated freely and established strong communities throughout the region. All these colonising groups added their own powerful linguistic and cultural heritages to most parts of the region, overlaying the indigenous languages and cultures. Added to this linguistic and cultural mix has increasingly been the global dominance of English for international and inter-community business and for other communication purposes.

It is the needs of this demographically, economically and educationally dynamic region that the Regional Language Centre was created to serve. For this region, language skills, ready communication across linguistic groups, and mutual understanding are not luxuries but are absolutely fundamental to the existence and co-existence of the countries of South East Asia and the development of their people and their economies. For practical purposes, the predominant linguistic interest of RELC is English, the language of highest demand in terms of international and inter-community communication in the region but, nevertheless and as already emphasised, the environment RELC serves is characterised by linguistic and cultural diversity and RELC's activities have to reflect the diverse needs this creates. It is significant in this regard that, though the acronym RELC has been retained, the original name of the Centre, Regional English Language Centre, was changed on 1 January, 1977 to Regional Language Centre (RELC 1992:5) and, in addition to strong interests in the teaching of English, the Centre has staff with interests in Asian (especially South and

South East Asian) languages such as Chinese, Bahasa Malaysia, and Bahasa Indonesia, and it also receives foreign experts in such languages as French and German. Thus, the Centre's concern is now the improvement of the teaching of both English and all other languages of national and international importance to the region (cf. RELC 1992:5).

The region served by RELC is diverse not only linguistically and culturally but also politically; hence, it is not feasible to think in terms of a single policy context or even a single language policy context in the region. Nevertheless, there are certain language and language education policy features that are commonplace across the region. These include such features as:

- acceptance of the importance of English as the first foreign language, the desirability of most children learning English as one of their languages, and the desirability of having vocational skills in English;
- the desirability of all children learning and being educated in their own first language for at least some of their schooling;
- the need for opportunities for all children to acquire one or more of the other locally spoken languages;
- the value of bilingual education;
- the need for some of the children to have the opportunity to learn other major foreign languages both from within Asia (such as Japanese) or from Europe or elsewhere (e.g., French or German);
- the importance of an early start to language learning, generally from the earliest years of Primary School, and the desirability of children being able to add other languages to their array of skills later in their schooling;
- the need to ensure that all teachers have the language skills, cultural knowledge, and competence in language teaching theory and methodology to enable them to teach effectively; and
- the high value placed on education but the insufficiency of resources to allow all children to fully pursue their education.

Most of the countries that are served by RELC also have certain difficulties in common (in many of these, the host country of Singapore, with its booming economy and high living standards, is an exception):

- financial resources which are stretched to the utmost in vigorous developmental programmes and which were further strained by the economic downturn of the second half of the 1990s;
- large population numbers in relation to the size of each country and substantial differences in standard of living, income, and level of health and education, across the various sectors of their societies;
- a gross under-supply of well-qualified, language proficient and skilful teachers and a high demand from elsewhere in industry for educated people with language skills (hence, severe difficulty in retaining language-proficient, competent teachers);

- insufficient good quality, region-relevant teaching materials and insufficient resources either to rectify this or to take advantage of the facilities offered by modern learning technology (e.g., computers, internet access, textbooks, multimedia resources, etc).

While maintaining their independence, the countries of South East Asia have come together in many fields in order to work together towards solutions for their problems and towards harmonious development. In the field of education, cooperation is pursued through the **Southeast Asian Ministers of Education Organization (SEAMEO)**, which was established on 30 November, 1965 to promote regional cooperation in education, science and culture amongst its members (cf. http://www.seameo.org/About/vision.htm). The member States are Brunei Darussalam, Cambodia, Indonesia, Lao People's Democratic Republic, Malaysia, Myanmar, the Philippines, Singapore, Thailand, and Vietnam (for further information on membership, see http://www.ait.ac.th/Asia/seameo/seameo.html and http://www.seameo.org/Members/index.htm: at the time of writing, the former site does not include Myanmar among the member countries but the latter does). Under its charter, SEAMEO offers "Associate Membership" to any country

> ...which is willing to promote cooperation among Southeast Asian nations through education, science and culture. (http://www.seameo.org/About/charter.htm)

There are six Associate Member countries: Australia, Canada, France, Germany, New Zealand, and the Netherlands. Japan is listed as a donor country.

The policy-making body for SEAMEO is SEAMEC (the Southeast Asian Ministers of Education Council), which consists of the Ministers of Education of the member countries, while its executive arm is SEAMES (the Southeast Asian Ministers of Education Secretariat), based in Bangkok. SEAMEO has some twelve regional "centres of excellence" located in its member countries to provide services in a range of areas covering health, education, agriculture, and culture; among these is the Regional Language Centre based in Singapore. (See the SEAMEO webpage at http://www.ait.ac.th/Asia/seameo/seameo.html and http://www.seameo.org/Members/index.htm).

SEAMEO operates under a charter which is available on its webpage at http://www.seameo.org/About/charter.htm. This document expresses the desire of the people of South East Asia to attain

> ...the benefits of peace, prosperity and security through an enlightened citizenry...

It goes on to spell out in some detail, *inter alia*, the purposes and functions of the organisation, its membership, its administrative bodies and their roles and functions, SEAMEO's relations with other organisations, and some of its modes of operating and decision-making.

According to its webpage and in accordance with its charter, SEAMEO provides expert assistance to governments and others in education, science and culture by providing policy advice, programme design, institutional development, staff training, and the design of learning materials. It also has a resources library and a virtual library. To its centres, it offers marketing services and information services (cf. http://www.seameo.org/Services/index.htm). In its webpage, its purpose is stated as:

> ...to promote cooperation in education, science and culture in the Southeast Asian region (http://www.seameo.org/About/vision.htm)

and

> ...to assist the governments of Southeast Asia to develop expertise and excellence in education, science and culture for the promotion of an enlightened and productive citizenry in their respective countries and for furthering the quality of life of all the peoples in the region. (http://www.ait.ac.th/Asia/seameo/seameo.html).

It asserts that its "strongest impact" is in the areas of tropical biology, Education Innovation Technology, Science and Mathematics, Language, Higher Education, Agriculture, Archaeology and Fine Arts, Tropical Medicine and Public Health, Vocational and Technical Education, Distance Education, and Human Resource Development in Indochina. SEAMEO states its vision as

> A dynamic, self reliant, strategic policy-driven and internationally recognized regional organization for strengthening regional understanding and cooperation in education, science and culture for a better quality of life. (http://www.seameo.org/About/vision.htm)

The SEAMEO mission is expressed as

> To enhance regional understanding and cooperation and unity of purpose among Member Countries and achieve a better quality of life through:
> – the establishment of networks and partnerships,
> – the provision of an intellectual forum for policy makers and experts, and
> – the development of regional Centres of Excellence for the promotion of sustainable human resource development.
> (http://www.seameo.org/About/vision.htm)

SEAMEO specifies its goals in these terms:

> – To develop regional Centres of Excellence of international standard,
> – To provide relevant and excellent programmes in training, research and development, information dissemination and policy analysis,
> – To provide the organizational capability to initiate and manage change and development,
> – To strengthen SEAMEO's management capability in order to meet Member Country needs effectively and efficiently,

- To promote Research and Development (R&D) in education, science and culture,
- To enhance collaboration among Member and other Countries and relevant organizations,
- To ensure continued financial viability by exploring alternative sources of funding. (http://www.seameo.org/About/vision.htm)

As noted above, SEAMEO has established Centres of Excellence as one of the means by which to pursue its goals. One such centre is the SEAMEO Regional Language Centre (RELC), which was conceived at the November 1966 meeting of SEAMEC and began operations in July 1968.

4. Geographical and administrative locations

When it commenced operations, RELC was housed in temporary quarters in Singapore and moved to its present site in the impressive RELC Building at 30 Orange Grove Road, Singapore, in May 1972. Its **geographical location** is almost ideal for a teaching institution serving a vast region in South East Asia. The Centre occupies the lower floors of an eighteen-storey building with the RELC International Hotel above it able to provide ample residential facilities for students, some staff and visitors at highly competitive rates. Though the Centre is not in the heart of "downtown" Singapore, it is within easy walking distance of another major shopping area in and around Orchard Road where there are also numerous hotels offering a wide range of accommodation and prices.

In addition, Singapore has always been a major transport hub, RELC staff are available for consultancy services in the member countries themselves, and so the Centre's activities readily extend beyond Singapore throughout the region. Non-member countries can also draw on them, subject to availability (cf. RELC 1992:27).

In brief, the geographical location of RELC in Singapore is ideal: as a major transport hub for the world as well as Asia, Singapore is readily accessed from, and readily accesses, all parts of the region the Centre serves; within Singapore itself, the Centre is conveniently located for students, staff and visitors; Singapore is technologically highly developed and so offers facilities of great value to the Centre in carrying out its regional and world role; to all visitors, Singapore is characterised by its super-efficiency, a quality that permeates all life in Singapore and is evident in RELC itself; and Singapore has an ethos that highly values education and linguistic skills and provides an appropriate setting for a language education centre such as RELC.

With respect to its **administrative location**, as already observed, RELC is a "centre of excellence" established by SEAMEO. It is not a part of a larger entity such as a university and is, to that extent, autonomous but it is a centre of SEAMEO (as its full name of the SEAMEO Regional Language Centre indicates) and its governing bodies are answerable to that organisation. In **governance**, RELC is administered by a

Director under a Governing Board consisting of one representative from each of the SEAMEO member countries appointed by SEAMEC on the recommendation of each country's Minister for Education. The role and functions of the Governing Board are described in RELC documentation thus:

> The Governing Board, under the broad policy guidance of SEAMEC, has the following functions: (a) formulation of policies; (b) nomination of the Director; (c) determination of programmes; (d) approval of the annual budget; (e) evaluation and review of programmes and activities; (f) maintenance of academic standards; (g) approval of the terms and conditions of service of staff. The actual appointment of the Director is made by SEAMEC. (RELC 1992: 4–5)

The plans for the Centre and the direction it is to take are laid out in five-year plans. Initially, its *Development Plan* set the scene for the period from 1968 to 1971. Since then, the Centre's work has been guided by five year plans in the *RELC Blueprints* (see RELC 1971, 1977, 1982, 1987, 1992). These publications typically contain an introduction setting the social and political context or reviewing the achievements of the previous five-year phase, a chapter on the historical background of the Centre, and an extended outline of the "blueprint" or next five-year plan. This "blueprint" covers such areas as the mission and objectives of the Centre and the teaching programmes it will offer, the research and development activities to be undertaken, the staff to undertake the work, the facilities and services to be available (including the library and information services), the Centre's publications, the conferences and workshops to be presented, and the "technical services" to be available to the member countries and educational institutions (cf. RELC 1992).

RELC's **autonomy** would seem to be similar to that of ECML, i.e., it is a centre independent of any other institution though it is funded by and answers ultimately to a multi-government organisation, SEAMEO, which appoints a Board to administer it. Though it is not a part of a university, it has some of the rights and privileges of a university as a result of its cooperation with the National University of Singapore, in conjunction with which and in accordance with the University rules, it offers graduate courses at various levels and grants graduate awards from the certificate level to Masters while a Ph.D. programme in Applied Linguistics was conducted in the period 1982 to 1986 (RELC 1992: 7; also personal communication from the Director, 17 July, 1999).

5. Purpose and mission of the centre

RELC's **mission** is stated in its webpage and in its 1992–96 "blueprint" as

> ...to respond actively to the growing and changing language needs of the SEAMEO member countries ... (http://www.relc.org.sg/noframe.htm)

> ...as articulated in their various human resource development programmes [in order] to contribute, ultimately, to an improved quality of life for all. (RELC 1992:6)

Elsewhere, in a 1993 publication marking the Centre's twenty-fifth anniversary, the Centre's mission is started thus:

> SEAMEO RELC is dedicated to the development of expertise and excellence in language education in the region, and the promotion of cooperation and contact among language professionals of the region and beyond.

Centre documentation available to the present author did not specify **goals**, as such, for the Centre though it did for the various programmes and activities that the Centre offers. General goals for RELC are, however, clearly implicit in the mission statements above and in a statement in the 1992–96 "blueprint" in which the Centre indicates that it aims to pursue excellence in all areas of language education in the region by offering effective training programmes, undertaking research, and disseminating information in order to benefit the language educators of the region who, in turn, are to be "catalysts and agents of change" in their own countries (cf. RELC 1992:6). In some of the documentation, the Centre is very specific on the nature of the participants in its training programmes: they are people who are able to effect change in their systems. In its 1997–2001 blueprint, it states about its teacher education programmes:

> ...RELC seeks to upgrade the skills and knowledge of professionals in specialised fields vital to the overall language curriculum development process of the region's educational systems. ...
>
> ... RELC's target participants will have to be key professionals engaged in specialized fields: language curriculum/materials development, language testing, language teacher education, etc. ...
>
> ...RELC recognizes that the aim of this kind of education is for the trained professionals to participate in their countries' language curriculum development process. ...
>
> ...These are professionals on whom the education systems of SEAMEO countries depend to write tests, develop the curriculum, write coursebooks, evaluate courses, train younger/fellow professionals, undertake research, develop theories and publish. (RELC 1997:3–4)

RELC's **functions and strategic approach** are determined by the fact that it is, essentially, a training institution and so its functions essentially orientate around the provision of a wide range and variety of training programmes both at its headquarters in Singapore and in the member countries. Though the functions of the Centre differ slightly from one five-year plan to another, the basic functions remain the same and take several forms including:

- provision of advanced training programmes for people involved in language education (including teachers, administrators, testers, curriculum specialists, and researchers);

- provision of short programmes for teachers to upgrade their teaching skills;
- provision of advanced courses leading to higher degrees;
- provision of courses by distance education where appropriate;
- undertaking and promoting research and disseminating the results of research relevant to language teaching (especially the teaching of English);
- provision of professional and administrative support to researchers and other scholars in South East Asia and beyond;
- provision of seminars, workshops and conferences to enable language educators in the region to keep up to date;
- the gathering of information on the teaching and learning of languages and its dissemination through the Centre library, information services and publications;
- provision of consultancy and advisory services in order to strengthen language teaching, language policy and its implementation;
- facilitating educational exchanges between the personnel of member countries and facilitating links between educational institutions;
- providing training and other support for English for Specific Purposes and related areas. (cf. RELC 1992:6–7; also RELC 1972:16; 1977:3–7; 1982:12; 1987:6–7; 1997:3 ff.)

6. Activities

The Regional Language Centre is essentially a **training** institution that carries out its mission directly by offering courses of various length in its own right, in conjunction with the National University of Singapore, and with institutions in the SEAMEO member countries, by mounting conferences, seminars and workshops, by offering a range of publications, and, indirectly, by gathering information and resources in its library and making these available to language educators. It is through these direct and indirect training activities that RELC exerts its undoubted influence on language education through the region.

Although RELC cannot be involved in the **language policy** of any member country, the Centre can assist in the implementation of language policy through its training, research and development, and clearinghouse/information service roles. Thus it can and does have a considerable indirect influence through these service roles. Some indication of such a role is given in the 1997–2001 "blueprint" where RELC states:

> RELC is dedicated to the continuing education of these professionals. These are professionals on whom the education systems of SEAMEO countries depend to write tests, develop the curriculum, write coursebooks, evaluate courses, train younger/ fellow professionals, undertake research, develop theories and publish. ...participants

in RELC courses will be required to design programmes as a follow-up to these courses and develop action plans to implement within specified time frames. (RELC 1997:4)

In the same way, though RELC would not be considered to have a specific or direct **think-tank** role such as that of the NFLC, it clearly generates such a role by providing training for those personnel from member countries who are or will be charged with language policy and language education planning roles in their own countries. Equally and similar to ECML, the proliferation of conferences, seminars, workshops and various forms of fellowships and guest lectures that RELC mounts brings together language educators and applied linguists from around the world to consider issues of substance directly relevant to the needs of South East Asia (the blueprints clearly demonstrate that the themes of such events are specifically chosen to respond to the needs of SEAMEO countries) and this activity creates a substantial, if *de facto* or indirect, think-tank role for RELC.

Again, it would not fit the political ethos of many of the South East Asian countries for a Centre such as RELC to arrogate to itself a prominent and direct **leverage** role such as NFLC has. It is a SEAMEO "centre of excellence" and, as such, its role is to assist in the implementation of the policies of the respective SEAMEO countries. Indirectly, however, it clearly has a substantial leverage role in the same way as its "think-tank" role has just been described.

RELC is essentially a service centre for the South East Asian region, providing **services** essentially growing out of its training activities. As, primarily, a training institute, the largest part of RELC's activities consists of the *training programmes* it offers. The nature of the programmes is summed up thus in the RELC webpage:

> The programmes focus on knowledge and related disciplines about language, language teaching and learning. This knowledge is of value to persons engaged in language research as well as those involved in language pedagogy, and language programme administration. (http://www.relc.org.sg/relc.htm)

The programmes are especially designed to impact on and strengthen training programmes in the member countries, in the spirit of RELC's catalytic role in training "agents of change". The programmes take, predominantly, two forms: short, specialist courses in "areas of practice-oriented language teacher education" and Diploma and Masters programmes in applied linguistics conducted, as noted above, in conjunction with the National University of Singapore (cf. http://www.relc.org.sg/relc.htm). The webpage lists the following specific courses:

> A. Degree of Master of Arts in Applied Linguistics
> B. Diploma in Applied Linguistics
> C. Specialist Certificate in Language Testing
> D. Specialist Certificate in Language Curriculum and Materials Development
> E. Specialist Certificate in the Teaching of English for Business and Technology
> (http://www.relc.org.sg/relc.htm)

The webpage goes on to provide entry requirements and course content. Elsewhere in the webpage, there is information on courses in educational technology, video production and word processing offered by RELC's Media Resources Unit. In addition, each of the "blue prints" provides details on the courses to be offered over that five-year period (e.g., RELC 1992: 8–12, 31–40; RELC 1997: 5–7, 20–35).

In addition to these courses, RELC offers two programmes by distance education in collaboration with local institutions, one aimed at High School teachers and offering a Certificate or Diploma in TESL/TEFL and an Advanced Certificate/Diploma in TEFL for tertiary English teachers (RELC 1997:7). Its 1997 2001 plan also indicates that RELC will conduct courses tailored to the special needs of member countries at their request and on topics they request. The courses are conducted when and wherever feasible (e.g., at RELC in Singapore or in-country) and under funding arrangements outside RELC's regular budgeting provisions. Courses shown as available in the 1997–2001 five year period (though others may be requested) include:

   a. Cross Cultural Communication
   b. Language and Culture
   c. Discourse Analysis
   d. Course Evaluation
   e. TESOL/French as a Foreign Language, etc
   f. Teaching of Grammar
   g. Media Technology in Language Teaching
   h. Research in Language Teaching
   i. Supervision of Language Instructors/Teachers (RELC 1997:6)

RELC offers a number of *scholarships and fellowships* to course participants and visiting researchers. Most of the course participants, especially "key personnel in language teaching, planning, administration and research" hold SEAMEO scholarships though fee-paying places are also available (http://www.relc.org.sg/relc.htm). RELC awards a limited number of research fellowships to researchers from the SEAMEO member countries who are undertaking research of benefit to the member country or the SEAMEO region. It also supports Research Scholars and Visiting Fellows from the SEAMEO countries or elsewhere who are undertaking research to fulfil postgraduate degree requirements, pursuing research relevant and beneficial to the member countries, or contributing in other ways to RELC through, for example, preparation of papers for RELC publications, giving public lectures or guest lectures to staff or students, or making video or audiorecordings for RELC use. Financial and other assistance may be provided with the extent of that support varying according to circumstances (cf. RELC 1992:14; 1997:8–10). Each five-year plan lists priority areas that are particularly encouraged for research during that period and so are more likely to receive financial support: in the 1997–2001 period, the areas listed include language learning strategies, textbooks, group work in language classrooms, language testing (especially issues of validity and new techniques), the language curriculum, and language teacher development (RELC 1997: 8–10). In addition, the Centre offers RELC Teaching Fellowships to enable suitably qualified persons from SEAMEO or beyond to teach at the Centre for periods up to six months. This scheme is designed to foster the exchange of ideas in RELC and to contribute to the professional development of language teachers in the SEAMEO region. Distinguished scholars are also invited to teach at RELC, especially during their study leave, and may receive a stipend or other assistance in order to do so (cf. RELC 1997: 10). Similar assistance is often provided, also, for plenary speakers at the RELC Seminar or other event. The present writer has, himself, been fortunate enough to benefit a number of times from one or another of these schemes.

As already indicated, RELC supports *research* activities in various ways. The prime role of RELC is, as we have seen, training and, consequently, the research undertaken at RELC seems largely to be within that context, i.e., research studies that are a part of degree programmes. The 1992–96 blueprint also indicates that staff are encouraged "to undertake research in their areas of specialization and interests" (RELC 1992: 14) but no statement of this sort appears in the relevant section of the 1997–2001 blueprint (RELC 1997: 8–10). The latter refers to assistance to self-supporting researchers to undertake research at RELC, assistance for institutional research commissioned and funded by Ministries of Education or other agencies, and a range of research fellowships to enable professionals from the region to undertake research at RELC provided that the research has been approved by the "proper authorities" and provided that the results are published in the *RELC Journal*. As noted above, each blueprint identifies priority research areas which, without excluding others, the Centre wishes to encourage during the five-year period. (See RELC 1997: 8–10, 1992: 13–17)

The Centre offers a range of *conferences, meetings, seminars and workshops* which attract participants from throughout the region and, in the case of the annual RELC Seminar, from around the world. Beyond the SEAMEO region, RELC is probably best known for its RELC Seminar, which has been presented annually since 1968 and, globally, has almost become the RELC flagship. Despite being called a seminar, it is probably the largest annual, international applied linguistics conference in the Asian-Pacific region, attracting each year a capacity audience in excess of 600 and offering a suite of parallel papers and workshops in addition to major plenary sessions relayed to several lecture halls. The themes for the RELC Seminar are decided in advance for each five-year plan though certain ones such as language testing and assessment recur regularly (e.g., RELC 1997: 10–11; 1992: 25). A "Post-RELC Seminar" is held in Bangkok immediately after the RELC Seminar using some of the speakers from the RELC Seminar and directed at delegates who were unable to go to Singapore for the RELC Seminar. In addition, RELC offers a variety of public, staff and guest lectures, joint symposia and other events mounted in conjunction with institutions around the region (see RELC 1997: 11, 1992: 23–24).

The various events may be held at the RELC headquarters in Singapore or in any of the SEAMEO member countries though the RELC Seminar is always held at the RELC Centre in Singapore where the Centre's own facilities in RELC International Hotel (with lecture halls, classrooms, accommodation and restaurants) together with other nearby accommodation ideally cater for a large conference. In the present writer's experience, if all the events are like the RELC Seminar, they are meticulously organised, highly efficient in their running, and very popular with the participants. They serve an important training purpose, attract senior personnel from the SEAMEO countries who are able to further disseminate their experience in their own systems, and attract into RELC respected applied linguists from around the world to contribute their ideas and further stimulate thought and discussion. Thus, in addition to their important training function, these events go some way to catering for a "think-tank" function in RELC, and add greatly to the Centre's prestige through the quality of what they offer and their efficient organisation. (cf. RELC 1997: 10–11)

Another development at the end of the twentieth century has been to facilitate exchanges between language educators and applied linguists in the region through the internet as part of RELC's Regional Schools Internet Project (see below and *RELC Newsletter,* Vol. 33, No. 1, March 1999: 4).

RELC has an important *information and clearinghouse* role in the region, carried out especially through its library. The Library and Information Centre is designed primarily to support the Centre's training role and to assist in such activities (whether carried out in RELC or across the region) as curriculum development, materials production, publishing, research, and advisory services (cf. http://www.relc.org.sg/noframe.htm; http://www.relc.org.sg/relc.htm). Information on the Library and Information Centre is available on the webpage at http://www.relc.org.sg/libinfo.htm. The aims of the Library and Information Centre are said to be:

> a. to support the training, research and development and other professional activities of the RELC;
> b. to serve as a valuable source of knowledge on language education, teaching and research;
> c. to provide information, facilities and services to various individuals and institutions interested in language teaching. (RELC 1997: 11)

In brief, the Library and Information Centre houses a multimedia collection which comprises over 60,000 print and non-print items (books, periodicals, video and audio cassettes, CD-ROMs, and microforms) and provides the usual array of library services including borrowing, reference and information services, listening and viewing facilities, internet access, and access to other libraries on-line through the Singapore Integrated Library Automation Service (RELC 1992: 18). On-line access is clearly important in extending the availability of the library across the SEAMEO region (and beyond, for that matter) and this service is increasingly being provided. The library allows free membership from the Centre's own staff and fellows, relevant staff in government departments or authorities and other institutions, and it provides a fee-based membership for relevant professionals in non-government institutions and corporations. (See RELC 1997: 11 and http://www.relc.org.sg/libinfo.htm)

The *Media Resources Unit* both services the Centre's training function and helps to disseminate information across the region. This Unit manages the Video and Audio Recording Studios, the language laboratory, and the computer laboratory. It provides services and equipment in support of the training activities, it produces material in support of the distance education programmes, produces video and audio material both to support the various training programmes and for wider dissemination (e.g., recordings of lectures by or interviews with visiting speakers), and conducts training programmes itself in such areas as educational technology, video production, and word processing. It also produces publicity material on the Centre itself (see RELC 1997: 12; http://www.relc.org.sg/relc.htm). The Centre has also supported the extension of educational technology into the schools of the SEAMEO countries through a major project, commenced in 1997, to link the schools via the internet. The "Regional Schools Internet Project" has enabled students in the schools of the SEAMEO countries to exchange information; it is also intended to provide opportunities for language experts, teacher educators and applied linguists to discuss language teaching issues (see *RELC Newsletter*, Vol. 33, No. 1, March 1999: 4).

RELC produces an impressive array of *publications* predominantly focussed on meeting the needs of practising teachers. The publications department produces information material on RELC, professional materials and distance education materials; it markets and distributes RELC publications; and it collaborates with institutions throughout the region to co-publish materials for teachers in the respective countries (cf. RELC 1997: 12–13). Materials produced by RELC include the five year plans or "blueprints", the bi-annual *RELC Journal*, the quarterly *RELC Newsletter*, *Guidelines* (a highly practical publication focussing on classroom practice), various reports (including the Seminar reports, Annual Reports, and reports of the meetings of the Governing Board), *RELC Anthologies*, the *RELC Occasional Papers*, and various instructional materials for class use and distance education (RELC 1997: 12–13; RELC 1992: 20–22; http://www.relc.org.sg/relc.htm).

As already noted, RELC is primarily a training institution and the *projects* it undertakes are mostly of this type (see above). In addition, the Centre is willing to undertake other projects (including consultancies). In its 1997–2001 five-year plan, the Centre indicates that it seeks to join in partnerships with institutions in developed countries to cooperate on projects in SEAMEO countries in language testing, language curriculum and materials development, distance education, and English for Business and Technology (RELC 1997: 7–8). These projects are seen as being transferable to other parts of the SEAMEO region and also provide RELC staff, who are charged with training persons from throughout the SEAMEO countries, with better knowledge of the local conditions encountered by their students. It seems that such cooperation is seen as a way of obtaining additional funds to expand the Centre's work through the region by involving foreign institutions that might contribute to some of the costs.

As noted above, RELC makes its expert staff available for *consultancy services* in the SEAMEO countries. The 1992–97 blueprint lists as one of the "Programmes", "Technical Services to National Programmes and Educational Institutions". Under this programme, RELC offers to make available to member countries the experience and expertise of its staff for consultancy and advisory work in the member countries with the aim of

> …assist[ing] and strengthen[ing] the development of language teaching programmes at the national level. (RELC 1992: 27)

It is not clear from the available documentation how large an activity provision of consultancy services has become. Informal discussion with RELC staffmembers suggests that it is quite substantial though undoubtedly the primary tool for change exercised by RELC is the training that it provides to teachers, administrators, policy-makers and others in the SEAMEO countries and the indirect "think-tank" role that has been referred to above.

The *RELC Examinations Bureau* administers regular and *ad hoc* examinations for a number of overseas organisations, institutions and professional bodies from such countries as Australia, Britain, New Zealand, and the United States. This service commenced in 1989 and, according to the webpage, now administers some 16 regular examinations to more than 30,000 candidates.

At RELC, there is also a *Language Teaching Institute* that offers courses in English and other languages to cater for the needs of Singapore and the other SEAMEO countries. Courses on offer include TESOL, General English, English for Business and Administration, Communication Skills, and English for the Professions. Courses in Chinese include General Mandarin, Conversational Mandarin, and Business Chinese. The webpage listing shows that the language courses range from 24 to 32 hours at a cost of ten to fifteen Singapore dollars per hour (see http://www.relc.org.sg/lti.htm). In its 1997–2001 blueprint, there is indication that the Centre's "direct language teaching" is seen as secondary to its teacher education role and that it commenced this activity to meet the needs of certain regional governments and for revenue purposes. It also provides RELC staff with classroom teaching experience. (see RELC 1997: 14)

In February 1999, the range of languages that RELC teaches was increased when the 34th SEAMEO Council approved "a new vision" for RELC as a centre for the learning of South East Asian languages. In addition to providing opportunities for the study of South East Asian languages at RELC itself, optional immersion programmes are to be offered in the countries of origin of the languages. The report in the March 1999 issue of the *RELC Newsletter* commented:

This was felt to be in line with SEAMEO RELC's mission of developing expertise and excellence in language education in the region, and the promotion of contact and cooperation among language professionals in the region and beyond. Public and private sector executives and professionals from the region and beyond who wish to study a Southeast Asian language will have the opportunity to do a course at SEAMEO RELC. The Centre, which has an established reputation as the English language centre of the region, will seek to establish itself as a centre for the study of Southeast Asian languages as well. (*RELC Newsletter*, Vol. 33, No. 1, March 1999:4)

7. Interactions and links

The basic link for RELC is with its parent organisation, SEAMEO, but it seeks to establish other links both across its region (in order to facilitate its work towards the improvement of language education in the SEAMEO countries and to maximize the effectiveness of its budget), and internationally (to involve worldwide expertise in its own on-going development and in its activities and also to seek to draw additional financial and human resources into its operations).

As a centre with a regional responsibility, we have seen that RELC, in many of its activities, seeks to reach out into the region, into, especially, the SEAMEO member countries to cooperate with their governments, institutions and organisations as well as with the other SEAMEO centres in order to be more aware of and able to respond to their needs and provide services where they are required or most likely to be effective. Thus, in emphasising RELC's regional role, the 1997–2001 five-year plan drew attention to its need for:

a. a greater capacity for regional work;
b. cooperation through institutional linkages;
c. partnership in regional projects; [and]
d. greater regionalisation of its courses. (RELC 1997:3)

We also saw earlier that, in some of its project work, RELC seeks to establish partnership arrangements with institutions in developed countries and to draw on both their expertise and their resources in order to undertake projects in SEAMEO countries (RELC 1997:7–8). Elsewhere in its 1997–2001 blueprint, there is reference to links with at least a dozen overseas universities in order to undertake projects in SEAMEO countries. This activity also enables staff from those universities to spend time working and researching at RELC. In the 1997–2001 period, the blueprint indicates that RELC will seek to establish linkages with universities with a view to cooperating in such areas as joint courses on language testing or TEFL distance education, in the development of distance education materials for teacher education, in running summer courses for language teachers, seminars and workshops, and in accepting staff attachments at

RELC (cf. RELC 1997: 13–14).

In the documentation on RELC's language teacher education programmes (undoubtedly the core of its activities), there is strong indication of the cooperation RELC seeks with regional institutions. Earlier we noted that the higher degrees it offers are offered jointly with the National University of Singapore. The Centre's 1992–97 blueprint also indicates that RELC has established professional links not only with institutions in South East Asia but also in Canada with the purpose of running joint programmes "and/or the sharing of academic resources" (RELC 1992: 7–8). Much of the training RELC offers is building on the basic training language teachers receive in other institutions and so the Centre seeks collaboration to ensure the most appropriate continuing education programmes. The other reason for this cooperation is, again, the need to maximise the funds available for RELC programmes. The Centre states:

> What RELC cannot offer on its own due to constraints[,] it has to cooperate with other institutions to offer in partnership with others. In this it is important that RELC is seen to work with local partners and not for them. There ought to be exchange of knowledge and skills between the partners resulting in benefits for both parties. Thus, such partnerships should be equal and mutually beneficial. (RELC 1997: 3)

As already observed, it is especially through the participants in its programmes that RELC seeks to create links with, and has its most decisive influence on, the education systems throughout the region. As noted earlier, its programmes target senior personnel or persons who are in positions to enable them to act as "agents of change" in their systems. Thus, through them, RELC has strong and influential links with most aspects of the education systems throughout the SEAMEO region (cf. RELC 1992: 6; RELC 1997: 3–4, 13).

The Centre seeks to continue its links with the participants in its training programmes after they have left the Centre. Thus, its webpage indicates that RELC fosters strong ties with its alumni in order to continue to develop their professional competence through workshops and seminars and to foster mutually beneficial exchanges (cf. http://home1.pacific.net.sg/~relcalum/). This approach also enables it to have further influence on the language policies and their implementation in the SEAMEO countries by influencing the personal thought and professional development of its former students who, for the most part, are key personnel in their own education systems. To the extent that such persons, as senior advisers in their own systems, are favourable towards RELC, the Centre itself, which is ultimately dependent on SEAMEO for its survival, becomes more secure. Clearly this use of alumni is a mutually beneficial programme.

Internationally, we have seen that RELC develops strong links beyond the SEAMEO region. Its Examinations Bureau, as we have seen, operates in cooperation with examination bodies, professional accrediting organisations, and institutions in several different countries. Its fellowship programmes allow foreign experts to visit

RELC in different capacities to pursue their own research and writing, to teach on RELC courses, or to participate in joint projects. In the last category, the 1997–2001 blueprint lists a number of courses and activities being conducted with foreign institutions including

- an M.A. in applied linguistics conducted jointly with the National University of Singapore;
- a distance education TEFL project conducted with cooperation from Canada and the Ministry of Education and other institutions in Thailand, Vietnam, Laos, and Cambodia; and
- an English language testing project, a materials development project, and a distance education project with Australian collaboration.

In addition, as noted earlier, RELC is making remote access available to the Library and Information Centre and, through it, to other libraries. This internet-based service enables RELC to maintain links with persons across the region and beyond and to provide a service of considerable value to their daily activities in the education systems of the region or in their academic programmes (whether as students, researchers, teachers or senior administrators) (RELC 1997:19).

All of these activities, the links the Centre creates, its maintenance of an alumni system based on the senior personnel who have attended its training programmes, its frequent invitations to applied linguists from within the SEAMEO region and worldwide, and its publications which are of interest to teachers, administrators, and academics have given RELC a high profile not only in the SEAMEO countries but amongst applied linguists and language educators in most parts of the Asian-Pacific region and, to no small extent, globally.

8. Staffing

RELC draws its academic and support staff from many different ethnic groups and countries: the staff, like the region, is ethnically, racially, linguistically and culturally diverse. Some staff (especially visitors and those on short contracts) live on site in rooms or apartments in the RELC building while others live elsewhere in Singapore. Staff recruited from within the SEAMEO countries are supplemented by persons recruited from elsewhere in Asia, are appointed under various cooperation agreements with foreign countries or institutions, or come for differing periods under one of the visiting fellowship schemes referred to earlier. The academic profile of the staff is comparable with that of similar institutions elsewhere, with most staff having higher degrees and about two-thirds with doctorates. The staff webpage at the time of writing (May 1999) listed seven academic staff, from some half-dozen countries, with qualifications ranging up to doctorates from seven different countries (including

Australia, Britain, India, Malaysia, New Zealand, Singapore and the United States), and with experience of one sort or another claimed in more than ten countries in addition to the SEAMEO region (see http://www.relc.org.sg/staff.htm). The webpage describes its staff in a way which, on the observations of the present writer when he has visited RELC, is not over-stated:

> RELC has reputable and well qualified staff drawn from various countries. With their wide expertise and specializations, they are able to tailor the training programmes to meet the needs of member countries effectively, while keeping themselves abreast of the latest developments in language education. (http://www.relc.org.sg/relc.htm)

The latter part of this claim seems also, from this writer's personal observations, to be accurate. Staff are expected to keep up with the literature but the manner in which RELC is funded and organised also helps greatly to ensure that staff maintain and develop their expertise and allows programmes and expectations to be put in place that assist in this, an essential, indeed pre-requisite, requirement if the claim of RELC to be a regional "centre of excellence" is to be justified. This is further discussed below in the context of the RELC budget (see Section X).

9. Facilities

Anyone who has visited RELC cannot but be impressed by the practical usefulness and quality of the facilities. They are not needlessly lavish but they are of good quality, comfortable, convenient, and flexible enough to cater for regular training programmes or a large conference. It has a 316-seat auditorium with modern lighting, video and sound equipment enabling lectures or conference events to be relayed to other parts of the building to cater for conferences of six to seven hundred participants. In addition, there are some 15 classrooms/conference rooms, meeting rooms, staff offices, administration offices, staff common rooms, recording studios for sound and video, language and computer laboratories, the Library and Information Centre, and a garden where several small conference or class groups can also meet (see RELC 1997: 11–12, 1992: 18–19; http://www.relc.org.sg/relc.htm and http://www.hotel-web.com/relc/singapor/index.htm).

RELC occupies the ground and lower floors of the 18-storey RELC Building, a facility that is part of the Centre's distinctiveness. This facility is open to tourists and other visitors to Singapore but is primarily used for students, staff, conference participants, and other visitors to the Centre. In addition to the facilities just described, the RELC Building accommodates the RELC International Hotel, which has 128 guestrooms, two restaurants, and the same array of communication and other facilities as one generally associates with a modern hotel (see http://www.relc.org.sg/relc.htm and http://www.hotel-web.com/relc/singapor/index.htm).

10. Budget

No information was available to the present writer on the size of the RELC budget though, as a frequent visitor to RELC over the years, the impression has been gained that it is financially secure. RELC itself generates most of the funds it uses: its capacity to do so is impressive and is based principally on revenue derived from the hotel and hospitality services provided through the RELC International Hotel but also from materials, publications, conferences, and services; in addition, students who are not on scholarships are required to pay fees; governments, organisations or institutions that request a programme or service not included in the Centre's budgeted programme may be required to meet the costs or RELC seeks resources for it from cooperating institutions in developed countries (see RELC 1997: 7–8); the Centre has some access to government funds through SEAMEO members and associate members, which provide funds for scholarships and fellowships, while the host government, Singapore, also provides some funds; and RELC seeks sponsorships for some activities from commercial and other organisations (see RELC 1992: 29). The Centre is also able to offer courses on a fee-paying basis, as was noted earlier in relation to certain activities (see also RELC 1997: 14). Finally, as already noted several times, RELC cooperates on projects with other institutions and organisations both within SEAMEO and beyond in order to maximise the resources available to support its activities and in order to include in its programme projects that it, alone, would be unable to finance.

The fact that RELC generates most of its funds itself undoubtedly gives it more discretion in identifying and responding to a greater range of needs than if it were wholly dependent on government funding or competitive project submissions. In this, it gains considerable strength from the diversity of its funding base. Of very considerable importance (and innovation in the funding of centres) is the RELC International Hotel, which is an important core source of funding and gives the Centre substantial independent and discretionary funding, providing a security and other benefits reflected in the nature of the Centre and how it operates, allowing it, amongst other things, to largely determine its own agenda (obviously within its founding terms of reference) and to manage such non-revenue-generating activities as staff development and related activities that maintain the academic excellence of the Centre. This contrasts with self-funding centres wholly dependent on a relatively narrow and inflexible funding base (such as student fees or competitive project funding). A wholly self-funding centre, even one such as CALL within a university supposedly dedicated to academic excellence, must, in contrast to RELC, generate all its revenue from the courses and services it sells or the projects it wins in competition with other university or commercial operators: in such circumstances, margins are, necessarily, small and funding, even for essential things such as staff development, continually becomes eroded. Where funding and funded programmes can be influenced by reasonable argument or where there is a substantial, recurrent and independent source of funding such as provided by RELC's hotel and hospitality enterprise, arguments can be successfully adduced and policies adopted that sustain the quality of the staffing and the centre operations without, for example, the academic maintenance and development activities or the projects and programmes undertaken being mechanistically tied to dollar-based output. This has, for example, enabled RELC to provide frequent seminars, fund visiting researchers and other fellowships, offer guest lectures, provide frequent seminars and conferences, and adopt a reasonable teaching or administration load in comparison with the working week, all of which contribute greatly to staff development, staff morale, and the responsiveness of the Centre's programme to the needs of the region it serves. This funding base also allows the centre to generate an informal "think-tank" role essential both to a lively academic atmosphere in any centre and to creative approaches to meeting the needs of the clientele, in the case of RELC, the region that it serves. Such features as visiting fellowships, guest lectures or conferences, that are of great benefit in terms of staff development, staff morale, maintenance of a high level of expertise, and a strong academic and public profile, are difficult to sustain in a project-funded centre in which each activity has to pay its own way and, indeed, they are impossible to sustain with any degree of frequency, since they generally bring little direct financial return (other than the relatively trivial sale of seats at public lectures or of conference registrations).

11. Constraints and opportunities

The Regional Language Centre serves a clearly defined purpose to seek to raise the quality of language education in the linguistically, culturally and racially diverse South East Asian region. This, in turn, sets certain constraints on the Centre since all its activities are intended to contribute to this common purpose. However, the very nature of that task gives it many opportunities to develop and to engage in interesting and rewarding activities in the broad area of applied linguistics. Like any organisation, it is constrained by what funds it can call on but, to the outside observer, it seems to be adequately funded and to be able to provide high quality service and to have available to it the human and other resources that enable it to maintain appropriate academic standards. The reputation it has gained over the three decades of its existence, the interest of its location in Singapore, the linguistic interest of the region it serves, and the quality of its facilities serve to attract to it expertise from around the world to contribute to and to supplement the Centre's own pool of expertise. The Centre serves a region whose linguistic needs are considerable: this ensures an important role for the Centre for the foreseeable future and provides worthy opportunities for a Centre and staff interested in the practical implementation of applied linguistics and language policy in language education. As the five-year plans reiterate, the challenge for RELC as it enters the new millennium is to meet those regional challenges and to enable the countries whose needs it serves in turn to meet the challenges of the increasing globalisation that now characterises all fields of human endeavour (whether in the area of economy, tourism, human resource management, cultural development or any other).

12. Uniqueness and impact of the centre

RELC has been in existence for more than thirty years. It has clearly established for itself an important role, responding to vital needs, in South East Asia. Its distinctiveness lies in the nature of the regional role it fulfills as a predominantly training institution serving the needs of a highly populous and diverse region. That distinctiveness also grows out of its strategic location, the quality of the services it has provided over the years, the exceptional and very Singaporean efficiency which all visitors encounter in the Centre, and the mode and apparent adequacy of its funding base. The concluding paragraph to the 1997–2001 five-year plan provides an appropriate summary of the nature of RELC, its role and its challenges:

> RELC will be able to fulfill its mission through cooperation and collaboration with language centres/departments in SEAMEO countries. It will stay relevant to the needs of the region if it strives towards greater regionalisation of its activities and finds a niche in the vast demands for improvement of language education in South East Asia. This niche is in language teacher education in specialised fields in providing the kind of education essential to those education systems of countries of South East Asia. For SEAMEO RELC the theme "Language Education for Regionalism" offers the best chance of staying relevant to the needs of SEAMEO countries. (RELC 1997:14)

In 1998, the work of RELC in the region was officially acknowledged when it was accorded the inaugural ASEAN Award of $US100,000 for "outstanding work and contribution towards the promotion and development of regional cooperation" (see *The Straits Times*, 18 November, 1998).

CHAPTER 6

The Centre for Applied Linguistics and Languages (CALL), Griffith University, Brisbane, Queensland, Australia

1. ## Address

   ```
   Centre for Applied Linguistics and Languages,
   Nathan Campus,
   Griffith University,
   Kessells Road,
   Nathan, Brisbane,
   Queensland, 4111,
   Australia.
   Telephone:   61-7-3875-7089
   Fax:         61-7-3875 -7090
   Email:       call@mailbox.gu.edu.au
   Website:     http://www.gu.edu.au/centre/call

   Gold Coast Branch:
   Griffith University English Language Institute,
   Australia Fair,
   Southport,
   Queensland, 4215,
   Australia.
   Telephone:   61-7-5571-4800
   Fax:         61-7-5528-0450
   Email:       call@mailbox.gu.edu.au
   Website:     http://www.gu.edu.au/centre/call
   ```

2. ## The centre

The Centre for Applied Linguistics and Languages (CALL) is different from the centres discussed in earlier chapters in being a university centre, a centre administratively within and answering to a university (viz., Griffith University in Brisbane, the capital city of the State of Queensland, in Australia). The Centre was established by Griffith to promote the teaching of English and other languages, to bridge full-fee paying overseas students ("FFPOS students") into its award courses, to promote research, consultancy services and teaching in applied linguistics, and to raise the University's profile in these areas. However, though established by and within Griffith University, CALL is not funded by it but is wholly self-funding and, indeed, pays substantial levies and other sums to the University. Thus, it is both an academic and a commercial centre.

The strengths of the Centre lie in the synergy and focus characteristic of language centres, as discussed in Chapters 1 and 8, and the flexibility that comes from being self-funding and standing somewhat apart from the "mainstream" of a university while being able to draw upon its academic traditions and aura. Its weaknesses come from the difficulties inherent in bringing together its academic and commercial requirements: on the one hand, it is incumbent on the Centre to pursue academic excellence and to operate within a university, meeting the same academic, procedural, administrative and industrial demands as any other element within the university and answering to an administrative system that is traditionally concerned less with commercial efficiency and competitiveness than with activities and procedures intended to support academic excellence and tradition irrespective of cost; on the other hand, it is equally incumbent on the Centre to be commercial, competitive and entrepreneurial, to raise all its own revenue through course fees and through grants won for research and consultancy projects, to pay substantial dues to the university, and to compete both with entities in its own and other universities that are wholly or partially funded by university grant and with private institutions that operate with lower salaries, overheads and infrastructure and a less complex administrative bureaucracy than exists in most universities. Thus, the Centre's weakness but also its exciting uniqueness comes from bringing together the dual requirements of academic excellence in the fields of language teaching and applied linguistics and its wholly commercial mandate.

The largest set of programmes and the largest revenue earner that the Centre offers is the teaching of English as a Second Language, principally to students from other countries, in the Centre's two branches on the University's main campus at Nathan in Brisbane and at the Centre's branch in commercial premises in Southport on the Gold Coast. The Centre's English language programmes are offered under the marketing name of the Griffith University English Language Institute (GUELI), which is an integral part of CALL and provides, as its largest programmes, English language courses for overseas students in both extended courses ranging upwards from five to forty-five or more weeks and short vacation courses known as Australian Study Tours. In addition, the Centre has provided English language programmes for migrants, English language support services for students in regular award programmes, it seeks contracts with government and industry for courses in languages other than English, it bids for research and consultancy projects in any area of applied linguistics related to second or foreign language education, and it offers courses in applied linguistics at all levels from short courses in language teaching and testing through to graduate courses and research-based degrees (including Ph.Ds.). The only constraint on what can be offered within applied linguistics and second language teaching is that any course or project must be financially viable as a result of attracting sufficient numbers of fee-paying students or of being offered on contract to some funding agency (e.g., a government department, a business firm, or a research or aid agency). The Centre also provides community services that have ranged, for example, across such areas as language testing, the monitoring of afternoon Chinese classes in a primary school, curriculum and syllabus advice through State and national committees, advice on language issues in the justice system, membership of the Advisory Councils of Primary and High Schools, and language education policy in Australia and other countries. CALL's services and programmes are diverse, its research and consultancy services are specialised in such areas as language assessment, language policy, or language-in-education planning but they also cover the full gamut of applied linguistics envisaged as the field that responds to language-related problems or needs in society (cf. Ingram 1980).

3. Background and origin of the centre

The establishment and continuation of CALL can be seen to grow out of the economic, tertiary education, and language policy contexts in Australia. The **export of education in Australia** is relatively recent. Prior to 1986, very few overseas students were permitted to come to Australia to study except on scholarships offered to developing countries under the Australian aid programme with the intention that, on completion of their university studies, the students would return home to contribute to the development of their own countries. Though the scholarship programme has continued in some form, in the mid-1980s, the Australian Government realised that this stance excluded Australia from a high potential export market, the restrictions were lifted, and Australian educational institutions (especially universities but also Technical and Further Education Colleges, schools, and private providers) were positively encouraged to seek full-fee-paying overseas (FFPOS) students. Before their potential clients can obtain student visas, universities and the other institutions have been required to show, first, that accepting overseas students in any field will not adversely affect either the chances of Australian students being enrolled or the quality of the education provided; second, that the level of fees they charge are sufficient to recover all costs (including those from teaching, resources, management and administration, and facilities); and, third, that appropriate steps are being taken to ensure that overseas students have sufficient English to be able to undertake their courses. To meet the English language requirements, overseas students have been required to take an English test (especially the International English Language Testing System, IELTS, which was developed for this purpose in a joint Australian-British project on which the present writer was the Australian representative); in addition, universities, colleges, schools and private providers have established full-fee-based English language teaching entities (usually termed centres or institutes) to provide English as a second language courses to intending students and to sell a variety of English language courses to anyone else who wanted them. The formal courses intended for students and others wishing to raise their English language proficiency for academic or other purposes have become known in Australia as "English Language Intensive Courses for Overseas Students" (or ELICOS). Thus, language centres have grown up in universities, colleges, schools and private institutions with the express purpose of selling English language courses to overseas students: most of these ELICOS Centres have done no more than that but a very few, including CALL, have been more diverse and have matched, to a greater or lesser degree, the type of language centre described in Chapter 1, Section II and the subject of this book.

The second element of the context in which CALL was created has been the Australian **language policy context**. Since the late 1970s, a great deal of interest had been generated in Australia in language policy and in an expanded and higher quality language education system. In 1978, the present writer produced the initial paper arguing the case for a national policy on languages in Australia (Ingram 1979) and, prior to publication, distributed it in mimeograph form to Federal and State government ministers, parliamentarians, and departments. This, together with other influences and other lobbying, eventually led, in 1982–84, to a Senate inquiry into the need for a national policy on languages (SSCEA 1984) and the adoption, in 1987, of the first national policy on languages (Lo Bianco 1987). The 1987 policy was replaced in 1991 by the Australian Language and Literacy Policy (ALLP), which, significantly, placed increased emphasis on economic factors and the enhancement of Australia's international trading competitiveness (DEET 1991 and 1991a). In turn, the ALLP was supplemented in 1994 by the National Asian Languages/Studies Strategy for Australian Schools (COAG 1994). In the meantime, every State and Territory in Australia developed and adopted its own language and/or language education policies, a great deal of money was poured by all governments into the provision of improved language education and other language-related services (e.g., advisory services to government and industry, interpreting and translation services, library support, and multilingual publications) and, not least, into research and development activities in support of the language and language education policies. Universities and other institutions, in their turn, re-examined their language education programmes and the teaching of applied linguistics and sought projects and established centres that might win some of the available funds to increase their own research and consultancy profiles.

Thus, through the second half of the 1980s and the first half of the 1990s, there was a strongly supportive environment for universities to foster teaching and research in applied linguistics, to use commercial ventures such as ELICOS and community language programmes to generate funds to further expand this activity, and to comprehensively market their available courses to overseas students. Regrettably, with the change in the Federal Government from Labor to the Liberal-National Coalition in 1996 and the subsequent demise of the National Languages and Literacy Institute of

Australia, research funding in the language and language education area virtually disappeared, language policy in the second language area has stagnated, and a major funding source for centres such as CALL has disappeared.

The third element in the creation of the Centre for Applied Linguistics and Languages and a strongly determining influence on how it operates is the **university context** in which it exists. Language centres in Australia, such as CALL, largely developed as one response to the increasing imperatives on Australian universities to generate more and more of their own revenue (especially by attracting overseas students) and to go beyond traditional government sources to expand their research programme. ELICOS Centres have generally, therefore, been required to recover all or most of their costs, to operate their courses profitably, and, in the case of university centres, to bridge overseas students into the more lucrative award courses. In some instances, such as CALL, they have, as already noted, broadened their activities into research, consultancies, and courses in applied linguistics that were either cross-subsidised from the profits on the English language courses or were, themselves, operated profitably. Thus, the creation of CALL by Griffith University was a response to the changing context of tertiary education in Australia in a period when funding pressures have risen dramatically and universities have been obliged by government to generate increasing proportions of their own revenue.

Griffith University was initially established in 1972, during a period of dramatic growth and considerable innovation in tertiary education in Australia, and it was something more than a decade later that the influences just described emerged. The creation of a unique element such as the Centre for Applied Linguistics and Languages, with its academic and commercial mandates within a wholly self-funding requirement, fits well, if innovatively, both within the broad context of tertiary education and with many of the features on which Griffith prides itself. Griffith has been, from its establishment, an innovative institution placing great emphasis on inter-disciplinary studies and on identifying and responding to societal need. The Foreword to its strategic plan states:

> Griffith University is widely recognised as one of the most creative and influential universities in the Asia-Pacific region.
>
> This reputation has its basis in the University's historical commitment to thinking "outside the square". Innovative courses, cross-disciplinary teaching and research, and flexible and entrepreneurial responses to community needs have characterised the University's work. ...
>
> ...it is our intention to continue building a University that can think and act both locally and globally. (Griffith University 1999: 1)

Elsewhere in its strategic plan, the University indicates that it will "increase the number of internationally recognised centres of excellence" across the University, it will respond "creatively to local, national and global change by embracing diversity and nurturing innovation to position the University at the forefront" of "research needs and opportunities", it will develop strategic alliances and partnerships "to enhance the quality and range of its work by building strong networks, both on-shore and off-shore", and it will seek to increase its income by, amongst other strategies, "increasing the number of fee-paying students" (Griffith University 1999: 2, 7, 12).

The Centre for Applied Linguistics and Languages (CALL) was established by the Griffith University Council as a wholly self-funding "allied centre" of the University in 1989 (see CALL Constitution, Document Number 97/0001 and Council minutes 14/89 of 7 August, 1989, 16/89 of 2 October 1989, and 1/97 of 3 February 1997). It commenced operations with the appointment of the founding Director (the present writer) on 12 February, 1990. Prior to this, a similar centre, performing similar functions, the Institute of Applied Linguistics, had been operating successfully since 1986 on the nearby Mount Gravatt Campus of the then Brisbane College of Advanced Education. In the lead-up to the major re-organisation of higher education that occurred in Australia around 1989–1990, Griffith had sought to take over the Institute but when this was prevented by government decision, the University created the Centre and advertised a Chair in Applied Linguistics, eventually appointing the then Institute Director as Professor of Applied Linguistics and Director of the new Centre for Applied Linguistics and Languages (CALL). CALL was originally established as a centre within the Faculty of Asian and International Studies but, from February 1997, it became an independent centre within the Arts Group of the University, answering to a Pro-Vice-Chancellor and, in practice, with the equivalent of School status (see CALL Constitution, Document 97/0001, issued 2/97, Clause 1).

Thus, the establishment of the Centre for Applied Linguistics and Languages with its broad terms of reference within applied linguistics and second language education (including teaching English to overseas students) fitted well with the national language policies, with Australia's broad economic and tertiary education contexts, and with the distinctive context and aspirations of Griffith University.

4. Geographical and administrative locations

The **geographical location** of CALL is, at present, in two branches: the main branch on the University's Nathan Campus in Brisbane and the other in the Australia Fair commercial complex in Southport on the Gold Coast, Australia's premier holiday resort, a hundred kilometres south of Brisbane. At the time of writing (1998–2000), CALL has also spent considerable time and effort in negotiating to open branches or provide some of its teaching programmes overseas (in such places as China, Hong Kong, India, Japan and Thailand) as joint venture operations with local institutions.

CALL's various locations have been chosen for several reasons similar to those discussed in Chapter 8 in terms of the locations of language centres in general. First, the main branch is on the main campus of the University because that facilitates interaction with the University administration and many of the Schools. Second, many overseas students prefer to be on campus for reasons of prestige or because they intend to go on to study in other courses and prefer the familiarity of having done their English studies on the same campus. Third, the other facilities of the University are readily available to the Centre and to its students (e.g., library, computer classrooms, sporting venues, student clubs, restaurants, and other services). However, the facilities that CALL has had to use on the Nathan campus have been inferior, the scope for expansion there has been limited by the limited availability of office and teaching space (the University generally has been pressed for space on all its campuses), and, when the Centre was persuaded to expand to service the needs of the University's Gold Coast campus, it became necessary to look off-campus to find adequate facilities. Consequently, CALL leased space in commercial premises, which it renovated to provide high quality facilities with a superb outlook over the "Broadwater", a beautiful inlet separating Southport and Surfers' Paradise, fringed on the other side by some of the Gold Coast's major tourist attractions, and with surfing beaches in the distance. Though such facilities are expensive to rent, because they are off-campus, the Centre pays lower overheads to the University for the students that are there and, indeed, when the Gold Coast branch is working to capacity, the per capita overhead costs (including rent) will be less than the Centre pays on the Nathan campus (further discussed in Chapter 8, Section IV, *Facilities*). Being off-campus, it also avoids some of the "hidden" but none the less substantial costs involved in being on-campus where, for example, even though the Centre is self-funding, it is expected to provide gratuitous advice on language matters to the University and its staff are expected to participate in the University's administrative and academic committee systems (or are vulnerable to criticism if they don't). In addition, having both on-campus and off-campus branches in the State capital and in a popular tourist resort enables the Centre to cater for a wider range of clientele.

As noted above, the Centre is also seeking to open branches or commence other operations overseas in order to extend its market, especially following the Asian economic crisis that erupted in 1997–98, and to provide an alternative way of responding to the large market potential of countries such as China, Hong Kong, India, Japan and Thailand. By opening branches overseas, it is possible for the Centre to allow students to learn English or study applied linguistics through the centre but at lower cost than if they have to travel to Australia. In addition, off-shore operations can cater for those students (whether in English or in aspects of applied linguistics) who wish to extend their skills for local purposes (e.g., to increase their local employability) and want an international certificate but do not wish or do not have the resources to travel overseas. The exercise of working in a joint venture with an overseas institution and responding to the distinctive needs of a foreign context also provides a powerful stimulus to the Centre itself and to its staff, raising new challenges, demanding new approaches to applied linguistics and its teaching, and helping to create a more lively and creative institution. One immediate effect of these developments, for example, has been to encourage Centre staff to make more of their programmes available by "flexible learning" methods using both hardcopy and internet so enabling overseas students to take applied linguistics courses through CALL without leaving their home countries.

CALL's **administrative location** is within the University's Arts Group, one of four groups of Schools, the focal administrative units in the University. In practice, CALL is equivalent in status to a School (but not in funding since it is wholly self-funding and pays dues to the University) and, like a Head of School, the Director answers directly to the Pro-Vice-Chancellor (Arts) (Griffith University Calendar: D64.14, CALL Constitution, Document Number 97/0001, issued 2/97, Clause 4). Though it has its own Constitution and governance arrangements, the Centre is required, under its Constitution, to operate

> within the general policies of the University and, in particular, the policy on "the Centres and Institutes — Organisation" (1373/77) and amendments made thereto. (CALL Constitution, Document Number 97/0001, issued 2/97, Clause 2(1))

It is thus integrated within the University's academic and administrative structures, which acknowledges the fact that, though it is a commercial centre required to generate all its own revenue and to be entrepreneurial in marketing its services and in responding to society's or potential clients' needs, it is also an academic element required to meet the same array of staffing, programme and quality assurance procedures as do all other academic elements.

CALL's status as a stand-alone centre dates only since February 1997 (see Griffith University Calendar: D64.14, CALL Constitution, Document Number 97/0001, issued 2/97). Previously, like most centres in the University, it was administratively within a faculty, the Faculty of Asian and International Studies (AIS), with the Director answering to the Dean of the Faculty. The principal reasons for this location were, first, a convention that existed at the time the Centre was founded that all allied centres would sit within a Faculty and answer to a Dean and, second, the fact that the Dean of AIS in 1989 had assisted in the creation of the Centre. However, the relationship with the Faculty of AIS became very unsatisfactory for many reasons including these:

1. The Centre had no specific role in the Faculty and had its own purposes, roles and functions, which were no more or less relevant to AIS than to any other Faculty in the University. The services the Centre provides to the University (in particular, the bridging of overseas students into degree programmes) are and were equally relevant to all Faculties.

2. Successive Deans and Faculty Managers lacked knowledge or experience of applied linguistics and of management of self-funding centres, the Centre was not represented on the Faculty Standing Committee or any other Faculty committee, but the Deans,

Faculty Managers and Standing Committee had the power to impose decisions on the Centre, did so regularly and, often, inappropriately.

3. Academic staff were appointed to carry out Centre duties as teachers, researchers, or support staff, their job descriptions were written by the Centre to fit their duties, but, at that time, they were appointed by the university to academic salary scales that carried academic work expectations (especially with regard to research and publishing) which, in the case of the English language teachers, were inappropriate and caused continual friction, especially with the Faculty Staffing Committee and Deans. More recently a separate "enterprise bargaining" agreement has been finalised setting special employment conditions for ELICOS teachers.

4. The Faculty required that the Centre's fully self-funding status be applied to each programme and each project individually with the adverse effects discussed more fully in Chapter 8, especially in preventing cross-subsidisation of research and precluding the Centre from bidding for major research grants which, in Australia, do not allow the charging of chief investigator salaries or infrastructure costs. It also meant that academic staff were discouraged from publishing significantly since project funding rarely covered more than preparation of a report.

5. In the first eighteen months of the Centre's existence, the Faculty supported the University in financial requirements on the Centre that were unrealistic and plunged the Centre into a heavy debt that it took several years to eradicate. The worst of these was to require the Centre to pay excessive commissions to a joint venture operation between the University and a foreign company intended to market the Centre's programmes. These commissions (40% of the fees from every student that entered CALL, irrespective of source) were contrary to the Centre's advice and meant that every student that entered CALL, whether recruited by the joint venture operation or not, put the Centre further into debt. That debt was further aggravated by the fact that part of the arrangement with the foreign company required it to provide establishment funds for the Centre, the funds were handed over to the University but not passed on to the Centre and, when the joint venture collapsed two years later, the funds were returned to the company together with commercial interest ultimately paid by the Centre.

6. Staffing decisions were made by a selection committee on which the Centre was generally represented though not necessarily in an effective majority, the decisions had to be approved by the Faculty, and, on a number of occasions, key appointments made proved to be very inappropriate and inevitably took years to correct.

7. The Faculty was responsible for the Centre's obligatory triennial reviews. These reviews invariably ignored normal procedures, demonstrated little understanding of the parameters within which the Centre was required to operate, tended to target key individuals, and made no attempt to verify assertions whatever their source. The result

was that the reviews, especially the one that preceded and triggered the Centre's removal from the Faculty, served no useful purpose, created a heavy additional workload as the Centre sought to correct the reviewers' errors, and caused bitter antagonisms between the Centre and the Faculty.

8. Decision-making and approval procedures were very slow and often failed to accommodate the Centre's needs for quick decisions to meet project submission deadlines, staffing requirements, or commercial opportunities. Very often, research and other projects had to proceed regardless and contracts were not agreed and signed off within the university until the project was almost over. On one occasion, for example, when it had become evident that the Centre had out-grown its original administrative structure, the Centre Director proposed a review: it took 15 months before approvals were through and the review commenced, the external consultant who conducted the review was recommended by the Faculty, and the outcome of the review was, it transpired subsequently, strongly dictated by the Faculty, proved inadequate, and was radically revised a short time later when the Centre became a stand-alone Centre in the Arts Group.

Despite such problems, the impression should not be left that Griffith University as a whole has been a deliberately inhospitable home for the Centre or for the type of commercial, academic operation that it is. On the contrary, the Centre has received considerable support and encouragement from most of the senior hierarchy of the University. The source of the difficulties (other than where antagonistic individuals might have been involved) has been the fact that the traditional management rules and procedures of a university often do not match the requirements of a wholly self-funding, commercial and academic centre such as CALL. The University has had to accommodate to this new entity just as much as staff working within the Centre have had to accommodate the requirements of a commercial operation to the rules and procedures of the university. In such circumstances demanding significant accommodation and change on both sides but especially by a university unused to commercial mandates and with a bureaucracy not unreasonably jealous of its traditional ways of doing things, tensions were inevitable, not so much with the senior management that had the broader vision but with the bureaucracy charged with implementing what (at best) it saw as the University's established ways of doing things. The fact that neither the University nor the Centre has chosen to weaken the relationship between the Centre and the University illustrates the fact that the relationship between the two has, overall, been satisfactory and mutually advantageous. In any case, though CALL is a wholly self-funding unit, operating along commercial lines, it has as strong academic interests as any School or Faculty in a university. Indeed, one of the distinctive features of CALL as an ELICOS provider is the fact that its language programmes exist within a strong academic context both in the Centre and in the University. Unlike commercial operations in some universities, the Centre has not been corporatised or moved outside of the regular university structure. It has remained within the regular university academic and administrative structure, not least (from CALL's point of view) in order to emphasise its academic interests in applied linguistics and the academic worth of all its courses (including its language programmes, the non-award courses in such areas as language assessment, and its graduate award courses which range from Graduate Certificates in aspects of applied linguistics to Ph.D. research degrees supervised by CALL staff). Its location within the University's academic and administrative structures also reflect the direct contributions that the Centre makes to the academic life of the University by cooperating with other elements in joint programmes of different sorts, providing advice on language matters, and bridging large numbers of FFPOS students into their award courses. In fact, the approval processes for courses within CALL are no less arduous than for award courses elsewhere in the University and, in some respects, are more arduous since there are external accreditation requirements that have to be met as well as the University's and the Centre's own internal demands. The same accreditation system is used for the Centre's award courses as elsewhere in the University since Graduate Certificates, Diplomas or Degrees are awards of the University and not just of any element within it, the Centre has its own internal accreditation or quality assurance processes through its own committee structures, and, in addition, English language courses for overseas students and the Centre itself (including each of its branches) are required, under Federal Government legislation and regulations, to be accredited and regularly re-accredited by the National ELICOS Accreditation Scheme (NEAS), which can (and does) make regular inspections and spot checks. In addition, like any other element within the University, the Centre is required to implement the University's quite arduous (and, therefore, for CALL, quite costly) academic and administrative performance review schemes which are an integral part of the University's productivity and quality assurance programmes. In brief, CALL's location within the University's academic and administrative structures emphasises the Centre's nature as an academic element and requires that it meet the same academic quality assurance standards as any other academic element and, indeed, it has other external quality assurance requirements to meet as the result of being an accredited ELICOS provider.

The model of **governance** for CALL has changed in recent years as it moved out of a Faculty to become a stand-alone centre answering to the Group Pro-Vice-Chancellor (Arts). The Centre, as noted earlier, is integrated into the University's academic and administrative structures and has equivalent status to that of a School of the University with the academic line of authority being from the Head of School/Director to the Group Pro-Vice-Chancellor for that broad discipline area, Deputy Vice-Chancellors and Vice-Chancellor while, on administrative matters, the Manager (who answers to the Director within the Centre) relates to the Pro-Vice-Chancellor (Administration). The University endorses participatory decision-making and problem-solving (see Griffith University 1999:3) but, within a School and within the Centre, the Head of

School or Director is empowered to act executively within University policies (CALL Constitution, Document Number 97/0001, issued 2/97, Clause 5(1)). Hence, all committees are essentially advisory to the Head of School or Director rather than deliberative but, in CALL, except where issues of commercial competitiveness or compatibility with the Centre's basic terms of reference determine otherwise, most issues are referred through committees to enable staff to contribute their knowledge and experience and be involved in the decision-making process, and the committee recommendations are generally respected. In addition to the decision-making structure, allied centres in the University are required to have an Advisory Committee, largely representative of actual or potential clientele of the centre and able to include persons from local industry, the education systems, the ethnic communities, students, and, in particular, the University. The Advisory Committee officially meets twice a year whereas the other committees in CALL meet either monthly or two-monthly.

The terms of reference under which CALL operates are laid out in the CALL Constitution (see Griffith University Calendar: D64.14) and in the Centre documents *Revision of CALL Administrative Structure: a Submission* and *Centre for Applied Linguistics and Languages [CALL]: Arrangements for Governance (Revised July 28, 1998–97/0291)*.

CALL is an unusually complex centre with a wide range of activities (see Section VI), two branches within Australia, and it is in the process of establishing joint venture operations overseas in collaboration with foreign institutions. Staff numbers (academic, teaching and administrative support staff) fluctuate through the year according to the size of the teaching programme and the other projects under way but average about 60. The committee structure (as elaborated in document 97/0291) has been developed to provide maximum opportunity for all staff to contribute their knowledge, insights and experience to the decision-making process and to encourage as much creativity and innovation as possible within the constraints of the Centre's terms of reference in applied linguistics and second language education.

The senior committee in the Centre, the one through which all other committees recommend to the Director, is the *CALL Committee*, which is responsible for overall Centre policy and management. The other committees operate officially as sub-committees of the CALL committee and are

- *Academic Planning, Teaching and Learning*, which advises on any matter that affects academic planning, the teaching programme, curriculum development, accreditation, staff development, and quality assurance;
- *Resources*, which monitors and approves the budget and any other matter that impinges on the financial, material, human, or other resources of the Centre;
- *External Relations*, which oversights CALL's relations with other bodies (including other elements in the University and external organisations such as professional

bodies, industry, government and the wider community) and, in particular, the marketing of CALL's programmes and services;
- *Applied Linguistics*, which oversights and advises on the Centre's research agenda and its non-award and graduate courses in applied linguistics; and, as noted earlier, the
- *Advisory Committee*, which seeks to draw on advice from the wider community in the University and beyond to whose needs the Centre seeks to respond, especially in relation to the Centre's strategic direction and its performance and public image.

At the time of writing, the Academic Planning, Teaching and Learning Committee and the Applied Linguistics Committee were in the process of amalgamation, partly to reduce the number of committees and partly to clarify responsibility for courses in the Centre. Other *ad hoc* committees are established from time to time for specific purposes (such as staff selection or management of a particular project) and meetings may also be called of all or a section of the Centre staff. All the committees comprise relevant *ex officio* staff with responsibilities in areas relevant to the committee's responsibilities together with elected representatives of academic, teaching and general staff.

This committee structure is relatively new in the Centre and was established after the Centre moved out of a Faculty to become a decision-making element in its own right within the Arts Group. Thus the decision-making and advisory process changed from an external one largely imposing Faculty decisions on the Centre whenever the opportunity existed to an internal one where the persons working in the Centre are integrally involved in the decision-making process, specifically advising the Director, who answers to the Pro-Vice-Chancellor (Arts). Though, under the University's governance model and the Centre's constitution, decision-making rests with the Director while the committees are advisory to the Director rather than deliberative, this committee structure was designed to implement, as far as practicable, a participatory or shared decision-making process. At the same time, it was designed to respect, as discussed in Chapter 8, the commercial need to have a process that is economical of time (and hence costs), that allows rapid decision-making, where that is required for commercial and competitive purposes, that respects confidentiality where that is necessary for reasons of personnel management or commercial competitiveness, and that facilitates, in the broad management and planning of the Centre, a broad vision of the Centre's role and potential and a readiness to grasp at new academic and commercial possibilities that, it is hoped, might permeate through the committees to the staff as a whole. Though the various committees recommend to the Director, this process can be short-circuited when decision-making deadlines are short or when (occasionally) confidentiality is paramount. Nevertheless, in practice, the Director and the Centre are not autonomous since the Centre has to operate within the University's rules, procedures, and hierarchy and decisions can be imposed by the Pro-Vice-

Chancellor and his advisers or by other elements of the University bureaucracy.

As an "allied centre" of the University, the Centre is also subject to formal triennial reviews which have the power, under the Centre's constitution, to determine whether it continues to exist and, if so, in what form. In principle, such regular reviews are important to assure the University, clients and the Centre itself that quality is being maintained, that administrative procedures are appropriate and efficient, that the Centre is identifying and meeting real needs, and, in the case of a self-funding centre, that it continues to be commercially viable. However, such reviews (and the other accreditation and quality assurance procedures that CALL goes through) are costly of time and, therefore, impose a substantial financial burden on the Centre's resources. Where they are carried out, therefore, it is essential that they make a real contribution to the successful operation of the Centre and, to this end, it is essential that they be carried out effectively, by competent and ethical persons capable of genuinely investigating and evaluating rather than basing their reports on empty, dishonest or untested hearsay, and by persons with expertise in applied linguistics and the management of self-funding centres. In CALL's experience, achieving such a balanced and competent review for a centre that is unique in its roles, functions and management expectations is very difficult.

The current **administrative structure** within the Centre was developed and progressively implemented from late 1997 to enhance the academic and research strengths of the Centre, to strengthen the inter-dependence of, interaction between, and shared values of the different but complementary sectors of the Centre, and to ensure adequate and flexible administrative support for all sectors (see Centre for Applied Linguistics and Languages: *Revision of CALL Administrative Structure: A Submission, Version 3, Revised February 1998*. Mimeograph). The integration of all sectors in the Centre, considered vital to the cohesion and competitiveness of the Centre, is underlined by the fact, unique in a University which has traditionally separated the academic and administrative lines of authority and accountability, that the Director is a senior academic (whose substantive position is at professorial level) but the Deputy Director and Manager, who is Acting Director in the Director's absence, is an administrative appointment. What positions are filled, whether the duties of two or more positions are merged, and whether positions are filled casually or on contracts of different lengths are determined by the level of the Centre's actual and prospective activities (and hence its finances).

The Centre's academic (including research and teaching) interests fall within two broad sectors "Language Programmes", staffed by language teachers (principally, teachers of English as a Second Language) and "Applied Linguistics", formerly known as "Research, Consultancies and Applied Linguistics" and staffed by academics with responsibilities for research, provision of consultancy services in applied linguistics, the teaching of award and non-award courses in applied linguistics, and the supervision of research higher degree students (including Ph.Ds.). In practice, there is no rigid barrier between the two sectors so that staff in one sector are able to contribute to work in the other as their regular duties, their interests, and Centre resources permit. The academic organisational model is shown in Chart One.

This academic organisation is complemented by an administrative structure comprising two functional areas: the Corporate Services Group and Business and Education Operations. The Corporate Services Group provides support for all the Centre's activities at both branches and includes the finance, media services, and, potentially, "commercial development and research" functions and relevant administrative assistants. The Business and Education Operations Group is directly responsible for the daily educational operations of the Centre's activities, giving administrative support to them. The administration organisational model is shown in Chart Two.

It should be emphasised that the boxes in Charts One and Two represent, in the first instance, roles, two or more of which may be undertaken by one person and become separate positions or merge again as changes occur in the level of the Centre's activities, the particular projects and programmes that are operating, and budget requirements. So, for instance, with the decline in language-specific research funding in Australia since 1996 and an increase in the number of graduate courses offered by CALL, the number of Senior Research Fellows was reduced to two, one with the specific duties of coordinating the Centre's Testing Services and the other with responsibility for the Centre's Postgraduate Studies. Both Senior Research Fellows and the Director also engage in research and consultancy activities, teach applied linguistics as required, and supervise research higher degree students.

The importance of centres having at least some degree of **autonomy** in decision-making and management is a recurrent theme throughout this book. A centre integrated into and answerable through a university's academic and administrative structures as CALL is cannot be considered autonomous: any decision made within the Centre can be overridden by others in the university hierarchy or administrative bureaucracy and the Centre is required to conform to the University's rules and procedures. Nevertheless, as the quite elaborate governance and administrative arrangements just described suggest, the Centre is largely self-sufficient in its operations even though it is required to pay substantial administrative levies to the University. It is vitally important for the Centre to be self-sufficient in its day-to-day operations (within the constraints of the University's procedures) since the Centre has to operate as a wholly self-funding, commercial and entrepreneurial academic centre in which courses and projects turn over at frequent intervals throughout the year, students enrol and graduate at frequent intervals, and there is a relatively high proportion of casual and short-term contract staff continually starting and finishing their employment in the Centre.

Such distinctive features of the administrative requirements of the Centre make for operational demands that are quite different from those in the rest of the University where courses are based, largely, around two semesters with comparatively long periods of reduced activity between semesters. This incompatibility is reflected in many aspects of the day-to-day management of the Centre including financial reporting, timetabling and room allocation, and student administration. Problems of student administration, for example, arose from the the fact that, for many years until a new University-wide database was developed, the University database could not accommodate the Centre's needs and a separate Centre database had to be maintained with difficult corollaries for such needs as the tracking of students through their time in the University and, consequently, for the University's ability to acknowledge the magnitude of CALL's role in bridging overseas students into degree programmes.

As discussed in Chapter 8 and elsewhere in this chapter, though there are advantages to be gained from being an integral part of a university, serious difficulties have, at times, arisen as a result of CALL's lack of complete autonomy and the *ex officio* capacity of persons with no knowledge of applied linguistics or of the management requirements of and constraints on commercial operations to impose decisions on the Centre. Not the least examples of these difficulties have been the disputes that have occurred following incompetent reviews, the heavy debts caused by early commission requirements (referred to earlier), and the temporary financial difficulties that followed a period when the accounts were not closely monitored at a time of rapid changes in the market that coincided with a demand from the University that Centre finance staff devote their time to matching the Centre's books with the University's own auditing and accounting requirements rather than maintain their regular detailed monitoring and reporting of the Centre's financial performance. Another persistent problem, making it difficult to maintain the Centre's national and international profile and hence its ability to attract and win research and consultancy contracts, has been the University's failure to accept that it is vital that funds be available to enable senior staff to present even plenary papers at national and international conferences or to accept international fellowship invitations, the University's attitude having been that such events may be personally prestigious but bring little if any benefit (i.e., no direct financial benefit) to the Centre or the University. In reality, such events are essential both for the maintenance of academic excellence and, from a purely commercial point of view, for the Centre to demonstrate its excellence, report on research undertaken, and keep its name before the clients (whether research funders, potential consultancy clients, or teachers of language students) who provide the Centre's business. Such problems, again, arose not from ill-will or incompetence on the part of the University bureaucracy but out of the tension between traditional management styles in a university and the distinctive requirements of managing a commercial, entrepreneurial and academic centre.

Nevertheless, the reduced level of the Centre's autonomy as a result of being within the University's administrative structures has, overall, been considered unavoidable (even if, sometimes, distressing), granted the importance of the Centre's academic status and activities and its status as a university entity. In any case, as stated earlier, despite the problems that have been referred to, especially those arising from the Centre's initial location within an irrelevant and intrusive faculty, Griffith University has, on balance, been a congenial and generally supportive home for the Centre. The problems and difficulties that have arisen have, as stated previously, generally occurred as a result of the University's unfamiliarity with and need to accommodate to the requirements of a different type of commercial, academic operation rather than as a result of any particular malevolence towards the Centre. The problems have largely arisen out of the tension between traditional academic management expectations and the requirements of a commercial, entrepreneurial and academic centre.

The University would probably also argue that the fact that the Centre is backed by a multi-million dollar institution has been of great importance when the Centre has experienced financial difficulties as occurred during its establishment phase and following the Asian economic crisis and that this benefit more than compensates for any loss of autonomy. On the other hand, CALL would argue that such support is appropriate when some, at least, of the difficulties the Centre has encountered were caused by the University's own decisions to impose excessive commissions, to require substantial levies, and to accept without acknowledgement the very large financial contributions that the Centre routinely makes to the University. These contributions, which underline the Centre's lack of autonomy and, conversely (and beneficially), the University's obligations to stand by the Centre during times of financial difficulty, have taken such forms as these:

- substantial *per capita* administrative and capital levies (between $¼ and ½ million annually) paid on foreign students;
- charges deducted from the tuition fees or grants paid by or for the overseas and Australian students in its Graduate Certificate and Ph.D. programmes;
- fees (originally 7% now 10%) paid on all project, consultancy or research contracts signed on CALL's behalf;
- other occasional payments such as a $20,000 contribution to outfitting a new building for the then newly established School of Languages and Linguistics;
- a favourable impact on the University's research quantum which is now passed on to the Centre but originally was retained by the host Faculty,
- the considerable services (gratuitous to the University but expensive to CALL) that Centre staff provide to the University in the form of committee activities and advice on language matters, and
- the very substantial fees the University receives from the award course students that CALL bridges into other Schools. (The actual level of this contribution is difficult to estimate because it depends on the number of ELICOS students who go on to award courses, the fees for the particular courses entered, whether the students end up attending Griffith or going elsewhere, and how long they spend in

their degree programmes but, on a conservative estimate, this contribution ranges upwards from about $1 million a year for each year that a cohort leaving CALL is in the University. In other words, in any one year, students that CALL has bridged into award courses are probably contributing considerably in excess of $3 million dollars to University revenue. Whereas CALL pays a marketing levy on students attracted by the University's marketing arm into Centre courses, no commission is paid to the Centre for students it bridges into courses elsewhere in the University.)

To sum up, though the Centre is essentially self-sufficient in its operations, its location within the administrative structure of the University means that it is not and cannot be autonomous. Decisions made within the Centre are subject to ratification or veto elsewhere in the University, substantial direct and indirect financial contributions are made to the University using funds generated by the Centre, and the tension between academic and commercial exigencies becomes great when administrative decisions are made by persons elsewhere in the University who may have the best intentions in the world but who have not understood the delicate balance required between commercial and academic considerations.

Apart from its integration within the University, the other major intrusion on the Centre's independence comes from the requirements of the National ELICOS Accreditation Scheme (NEAS). As noted earlier, NEAS has been established under Federal government legislation with the aim of ensuring maintenance of high standards in the ELICOS industry in Australia. Institutions that wish to sell courses in English as a second language to overseas students must meet NEAS requirements and be subject to regular reporting and inspection; overseas students wishing to attend an institution that has not gained NEAS accreditation will simply not receive visas to allow them to enter Australia. Though meeting NEAS requirements may be seen as an intrusion on the Centre's autonomy, the requirements are not arduous and would be readily exceeded by most language teaching institutions wishing to provide a high quality programme. In any case, the requirement to hold NEAS accreditation is a limitation that has more advantage than disadvantage in that it provides potential clients with an assurance of quality and, under the Australian Government's student visa rules, without NEAS approval, the Centre would not receive students into its ELICOS programmes. In fact, NEAS accreditation has been seen as sufficiently advantageous as a demonstration of quality that the Centre has, at times, voluntarily sought its approval of programmes (such as short introductory language teacher education courses and vacation English courses) for which such approval has not been mandatory.

5. Purpose and mission of the centre

The purpose and mission of the Centre are laid out in the Centre Constitution, as approved by the University Council on officially establishing the Centre in 1989 and as subsequently amended in February 1997 to allow the Centre to move to its current administrative location as a stand-alone centre answering to the Pro-Vice-Chancellor (Arts). Under the heading of "Functions", the Constitution states:

> 3 The function of the Centre is to offer language training and development programs and to undertake research and provide consultancy services in applied linguistics with a view to becoming self-funding and, in the long-run, to generating income and facilities for the University. Without limiting the generality of the above, the Centre will —
>
> (1) provide a facility and an institutional base in the field of language education from which the University could respond to, and show national leadership in meeting the demand for special purpose language training, with particular but not exclusive emphasis on Asian languages;
>
> (2) develop as a centre of excellence in applied linguistics with special but not sole reference to the second language area (i.e., the learning, teaching, use and functioning of English as a Second Language (ESL)/English as a Foreign Language (EFL) and other second or foreign languages in any individual, group, societal or international contexts;
>
> (3) provide a capacity for the University to build and engage in external relationships; and
>
> (4) interact with other parts of the University in pursuit of its objectives. (*Griffith University Calendar*: D64.14, CALL Constitution, Document Number 97/0001, issued 2/97, Clause 3)

The 1999 business and strategic plan states:

> The mission of the Centre for Applied Linguistics and Languages is to serve Griffith University and the wider community of language interests through
> - the development of high quality second and foreign language learning programs,
> - excellence in the development and implementation of applied linguistic theory and practice, and
> - the promotion and development of applied linguistics through the provision of high quality training programs, research and consultancy services.

The Centre exists within a University which, according to its strategic plan, has always sought to combine "the best university traditions and values with the innovation necessary for success", to foster cross-disciplinary teaching and research, to make "entrepreneurial responses to community needs", to "think and act both locally and globally", to embrace diversity, and to nurture innovation (see Griffith University 1999:1, 2). In that context, the Centre has always sought to be innovative and to identify and respond to the needs of the local, Australian, and overseas community in which it sees its market opportunities; in doing so, it is mindful both of its own terms of reference and the University's aspirations and also, as the introductory paragraph in Clause 3 of the Constitution cited above indicates, it is required to be self-funding and to generate revenue for the University. Though the wording above implies that self-funding is a long-term goal, the Centre has never received funding from the University but has always paid money to the University in the form of contract levies and administrative and capital overheads based on the number of students in its ELICOS and graduate programmes. In the years when overseas student numbers have been strong and there has been liberal funding available for second language research and consultancies, the self-funding mandate has not been unduly harsh but at times when overseas students have been difficult to recruit because of international economic or political turmoil and when governments have reduced the funds available for language research, the self-funding requirements became very difficult to sustain. In addition, though the University may aspire to be innovative and entrepreneurial, its bureaucracy has always been traditional, conservative and slow to approve new ways of acting even where they are essential to allow the Centre to respond quickly to commercial opportunities, to finalise contracts with outside agencies, or to take advantage of new market opportunities (such as the establishment of overseas branches would allow). Such carefulness in the bureaucracy that underlies and supports university activity provides a balance against insubstantial innovation, ensures that innovation and "entrepreneurialism" are tested against traditional standards, and undoubtedly helps to ensure that high standards are maintained in both the academic and management functions of the University. However, that same carefulness can become stifling in an entity such as CALL which, under its Constitution, is required to find new ways of funding and is required to operate under commercial exigencies which impact on all aspects of its management (not least on the management of its human and other resources) and which often require that it be able to respond quickly to market opportunities and to changing market conditions.

In implementing its terms of reference as laid down in its Constitution, all the Centre's activities have been dependent on the basic necessity to generate sufficient revenue to be able to survive: it does not have the opportunity available to other elements in the University to argue the desirability of, for example, academic activities that serve the goal of academic excellence rather than immediate market success. Though this seems arduous in a traditional university context, in the reality of the present trends in university funding and accountability, such requirements probably put the centre just a little "ahead of the field"; in addition, the discipline that such requirements place on an academic unit is salutary in that it makes all players aware of the actual cost of academic programmes and other academic activities. Nevertheless, the nexus between commercial profitability and academic excellence often leads to serious, seemingly irreconcilable, conflicts: the example was quoted earlier of how the

University has sometimes denied the use of even small amounts of Centre resources to allow senior staff to give even plenary papers at major world conferences even though such presentations would seem to be of vital importance in maintaining the profile of the Centre and the University, in winning research and consultancy contracts, and even in attracting fee-paying students into Centre programmes.

In summary, both because of the revenue-generating opportunities provided and because of the Centre's interests in language education and applied linguistics, a core function of the Centre has been the provision of second language programmes, predominantly the provision of English as a second language to overseas students in the form of long-term ELICOS courses and shorter vacation courses but also programmes in other languages offered generally on contract to government departments and to industry. The Centre's other core function is the provision of courses, research and consultancy services in applied linguistics. These include short and non-award courses of different sorts in areas of applied linguistics for which there is a fee-paying market (especially in language assessment and language policy) and full-fee paying award courses at the graduate level in applied linguistics (including a Graduate Certificate in Language Assessment, a Graduate Certificate in Second Language Teaching, and research higher degrees at the M.Phil. and Ph.D. levels). In addition, the Centre bids for research grants and consultancy contracts. Student fees and other charges are necessarily calculated to cover all the costs involved (including teaching, research, materials, and all infrastructure including administration, equipment and facilities) and activities can only be undertaken if they can recoup their costs (and, desirably though rarely except in ESL courses, provide some profit margin). Thus, the Centre's goals and functions are to promote the area of applied linguistics through excellence in language teaching, research and consultancies but, at the same time, to generate the revenue required to fund the Centre and meet its obligations to its own staff and to the University. The next section elaborates on the Centre's activities.

6. Activities

The Centre for Applied Linguistics and Languages differs from the other centres described in this volume in being essentially a university centre with the tripartite role characteristic of Australian universities: teaching, research and community service. Its daily activities fall into two broad areas, as indicated on Chart One: "Language Programmes" and "Applied Linguistics". In addition, there are activities that relate to the Centre as a whole rather than falling clearly under one of these two broad divisions.

Under **Language Programmes**, English as a Second Language (ESL) courses are offered to overseas students in four forms. First, the largest programme in the Centre is the programme in *English Language Intensive Courses for Overseas Students* (*ELICOS*), which are offered in four ten-week modules and a five-week module spanning the year. Students are accepted at any proficiency level and are able to take as many modules as they wish in order to achieve their own particular goals. For about half of the students, that goal is to enter award courses at the undergraduate or graduate levels in Griffith University or elsewhere; the other half come just to learn English for personal, vocational or some other reason and then return home. The Centre emphasises the importance of a needs-based approach to the development of syllabuses and work programmes and so it is willing, whenever student numbers make it viable, to provide courses that are tailored specifically to the students' needs and interests; however, the majority of students take General English while students wishing to enter award courses and who enter with moderate proficiency (about ISLPR 2 or IELTS 4.5 to 5) or attain it while in CALL are also able to take courses in English for Academic Purposes. Many students on exit from their English courses (especially those going on to other studies) take an exit test such as IELTS or the ISLPR and so they are also offered the chance to take IELTS or ISLPR Preparation courses, generally as a component of their other English studies.

Another major programme provided by the Centre is known as *Australian Study Tours (ASTs)*. These are generally short courses, averaging about 3 or 4 weeks but ranging up from about two weeks to as much as ten or more. These courses generally combine English with some other activity such as recreational activity, tourism, work experience, or, increasingly, an academic programme with the distribution being about half-time to English and half to the other activity. Though the Centre offers some standard packages that agents and others market to individual students, most AST programmes are arranged on contract with a foreign institution and the content is negotiated with that institution. Sometimes a group of students comes in under this programme but for a longer period with a major focus on English and sometimes, for both shorter and longer courses, with a requirement for formal assessment so that their work can be credited to their home degree programmes. The essence of the ASTs is flexibility to meet the precise needs of the students and their home institutions. It is especially in the AST programme that most students or their institutions request "homestay" (under which they are billeted with an Australian family) so as to maximise their exposure to English and to Australian culture.

The third ESL activity is the provision of *English language support* to "non-English speaking background" (NESB) students in award courses. NESB students may be either Australian residents with English needs or overseas students. This support is generally the result of negotiations with the NESB students' host School, which pays for the service, and is offered in small groups of two or three students once or twice a week on a largely needs-basis. In other words, the ESL teacher assists the students with English language aspects of their immediate studies: preparation of seminar papers, assignments, general language and cultural advice, or whatever other language or culture needs they have to assist them to cope with their studies.

The fourth ESL activity is the provision of *ESL within other courses* elsewhere in the University. The nature and level of these courses differs according to the particular programme being serviced but generally they provide "specified purpose" English language related to the nature of the rest of the students' programmes and usually include some attention to English for academic purposes, all designed to assist the students' other studies. One such course, termed English for Business, provides English language tuition in support of certificate and diploma courses in Golf Management. In 2000, Griffith University also established its International Institute of Sport and CALL was asked to provide both the pre-sessional ELICOS courses and some English language units for the award courses that students undertake through the Institute. These courses, like those for the Golf programme, concentrate on the language relevant to the students' sporting interests and also support their academic programme.

At various times, CALL has also offered a fifth ESL programme, viz., courses in *English for immigrants*, both under Federal Government programmes for the provision of English instruction to overseas-trained professionals and as week-end, fee-based courses to local immigrants.

From the beginning of 2000, the University transferred to CALL responsibility for two popular *bridging courses* that combine English with other studies and are designed to bridge overseas students into the University's degree programmes: the "Foundations" course, which provides both English language and some academic coursework for students whose academic qualifications and English proficiency require further development before they can be accepted into undergraduate courses, and the Postgraduate Qualifying Programme, which operates similarly for graduate students.

The Centre's English language programmes are marketed under the general rubric of *Griffith University English Language Institute*, that being a more informative name for intending students than "Centre for Applied Linguistics and Languages".

In addition to English language courses, CALL provides programmes in *languages other than English*, generally on contract to government departments or industry. So, for instance, it has provided a 12 months course in Korean for staff of the Australian Trade Commission, one in Italian (including a period in Italy) for an officer of the Australian Federal Police, courses in Indonesian for AusAID (the Australian Government's foreign aid organisation), a course in Thai for a drilling company operating in Thailand, and an extended programme in Asian-Pacific cultures for staff of the International Food division of the Queensland Government's Department of Primary Industries.

Under **Applied Linguistics**, the Centre engages in research, bids for consultancy contracts from Australian and overseas sources, and teaches a wide range of programmes in the broad area of applied linguistics. In this area, as in all CALL's activities, what is undertaken depends on what financial support is obtained through research grants, consultancy contracts, or the sale of courses to individual students or their funding agencies.

The actual line between research and consultancy is often fuzzy. Research projects may result from successful bids for funds from research agencies to investigate some issue (such as the effect of language teaching on cross-cultural attitudes). Consultancies may involve providing advice in relation to some issue (for example, to review a university language department and advise on its future direction). However, since applied linguistics can be seen as the field that seeks solutions to language-related problems in society (cf. Ingram 1980), the border between research and consultancy in applied linguistics is often not so clear and many consultancy projects have included significant research activity.

In the area of *research*, CALL and its individual staffmembers bid for whatever research funding is available, either through the major Australian research grants available to all fields or to language-specific research opportunities that have become very rare in Australia since 1996. Prior to the change of Federal government in 1996 from Labor to the conservative Liberal-National coalition, considerable funds were available for research and consultancy activities in the area of language policy and language education. Those widely available funds have almost entirely disappeared (at least in the second and foreign language area) and language researchers have been reduced to bidding through the major research grants. In principle, that would seem to give them the same opportunities as researchers in other disciplines but, in fact, in many other fields, the index of funding opportunities beyond such general grants as the Australian Research Grants (ARC) is quite substantial whereas there are none specific to applied linguistics. In any case, most of the major funds such as ARC are inappropriate to CALL because of CALL's required costing arrangements as a wholly self-funding centre: many grants do not allow infrastructure costs or full chief investigator salaries and, in some cases, require that the institution contribute a substantial portion of the funds required. Consequently, though CALL had a vigorous research involvement from 1990 to 1996, since 1996 research funding has been minimal and the number of research staff has been more than halved.

Throughout its history, CALL has shown particular interest in the areas of language and language education policy and language assessment. During some of that period, funds for language assessment and language curriculum activities were gained through the National Languages and Literacy Institute of Australia (NLLIA) by a sister centre in Griffith, the (NLLIA) Language Testing and Curriculum Centre, which the Director of CALL administered as a separate centre (the advantage to LTACC in this dual directorship was that CALL provided LTACC with support services largely gratuitously). When funds from NLLIA dried up, LTACC, its staff, and the few self-funding programmes it operated were absorbed into CALL. For convenience, no distinction will be made here between CALL and LTACC even though, when the two centres co-existed, a clear distinction was always made in their activities, in their funds, when and how they bid for projects, who prepared the bids, and the responsibilities of the staff: this very strict differentiation was made so that the centres and their shared Director could not reasonably be accused of conflict of interest.

The *research and consultancy activities* undertaken by CALL have been wide-ranging and have covered (amongst many others) such areas as advice on national

Asian language curriculum development, English proficiency levels and testing requirements of Australian institutions for overseas students, the development of competency specifications for language teachers, the mapping of on-shore and off-shore courses for teachers in languages other than English, advice to the Queensland Government on a new language education policy for Queensland schools, advice to the New South Wales Ministry of Education on foreign language education policy in New South Wales, and the comparability of literacy measures used by all Australian States and Territories. A major interest of key research staff in CALL, an interest that goes back many years prior to the commencement of CALL, has been language assessment. In particular, the present writer and Elaine Wylie, a Senior Research Fellow (Testing Services) in CALL, developed the Australian (now International) Second Language Proficiency Ratings (ISLPR) in 1978; since then, a great deal of their research and development effort has been spent on the concept of proficiency, its measurement, and its application to language teaching (syllabus design and methodology). Their language assessment research has included such issues as the measurement of proficiency in different languages, for different purposes and by different modes, resulting, for instance, in different versions of the ISLPR for English as a Second Language, Japanese, Chinese, and Indonesian as Foreign Languages, special purpose versions for English for Engineers, English for Business/Commerce, English for Academic Purposes, Indonesian for Language Teachers, a generic ISLPR for Language Teachers, and several self-assessment versions used for different purposes with different learner groups. The self-assessment versions include a short form able to be administered by telephone and used in a community survey of language resources and several versions in English and other languages administered by computer. In 1999–2000, the Centre cooperated with the Faculty of Arts at Chulalongkorn University in Bangkok, Thailand, to develop a test of Thai writing for Thai students entering that University. In 2000–2001, the concepts of proficiency, its development, its assessment, and "community involvement" (cf. Ingram 1978a, 1980a) were applied in a major project on language teaching methodology funded by the Australian Government's Committee for University Teaching and Staff Development (CUTSD) and based around the main languages taught in Griffith's School of Languages and Linguistics (Japanese, Chinese, Korean, Indonesian, Italian and Spanish). Another consultancy project which included substantial research and development activity was one to develop vocational language competency specifications for the Australian tourism industry.

    The Centre has always had a strong interest in the International English Language Testing System (IELTS), not least because the present writer had been the Australian representative on the joint Australian-British team to develop the test in 1987–88 (just before the establishment of CALL) and was Chief Examiner (Australia) from 1989 to 1998. In addition to the Director's involvement, other staff have undertaken a variety of research and development projects in relation to IELTS and its performance. In addition, Griffith University (through the Centre, which paid for the shares and receives the dividends) is a shareholder in IELTS Australia, the consortium that represents Australia's financial interests in the test, and in 1998 the Centre Director became a Director and Board Member of IELTS Australia.

Consultancy services, in addition to some referred to above under "Language Programmes", have included formal contracts for such activities as the provision with UNESCO funding of a Graduate Certificate in Second Language Teaching for staff of the Yunnan Normal University in Kunming, China, and middle school teachers from surrounding provinces, English language training funded by UNDP for staff of an Embassy training centre in Beijing, advice on language teacher education requirements for Catholic Education in Queensland, evaluation of the assessment procedures in the language training programme of the Federal Department of Foreign Affairs and Trade, preparation of an Indonesian syllabus for business purposes for the Australian Institute of Exports, review of the language departments in two Australian universities, preparation of a language curriculum and related materials for a Korean university, and advice on communicative methodology to a Korean language multimedia project. The very first consultancy project undertaken by CALL was one of the most influential locally when, in 1990, the Centre was contracted by a recently elected Queensland Labor government to provide advice on a new second language education policy for Queensland schools. This advice led to major changes in the provision of education in "languages other than English" (LOTE) in Queensland schools with, amongst other initiatives, LOTE learning being progressively extended down through all Primary Schools, with the eventual aim being for it to commence no later than Year 3, and with the introduction of a number of partial immersion programmes in State High Schools. Undoubtedly the largest consultancy undertaken by CALL was the academic management of the Federal Immigration Department's "ACCESS" test, the test of English required of applicants for immigration to Australia and administered around the world until mid-1998 when, for government financial reasons, it was replaced by the IELTS test.

In addition to such funded consultancy projects, the Centre is continually called on for advice on language education matters, especially in such areas as language education policy, the implementation of language teaching in schools, and language assessment at all levels. Various CALL staff also serve on a variety of advisory committees: the Director, for instance, was a member of the Australian Language and Literacy Council (the principal advisory body on language policy to the Federal Education Minister) throughout the life of the Council from 1991 to 1996. He is also the longest-standing member (for more than 25 years, less absences on assignments inter-state or overseas) of the Languages other than English (LOTE) Subject Advisory Committee of the Queensland Board of Senior Secondary School Studies and its predecessor, the Queensland Board of Secondary School Studies.

Courses in applied linguistics range from short, non-award courses to research Ph.D. degrees. Short Introductory and Advanced courses on the International Second

Language Proficiency Ratings are offered several times a year from one of the Centre's branches, inter-state or, occasionally, overseas, wherever contracts are obtained or fee-paying students are attracted. Two introductory courses to language teaching, together adding up to about 100 hours of instruction, have also been offered and accredited by the National ELICOS Accreditation Scheme as providing the basic training required for teachers to teach in ELICOS centres. A Graduate Certificate in Language Assessment is offered to students around the world by flexible learning methods (i.e., distance education) using both hard copy and the internet. The Graduate Certificate in Second Language Teaching that was initially developed and accredited for the UNESCO contract referred to earlier has been updated and re-accredited for flexible learning and has attracted substantial student numbers from around the world. Ph.D. students in applied linguistics have covered a broad range of applied linguistics from theories of translating, to the use of concordancing in second language teaching, computers and reading, learning strategies in immersion French programmes, phonological aspects of learning to read, special purpose syllabus design in English for Korean businesspeople, and language education policy in Senegal.

In addition, the Centre bids for any available training contracts in the broad area of applied linguistics, sometimes using such a contract to develop a package that can be marketed more widely and used to attract students into one of the graduate courses, sometimes, with advanced standing. Thus, for instance, in the course of 1999, contracts were won to provide a short training programme in language testing that would prepare some of the participants to develop a test of Thai writing for university entry in Thailand while at the same time attracting other students into the Graduate Certificate in Language Assessment. Another contract was obtained to provide basic language teacher education to teachers in a private language school in China: the total "professional programme in second language teaching" offers both face-to-face tuition at the participants' own school, additional work through flexible learning, and advanced standing (equivalent to one of the four units) into the Centre's Graduate Certificate in Second Language Teaching. Occasionally, also, CALL has mounted short seminars or courses on topics of general interest at the time and for which a potential market has been identified. On two occasions, for instance, it has offered short courses conducted by eminent international scholars on language policy and language education planning.

The Centre also provides a *testing service*. The short courses in the ISLPR are offered under this service but, in particular, advisory services are provided to institutions and the general public, second language learners are able to have their proficiency assessed using the ISLPR (especially in English but also in other languages), and ISLPR assessors are able to participate in an ISLPR assessor registration system that monitors the quality of their assessments and issues certificates to assure their clients of the tested competence of the assessors and the reliability of their assessments. The advisory services provided have included general advice on language requirements for courses and other activities and, in a number of instances, on language matters relevant to legal procedures or the needs of business and industry.

Under **other activities**, are grouped activities that don't fall clearly under either of the two broad sections of CALL. Though the Centre had offered public seminars on an occasional basis throughout its existence (generally on a fee-for-entry basis), in 1999, it formally commenced the *CALL Seminar Series* under which staff, visitors and invited guests offer a public lecture (open to university staff, students and the general public) on some topic of interest. In some cases, this has provided an opportunity for staff to give further airing to a conference paper, to "practise" a presentation for a major conference, or to provide a report on a recent research project.

Though CALL staff have been active in *conference presentations* and the Director and other staff have been frequent speakers (often by invitation) at conferences around Australia and overseas, the nature of the Centre's funding has been a major inhibition in this area. The Centre's funds, as already noted, come from project funding and student fees for intensive and relatively high cost language courses, on both of which margins are always minimal, not least during an era of subdued market activity and intense competition from other institutions. Consequently, unlike research centres funded by government grant or by universities in which it is always open to staff to argue that the work of the centre is enhanced and disseminated through attendance at significant conferences, CALL has had limited funds to support staff attendance at conferences. Consequently, what funds have been available have been used as part of staff development for the cross-section of the staff and the senior academics, such as the Director and Senior Research Fellows, have largely had to limit their conference attendance either to those events where the organisers were paying travel and other costs or where they themselves could meet the costs. At times, even the limited funds available for conference attendance and staff development have had to be cut when government policy or economic downturn in the market countries has reduced the Centre's revenue or squeezed already minute margins still further. The limitations on the involvement by senior staff in major conferences has been aggravated, as already noted, by the stated attitude of senior University personnel that even the presentation of plenary papers at major world congresses may add to the individual's personal prestige but brings few benefits to the Centre or the University and that consequently Centre funds should not be used to support such activity.

Such practices and attitudes raise, again, at least at a superficial level, the difficult nexus between academic and commercial interests. Other than considered in terms of short-term cashflow, however, both academic and commercial interests are very much put at risk by such practices and attitudes, which pose the very serious danger, in the long term, of academics' failing to maintain the currency of their expertise and of the Centre's name not being made sufficiently well known across the field for it to be able to maintain a flow of research and consultancy projects (i.e., conference attendance is not a luxury but a fundamental requirement for the survival of a centre of excellence).

However, the practice is unavoidable in academic units where host institutions or funding agencies fail to take account of the importance of centre staff being seen and heard at major events in their field and where essential academic activity is subordinated to the necessity for each individual project or centre activity to cover its own costs. The solution is for a university (or other host or funding agency) to recognise that there are essential academic activities (such as conference participation or personal research and writing) that cannot be made revenue-generating, certainly not profit-making, in the short-term and an academic centre must be allowed either to bid for the necessary core funds or to retain and accumulate surplus resources to fund such activities itself and to maintain reserves against market fluctuations.

Because CALL is self-funding with little margin on its operations and because in Australia, unlike the United States, there is relatively little involvement in education and research funding by private enterprise or philanthropies, the Centre has been unable to offer fellowships to attract scholars into the Centre in the highly successful way this has occurred at the National Foreign Language Center (see Chapter 2). However, CALL receives numerous requests from scholars to come to the Centre as Visiting Scholars or Visiting Researchers. Under Griffith University's arrangements, such visitors are encouraged subject to certain conditions, including the willingness of the element to provide certain support. Since CALL is unable to provide such support, it accepts what it terms *CALL Visitors* on condition that there is no financial liability of any sort to the Centre other than the Visitor's using space in the Centre, accessing limited equipment (such as a computer, telephone, and photocopying facilities), meeting occasionally with Centre staff or observing Centre classes, and accessing University facilities such as the libraries and the electronic networks. This programme has proved quite popular, with one or two Visitors being present for extended periods much of the time (though obviously it is limited to those persons who are able to obtain financial assistance from other sources). For the Visitors, this opportunity provides a congenial atmosphere, a place to pursue their own research or writing undisturbed if they wish, and colleagues with whom they can discuss their ideas and from whom they can receive informal guidance; for the Centre, the scheme provides intellectual stimulus and the discussion of different ideas, the opportunity to create links with colleagues in different institutions in different parts of the world, and the mind-broadening effect of discussing different points of view from new sources. In addition, a CALL Visitor is asked either to provide a seminar in the CALL Seminar Series or to provide a less formal presentation to CALL staff and, if possible, to produce at least one significant paper for refereed publication during their stay in the Centre.

CALL was not founded to provide the sort of *leverage* that other centres in this book provide at the national and international levels. However, indirectly, it has done so to a considerable extent through the research and consultancy projects it has undertaken and, in particular, through the individual activities of some of its staff. As noted above, the Centre's first major project was to provide language policy advice to the then newly elected Queensland government in 1990, advice that led to the adoption and implementation of a new State language education policy which, in subsequent years, became somewhat exemplary for the rest of Australia. As also noted earlier, Centre staff, especially the Director, have also been actively involved on major language or language education advisory committees, in particular the Australian Language and Literacy Council and the Languages other than English Subject Advisory Committee of the Queensland Board of Senior Secondary School Studies. In addition, consultancy projects and invitations to visit other institutions and countries as visiting fellows have led the Centre to have some leverage effect on language education not only around Australia but in such countries as Singapore, Thailand, South Korea and the United States while work on the IELTS and ACCESS tests has influenced ESL education worldwide.

To the extent that such direct and indirect leverage activities and the Centre's research and development projects require Centre staff to address significant issues in language policy and language education, the Centre has acted as a *think-tank* in such areas as language policy, language education planning, curriculum design, and language assessment. However, the nature of the Centre's funding is a major inhibition on its serving such a role in the more abstract or innovative way that has been open to, for example, the National Foreign Language Center, which was specifically designed to have a "think-tank" role with core funding unrelated to specific projects. Where centres are dependent on project-based funding or the sale of student places on courses, activities inevitably become limited to those which directly generate funds and, in CALL's experience, even the formal publication of articles and books that could come out of research and development projects is very difficult to achieve when academics are required to move from the preparation of the final report for the funding agency to the next project or to the preparation of the next set of submissions to win subsequent projects (and hence Centre funds). Thus, the very nature of CALL's funding has meant that its leverage and think-tank roles, even though considerable, have been incidental, rather than central, to its activities and have largely been the result of the commitment, energy and effort "beyond the call of duty" of its staff.

The same factor has limited CALL's capacity to produce its own significant *publications* and to commercially distribute those it does produce. The Centre has a substantial list of publications produced by its staff (mainly in the form of journal articles, research reports, or monographs published under the auspices of such agencies as the Australian Language and Literacy Council). It produces an occasional *CALL Newsletter* and an array of marketing materials such as brochures, videotapes and posters. A number of projects have led to the publication by the Centre of reports and other volumes (in particular, the various versions of the *International Second Language Proficiency Ratings*: e.g., Ingram and Wylie 1979/99, Ingram and Wylie 1995, 1995a, and 1995b; Ingram, Wylie and Maclain 1995; Ingram, Wylie and Commins 1995; Ingram, Wylie and Hudson 1995; Ingram, Wylie and Grainger 1995; Ingram,

Wylie and Woollams 1996, and Wylie and Ingram 1995). In addition, the Centre has cooperated with colleagues elsewhere to publish their material where financial assistance to cover the cost was available (e.g., Brändle 1993, 1996) and, in 1999–2000, the Centre joined with the National Foreign Language Center to jointly publish a monograph based on research undertaken by the CALL Director as a Fellow at NFLC in 1993–94 and 1998 (Ingram 2000). Increasingly, also, use is made of the CALL website as a means by which to make research reports and papers produced by CALL staff more widely available at minimal production cost.

As a commercial entity that survives on the students it can attract and the projects it wins, CALL necessarily invests considerably in *marketing* activities. For this purpose, it cooperates with the University's marketing arm, the Griffith University International Centre (GUIC) but, for several years, it also employed its own marketing manager, ran its own marketing activities, and used an array of marketing agents in all its target countries. In this context, it has also been able to take advantage of many of its other activities (e.g., overseas conference attendance, the global travel associated with the academic management of the ACCESS Test, and occasionally other research or consultancy projects) to extend the Centre's contact with its marketing agents or to attend additional educational fairs. The Centre also combines with a variety of other organisations to promote their common interests; so, for example, as an ELICOS institution, the Centre cooperates with the ELICOS Association, a grouping of ELICOS schools renamed in 2000 English Australia, that carries out some marketing activities for its members. Similarly, because CALL has a branch on Queensland's Gold Coast, it participates in the Gold Coast Education Network, which markets the educational services available on the Gold Coast. The advent of the internet is also changing CALL's marketing focus: increasing importance is being attached to the Centre's website and computer-based facilities are being continually extended to improve the effectiveness of the website and to enable applications for enrolment to be processed entirely through that medium.

As noted earlier, the third obligation of Australian universities beyond teaching and research is **community service**. Some of the Centre's consultancy projects clearly constitute community service but this term more usually refers to the expert but gratuitous services that university staff provide to the community. This is a more arduous task for a self-funding element such as CALL than for other parts of the University since there is no general or core funding available to cover staffmembers' time or infrastructure costs and the Centre's commercial mandate, especially at times of financial stringency resulting from depressed markets or limited research funding, means that any effort directed towards community service has to be paid for out of fees from student programmes or contracts, which in turn increases their costs and reduces the Centre's competitiveness. Nevertheless, Centre staff have provided numerous forms of community service. These have ranged from advice on language matters to individuals and organisations (especially on language proficiency and language policy issues), to leadership roles in professional organisations (the Centre Director, for example, was national President of the Australian Federation of Modern Language Teachers Associations for fourteen years and world Vice-President for some six years), service on advisory councils (such as the Australian Language and Literacy Council or the LOTE Subject Advisory Committee of the Queensland Board of Senior Secondary School Studies, as noted earlier), or involvement in local schools and their organisations.

7. Interactions and links

The Centre for Applied Linguistics and Languages has actively created linkages with other parts of Griffith University and with organisations within Queensland, across Australia, and overseas. The list of such linkages is too great to provide exhaustively here and the following is intended to be indicative of the approach that the Centre has undertaken. Such linkages have been of very considerable importance in the success of the Centre, not least in a context where the self-funding nature of the Centre limits the level of funds that can be put into commercial marketing activities.

University linkages arise largely out of CALL's efforts to provide services to other elements in the University, to cooperate with them, and to draw on their expertise in relevant research, consultancy and teaching projects. Administratively, CALL is a stand-alone centre within the Arts Group of Griffith University with much of the status of a School. In that sense, it is an integral part of the University's academic and administrative structure with the Director answering to the Pro-Vice-Chancellor (Arts) and with the same accreditation and other administration processes applying to it as to a School. The Centre Director is a member of the School Committee of the School of Languages and Linguistics, the Head of that School is able to sit on the CALL Committee, and the Centre Director attends on an "as needs basis" the Faculty of Arts Board for the Arts Group. In addition, as already noted, as a Centre whose major revenue source is from overseas students, it must abide by the accreditation and other approval processes imposed by the Australian and Queensland governments for the export of education, in particular, it is subject to initial and on-going accreditation and monitoring by the National ELICOS Accreditation Scheme (NEAS).

As a university centre, as already noted, CALL provides considerable services to the rest of the University by bridging large numbers of overseas students into its award courses, by providing gratuitous advice on language matters, and by cooperating with other elements in research, consultancy and teaching projects. Consequently, a continual activity for senior staff in the centre is to liaise across the University with Schools and other elements to explore their needs and opportunities for cooperative activity.

The Centre has regularly cooperated with other elements in the University and with outside bodies in research and consultancy activities and in the preparation of bids for other projects. Some of these have been referred to earlier. Reference was made to the large project focussing on language teaching methodology in the School of Languages and Linguistics. Bids for most overseas aid projects are made in collaboration with the International Projects unit within the Griffith University International Centre and CALL has cooperated with other elements in the University to offer English language programmes, for instance, as part of the golf management awards and as part of the various awards offered by the International Institute of Sport established in 2000.

External linkages are fostered in a variety of ways. The major project on the administration of the ACCESS Test mentioned earlier was conducted in collaboration with IDP Education (a consortium of Australian universities), with CALL being responsible for the academic management of the test and IDP for the administration of the test around the world while CALL has also cooperated on a range of projects with such organisations as the International Projects Unit of the Northern Territory Government, with other universities, with government departments, and with the National Languages and Literacy Institute of Australia (as referred to earlier). The various initiatives aimed at establishing operations in China, Hong Kong, Japan, Thailand and India are all being undertaken as joint projects with overseas institutions. Obviously the marketing activities of the Centre, as described earlier, are designed to bring CALL's activities to the notice of outside bodies and individuals and to utilise external commercial entities to promote the Centre. The University (often as a direct result of CALL's activities and with CALL as the prime focus of the relationship) has signed "sister institution" and similar agreements with overseas universities, especially in such countries as Japan, Thailand, Korea and China: though many such agreements seem to be purely formal, a token of friendship which goes little further, many are integral to programmes that CALL operates with the other institution, very often for Australian Study Tours. One increasingly significant link has been as a member of the Gold Coast Education Network, a cooperative activity of most of the significant educational providers on the Gold Coast together with the Gold Coast City Council to cooperatively market the Gold Coast as an educational site.

Other activities that have been described earlier also serve to create links with other organisations: the Advisory Committee is structured to strengthen CALL's contacts with other university elements and with other potential clients, the CALL Seminar Series attracts attendees from both within the University and the wider community, the CALL Visitor scheme creates favourable linkages with the Visitors' own institutions and extends the Centre's reputation, and many of the consultancy services serve similar purposes (e.g., membership of the various language policy and language education advisory bodies referred to earlier). In the opposite direction, CALL staff have been invited as visiting fellows or visiting researchers to other institutions: in particular, the Centre Director has been a frequent visitor to the Regional Language Centre in Singapore, he was an Andrew Mellon Foundation Fellow at the National Foreign Language Center, Washington DC, in 1993–94, and he has been an Adjunct

Fellow of that Center since 1994. In addition, one of CALL's terms of reference requires its active involvement with professional associations, in particular with such organisations as the ELICOS Association, the Queensland Association for Teachers of English to Speakers of other Languages (QATESOL), the Modern Language Teachers Association of Queensland (MLTAQ), the Australian Federation of Modern Language Teachers Associations (AFMLTA) of which the Centre Director was national President for fourteen years, and the Fédération Internationale des Professeurs de Langues Vivantes (FIPLV — the World Federation of Modern Language Teachers) of which the Centre Director was Vice-President and Regional Representative for South East Asia and the South West Pacific for some six years.

8. Staffing

The nature of the Centre, its self-funding status, and the inevitably fluctuating nature of its activities mean that there must be considerable flexibility in its staffing. The Centre's dependence on bidding for and winning research and consultancy projects means that the small core of applied linguists has to be supplemented with other short-term or casual staff when particular projects commence. Student numbers in the ELICOS programme tend to follow a common pattern increasing from the January intake through to the October intake with a dip in mid-year whereas Australian Study Tours are heaviest from July to September, reflecting the university vacation period in the Northern Hemisphere.

Staffing is one of the areas where the Centre's integration into a university with its obligation to observe the University's industrial arrangements impose a severe drain on centre finances and prevent it from operating under normal commercial conditions in competition, for example, with private language centres or even corporatised commercial units associated with some other universities: though, for example, the University's provisions for staff security, redundancies, and severance payments provide attractive security for academic and support staff in regular University elements, they make it very difficult for the Centre to respond to market fluctuations (whether caused by regular cyclic changes or changes in overall market conditions) and are extremely costly for a self-funding element running relatively high-cost, low-margin programmes. For these reasons, it is necessary for the Centre to employ a much higher proportion of casual staff (both teaching and administrative) than elsewhere in a university: to minimise the high cost of severance and other payments as workloads fluctuate, for most of the Centre's life, only the Director and Manager have been tenured staff of the University and all others have been either on fixed-term contracts or casual. However, under recent arrangements with the relevant industrial unions, the University has agreed to greatly increase the proportion of administrative staff on "continuing appointments" and to provide generous severance payments to most contract staff (both academic and non-academic): such agreements provide increased stability and higher levels of productivity in university staffing but they also restrict the flexibility needed in staffing the Centre's programmes and projects, add considerable cost to the Centre, and reduce its competitiveness with private centres.

In Chapter 8, there is reference to important considerations in staffing language centres, especially those like CALL that are considered to operate on "soft money" generated from the sale of student places and project funds rather than received from government grant. A centre such as CALL depends for its survival on the willingness of the market to buy its courses and to fund it for research and consultancy activities. Consequently, it requires high quality teaching and academic staff capable of providing high quality services and yet the conditions that CALL is able to offer (even within university industrial agreements) are considerably inferior to those available elsewhere in universities. For staff to be employed in CALL, they must have relevant skills, they must understand and accept the constraints on a self-funding centre, and they must feel a high level of commitment to their field and to the mission and vision of the Centre. Because of the fluctuations in the Centre's level of activity, they must be willing to be flexible in the duties they undertake and, for instance, research staff must be willing to fill up their workload doing other things when research funding is insufficient to justify their salaries. Consequently, most CALL staff over the years have shown a remarkably high degree of commitment to their field and a willingness to forgo employment benefits (tenure, study leave, long service leave, and private consultancy rights, for instance) for the satisfaction of working in an area to which they feel committed.

The staffing structures are shown in Charts One and Two: Chart One for academic or teaching staff and Chart Two for administrative staff. As noted earlier, not all the positions shown are filled at all times, those being filled depending on the level of Centre activity with some being left vacant or the duties combined with other positions if the level of activity (and hence the number of students and projects) is insufficient to pay for them.

9. Facilities

As already noted, CALL has facilities on the main Nathan Campus of Griffith University and in commercial premises on the Gold Coast. Though it was a decision of the University to establish CALL and for it to operate as a commercial entity competing with other universities and private schools for students and projects, the room allocation rules in the University generally give the Centre lowest priority for teaching space. Space constraints have, in fact, posed significant problems for the Centre's research and teaching programmes and its support services throughout most of its existence and have, on occasions, led to ceilings being placed on student numbers, with corollary limitations on Centre revenue and on the overseas students flowing through to degree programmes. Apart from the very limited space around its own offices, the classrooms allocated to the Centre have generally been those that were unpopular with other elements and were scattered across the campus, making it necessary for students and teachers to walk considerable distances between classes (a more significant problem for Centre students, who spend 25 hours a week in class, than for degree students who generally spend no more than half that time). The situation has improved with the advent of improved computerised room allocation methods but the Centre's priority for teaching space remains low. In the period when overseas student numbers expanded rapidly following the Asian economic downturn of the late 1990s, the lack of teaching space forced the Centre to cap its student numbers and so prevented it from expanding as rapidly as the demand for its services would have allowed. Consequently, CALL's Nathan facilities pose a serious threat to the Centre's expansion and remain inferior in quality to those of most of its competitors and even to those that many students are used to in their home countries. In contrast, the campus as a whole is exceptionally attractive with well-designed buildings set in the middle of a State Forest, which still covers the campus, penetrates between and around many of the buildings, and regularly reveals to overseas students some of Australia's smaller "exotic" wildlife.

Though CALL's funding base limits its capacity to invest in its own equipment beyond the basic necessities for teaching in a modern, language centre, the Centre also has access to the full array of equipment of a modern and well-equipped university, its library, sporting facilities, computer and multimedia laboratories, telecommunications networks, and so on. It also has access, in principle and when available, to all its facilities (classrooms, libraries, theatres, meeting rooms, and sporting and recreational facilities). The University's residential services are also available to the students with assistance being given to them to find accommodation elsewhere if it is not available on-campus and, in particular, to find "homestay", which tends to be the preference of language students because of the incidental language and culture learning gained from living with an Australian family.

The facilities for the Centre's Gold Coast branch contrast somewhat with the main Nathan branch. Since sufficient space was not available on the University's Gold Coast campus, the Centre leased facilities on the top floor of a major shopping complex in Southport, one of the principal beachside suburbs of the Gold Coast. The outlook over the "Broadwater" towards the surfing beaches is superb and the centre facilities are modern, purpose-designed, well-equipped and, overall, very attractive and conducive to good language teaching. The branch is linked into the University's computer network, giving it the same email and internet access as elsewhere in the University. Though the branch is ten minutes by car or bus to Griffith University's Gold Coast Campus, from the centre there is ready access to all amenities that staff and students could require: ample parking, hundreds of shops, entertainment such as cinemas, tourist offices, and, not least, the town library, all in the same complex. Across the road are parklands, enclosed swimming areas in the Broadwater, and, a few minutes further away, surfing beaches. The Centre provides an accommodation service, based principally (and by demand) on homestay with Australian families living in nearby parts of the Gold Coast.

In the long term, the Centre will be best served by the provision of its own buildings on the Nathan and Gold Coast campuses of the University. Discussions aimed at this solution were well advanced until the Asian economic downturn in the late 1990s adversely affected the market for overseas students and was accompanied by a change of government in Australia with the adverse effects already noted on funding for language education policy, research and development. Undoubtedly, as the market recovers, the previous building and funding plans will be revived and the Centre will seek to construct its own purpose-designed buildings with the assistance either of the University or of private enterprise. Probably, like RELC and because the Centre is self-funding and must raise the cost of any building, CALL buildings will be multi-purpose with the office and teaching space being accompanied by facilities for other purposes such as student accommodation that can generate additional revenue to contribute substantially towards the cost of the new facilities.

10. Budget

In Chapter 8, budget issues and alternatives, together with their strengths and weaknesses, are discussed at some length and the CALL situation is referred to extensively.

As already noted, CALL was established and has always operated as a wholly self-funding centre with strong academic interests but it is required to operate commercially within the constraints of university procedures. Rather than receive financial support from the University, it pays substantial sums in the form of levies and fees to the University and makes other very substantial contributions to University revenue. As already observed, the nexus between commercialism and academia creates significant tensions, which have to be negotiated on a daily basis though, overall, the Centre has been financially successful for most of its existence. The greatest tensions arise from the necessity for the Centre, as a commercial, competitive and necessarily entrepreneurial entity to respond quickly to market opportunities, to operate efficiently and cost-effectively, and to be flexible in its programmes and its staffing. Such features match with some difficulty the usual university bureaucracies that have evolved, presumably, to support academic excellence, to maintain university traditions, and to allow change that might (though not necessarily) reflect adversely on those traditions to occur only slowly and after prolonged consideration through a variety of committees and hierarchical levels. It was also noted earlier that serious tensions also arise at points where the demands of academic excellence (such as conference attendance, personal research, reading and writing) conflict with simplistically interpreted demands of commercialism to make immediate profits.

CALL sets its fees to cover all direct and indirect costs (including all ancillary benefits paid to staff whether casual, contract or tenured). Under Federal Government regulations in order to ensure that government-funded institutions intended for Australian taxpayers and their children do not subsidise overseas students, all overseas student programmes in universities are required to charge administrative and capital levies calculated to cover the cost of the facilities and services used by overseas students. Such levies have both their positive and their negative sides. Positively, they can be regarded as a legitimate rental payment to the university for the use of the facilities and for any administrative services provided (though, in reality, CALL is largely self-sufficient administratively). While student numbers are small, it is advantageous for these payments to be *per capita*-based but, as student numbers grow, it becomes increasingly cheaper to use leased premises; so, for instance, if CALL's two branches each averaged 170 ELICOS students or more throughout their 45 weeks of courses, the more luxurious Gold Coast premises paying commercial rent would be somewhat cheaper to use than the lesser facilities on the Nathan campus.

The University is obliged to require the payment of capital and administrative levies. However, in some institutions and in certain programmes in Griffith, some or all of these levies are returned to the programme in reimbursement of other costs not recouped through the overseas student programme or incurred in supporting some aspect of the university's activities. That has never applied to CALL, which pays all levies and contract fees in full and, on occasions, has paid additional amounts for particular purposes. So, for instance, on one occasion when the University was wishing to construct and equip a building for the new School of Languages and Linguistics, CALL contributed a sum of $20,000, supposedly against some dedicated space in the building vacated by the University's languages programme: between the transfer of the money and occupation of the building, however, plans were changed and the transfer became a contribution to the building without space being allocated. For some time, also, at the height of the Centre's research activity, the "research quantum" it received was retained by the host faculty. Again, in some institutions, the Director's salary is paid in recognition of the very substantial contribution to university revenue that comes from the full-fee paying overseas students bridged into university award courses but this is not the case in CALL, where the Director's salary and all ancillary costs including superannuation, all leave, and "sabbatical" (or "outside study and research programme") are paid by the Centre.

In addition to the financial contribution in the form of contract fees and *per capita* levies that CALL pays and other occasional payments, the University also receives the benefit of interest earned on any cash-in-hand that the Centre has as a result of advance payments of student fees and project funds. Such temporary cashflow surpluses have been well in excess of a million dollars which, when invested on the short term money-market, provide a useful additional revenue to the University, revenue which, in a non-university commercial operation, would be available to the Centre to extend its activities or to keep in reserve against market fluctuations. As noted in Chapters 2 and 8, the usefulness of such income is reflected in the National Foreign Language Center's Adjunct Fellowship programme, which it was able to fund from such sources. On the other hand, Griffith would probably argue that, though the Centre does not receive the benefit of interest earned on funds held by the University, whenever the Centre's cashflow is in deficit, the University covers the deficit until the Centre works back into "the black" (though the Centre is also liable for interest at commercial rates on any cashflow deficit). As noted elsewhere, the main (and very substantial) financial contribution from the Centre to the University comes from the large number of full-fee paying overseas students recruited and bridged into the University's degree programmes.

As discussed in Chapter 8 and earlier in this chapter, the self-funding requirement on CALL is manageable even within the demands of a high quality academic programme. However, for such a centre to be successful, it is essential that the full corollaries of being self-funding, commercial, and academic be followed through. This is discussed at greater length in Chapter 8 and here reference will be made only to three critical examples of the issue as it has confronted CALL. First, decision-making must be expeditious so as to enable market opportunities to be grasped; second, the Centre must be able to cross-subsidise within its programmes so that high-cost, low- or no-margin projects (e.g., projects funded by government research grants), the marketing of Centre services, or on-going staff development and academic maintenance can be supported from revenue generated from more profitable activities; and, third, the University itself and all its elements must accept the corollaries of the Centre's being commercial and self-funding when it comes to paying for the services CALL provides.

First, decision-making in the University has invariably been slow and careful, for undoubtedly defensible reasons already referred to, but the effect has often been that CALL has lost substantial opportunities, especially overseas, partly because the project has gone outside the University's traditional operational parameters and so has caused bureaucratic anxiety that has led to delays in decision-making. In particular, such delays have occurred either because of arguments over the wording of contracts (especially in relation to intellectual property and so with potential financial implications) or because such financial issues as tax liability and the return of funds to Australia have caused protracted delays in the University's approval processes, sometimes leading to the overseas partner's turning to universities elsewhere where the decisions were made more expeditiously.

Second, cross-subsidisation has not been possible to any significant extent in CALL because the requirement has usually been imposed for each activity to cover its own costs. This requirement has a number of effects including that of precluding CALL from bidding successfully for major Australian research funds (since these do not generally allow for full infrastructure and salary costs to be charged). Rejection of cross-subsidisation has also made it difficult for most research staff to engage in such normal academic activitiy as writing for publication even where the papers or books would be based on funded projects since project funding usually stops at the project report without supporting subsequent publications.

Third, for a commercial centre to survive in and provide services to the host university, the university itself and its elements must understand and accept the real nature of costs and realise that, if the centre is to provide services to the rest of the institution, it is legitimate and indeed necessary for it to charge real costs rather than the deflated costs that most academic staff are used to when, because their Schools are funded by university grants, they are able to ignore staff salaries and infrastructure costs on what, to them, may be peripheral projects. Too often, CALL has been criticised for "over-charging" other elements with, for instance, the result that some elements have provided their own ESL support services when, in reality, those services, if fully costed to include real management costs, materials, staff, staff on-costs, and infrastructure would have been no less expensive than CALL's fees and considerably less expert. This was dramatically illustrated on one notable occasion when CALL was awarded a small university research grant. The proposed project had initially been planned as a major research project costed at over $250,000, this was reduced to $25,000 for the bid to the university research fund, but the allocation provided was less than half this because the academics on the research grant committee thought it was over-costed, "couldn't understand" where the costs came from, and clearly were entirely unaware of the real cost of academic activity. On the other hand, CALL's experience is that university bureaucracies are often naive about the costs that outside clients will bear and the Centre has, on occasions, missed out on contracts because CALL's charges were substantially increased elsewhere in the University before the project submission was approved for transmission to the client.

As discussed in Chapter 8, it is essential that a commercial element such as CALL adopt strict budget processes and monitor its financial activities strictly. CALL is required to work in conformity with the University's accounting system but, for most of the Centre's existence, this system, if it had been relied on entirely, would not have provided the sort of detailed and comparative information that a commercial centre, properly monitored, requires. In addition, the University's priorities are often not identical with those of a Centre with commercial exigencies and a rapid turn-over of projects, programmes and staff. The period when the Centre most suffered financially followed a time when the University insisted that certain serious but, in comparison with the ultimate effects, relatively minor accounting defects caused by an inexperienced Finance Officer be rectified and that the regular budget monitoring be put on hold. CALL's management normally requires detailed monthly financial reports, annual projections based on the year's adopted budget and the performance to date, and charts that show comparisons with previous years in terms of revenue and expenditure, cashflow, and projected profitability. The effects when this detailed level of reporting and monitoring does not occur can be serious indeed, especially in a fluctuating market situation.

11. Constraints and opportunities

The Centre for Applied Linguistics and Languages has shown considerable resilience over the years and an ability to work through difficulties often incurred by unfavourable University requirements, market fluctuations, or the drying-up of language-specific research funds. It has shown a ready willingness to adapt when market conditions have changed or other issues have arisen to which it needed to respond. Its staff have generally shown a high degree of commitment to their field and to the Centre itself: undoubtedly and with only very few exceptions, the staff have been the greatest asset of the Centre. The constraints on the Centre are those imposed by its self-funding, commercial but academic mandate and the tension that this creates with the University bureaucracy and its traditional, academic procedures. On the other hand, Griffith, like all Australian universities, has had to adapt and is adapting to the financial exigencies and management expectations that have become increasingly demanding through the 1990s and, in some respects, the *modus operandi* of CALL is that which Australian universities as a whole are having to learn. As already noted, it is the tensions that occur between academic demands and traditions, on the one hand, and commercialism, on the other, that underlie the major, though by no means unrecoverable, constraints on the Centre.

One significant area of constraint which, at present, seems almost irreconcilable, is the difficulty, inherent in a centre funded by student fees and projects, of finding a way to allow sufficient focus to be placed on staff development (both on-going teacher development and the regular reading, personal research, writing and conference participation required by academics), on think-tank activities, and on the dissemination of research through conference participation and publications. A major constraint, in other words, is to find a way to fund those academic activities that do not directly generate revenue but which are essential to maintain a lively academic centre and, in the long term, are essential for the Centre's on-going commercial success. If the full implications of commercialisation were to be followed through so that the Centre was not only charged for services provided to it but was able to charge for all the services it provides, this problem may be resolvable. The need remains, however, to convince University authorities that the gratuitous services provided, the substantial and financially valuable numbers of students bridged into award courses, the direct monetary contributions, and the less tangible but no less real contributions through the enhanced reputation of the University should be acknowledged through a return of funds that, in particular, would allow these non-revenue generating academic activities to take place. In addition, as discussed earlier, cross-subsidisation within CALL from more profitable activities would allow other academic activities to be continued. Alternatively, the need is for a source of core funding to be found (as was obtained for many years by the National Foreign Language Center from American philanthropies). The prospect of any of these options being realised seems unlikely: in an environment of heavy financial pressures on all Australian universities, Griffith is understandably unlikely to forgo any of its revenue from CALL or to allow the full corollaries of CALL's commercial exigencies (including cross-subsidisation of some activities) to be followed through in the ways discussed earlier. Thus, in the face of short-term financial demands, it is difficult to win agreement that some funds must be allocated for the maintenance, development, and promulgation of the Centre's academic expertise or else that that expertise will dissipate. The prospect of core funding from a philanthropic organisation is even more unlikely because the funding of educational activities, including research, by the private sector in Australia is rare, if not entirely unknown.

In addition, CALL was established in an era when language policy and language education were of high priority in Australian politics and education and when the importance of language skills for their contribution both to "the clever country" and to Australia's export drive was strongly realised (e.g., see DEET 1991, 1991a). At that time, there was considerable funding available for applied linguistic research and development activities. Since 1996, however, as already noted, those funds have almost entirely disappeared and the lack of specific language research funding outside of the major research grants (with their limitations on what can be costed) poses a serious constraint on CALL's future development. Nevertheless, the applied linguistics area of CALL is adapting, it is focusing increasingly on the provision of training programmes in applied linguistics (both in Australia but especially overseas where language issues continue, rightly, to be regarded as of great importance), and on bidding for projects that don't ignore but broaden beyond language matters into other areas of education and social development. In order to attract more training programmes and a wider range of students, the Centre is also making use of more flexible teaching and learning methods and is offering programmes to be taught overseas either wholly or partially using distance education methods through the internet as well as by hardcopy and reduced face-to-face tuition.

The decline that occurred in the education markets in Asia during the economic crisis of the late 1990s and the effects that had on educational providers in Australia demonstrates how important it is that CALL market its programmes and services worldwide and diversify the ways in which it offers its services. Amongst other things, this consideration has led to the Centre's interest in establishing branches and other operations overseas but it also has implications for the way in which it markets its services and programmes. The limited resources that CALL has available for marketing purposes make it essential that it take maximum advantage of the wider marketing services offered by the University's marketing arm, the Griffith University International Centre (GUIC). This, in turn, necessitates that GUIC actively target CALL's programmes and services and that they not be marketed only as an incidental part of the University's education package for students wishing to undertake degree programmes. Previously, when the Centre relied on GUIC, it proved impossible to obtain an adequate marketing plan, only ELICOS was promoted, and that only incidentally to the University's degree programmes. The GUIC regime has now changed, there is greater realisation of the global market that should be addressed, the marketing plan is much more thorough and systematic, and there is a greater willingness to promote CALL specifically in its own right as well as part of a degree package. However, this enhanced marketing activity together with the rapid recovery in the main markets following the Asian economic slump of the late 1990s has brought to the fore another constraint on the Centre's operations, viz., the lack of sufficient, suitable teaching space at its main, Nathan campus branch, a problem which highlights the effects of the limited capital expansion permitted in Australian universities under the Federal Government's funding regime in the last decade of the 1900s.

Nevertheless, the opportunities for CALL remain considerable. The marketing of CALL's programmes and services has become much more professional and thorough and this has undoubtedly contributed to the rapid recovery and subsequent expansion the Centre experienced following the Asian economic crisis of the late 1990s. Changes in the Australian dollar in relation to the currencies of its main competitors in Europe and North America have also tended to make it much more competitive and able to hedge against some of the adverse market conditions. In addition, the Centre, in cooperation with GUIC, has broadened its marketing to other parts of the world beyond Asia, it is seeking to establish joint venture projects overseas, and it is diversifying its teaching modes in order to reduce the cost to overseas students of taking its courses and so to maximise the Centre's market potential. In other words, the future prospects for CALL's teaching programmes both in language and applied linguistics seem to be very good. So far as its research activities are concerned, as the general level of its activities continues to rise and provided that cross-subsidisation of less profitable activities should be permitted, it is expected that the Centre will be able to replace some of the external research funding that is no longer available with limited funds from its own resources. Under those conditions, CALL should also be able to maintain and perhaps gradually expand its research agenda, as was always intended under its founding mandate and constitution.

12. Uniqueness and impact of the centre

CALL is unique as a language centre, especially a university language centre, in its diversity of interests and its wholly self-funding, commercial mandate. Despite the tensions created by this, it has been successful beyond the levels envisaged at the time it was founded: it has enrolled more students, undertaken more research and consultancy projects, generated more revenue, bridged more students into University award courses, and created a stronger national and international reputation for itself and the University than had been envisaged when it was founded. Financially, it has paid its own way and contributed very substantially to the University; even when its finances have been under strain, it has worked through the difficulties while continuing to contribute financially to the University. Its founding constitution required it to undertake research and other activities "with a view to becoming self-funding" (CALL Constitution, Griffith University Calendar: D64.14, Clause 3) but, in reality, it has always been self-funding, any loan arrangements or underwriting with bridging finance have been repaid, and there is every reason to believe that the Centre will continue to be financially successful while, at the same time, fulfilling its academic mandates.

As already observed, in many ways, CALL is showing the way for other elements in Australian universities as they increasingly confront demands that they become more commercial, that they generate more of their own revenue, and that every element exert stricter budget control and become more accountable to their clients, to the university hierarchy, to the governments, and to the community as a whole. The majority of the problems that CALL has encountered have arisen from the tension between the traditional purposes, operational style, and management procedures of a university, on the one hand, and the need, on the other, for the Centre to be commercial, entrepreneurial, but nonetheless academic. In this regard, the CALL experience has a number of lessons for university administration as institutions confront the new exigencies arising directly or indirectly from the imposition of economic rationalist policies on academic institutions. Many of these issues have been referred to in passing but, in closing this chapter, it is worth briefly noting again some of those lessons, not presented in any priority order since they are all important:

- The issue of synergy in a language centre is fundamental and has implications for all aspects of a centre's management. Staff, for example, must be compatible, competent in applied linguistics, and willing to accommodate to the demands of working in a self-funding centre with its commercial constraints, the need for flexibility, and the need for rapid decision-making. There are also important considerations in terms of the facilities: the availability of commonrooms and meeting spaces should be seen as essential, not as luxuries that either do not exist or are shared with students or with everyone else in the university.

- Employment conditions in a self-funding centre relying on "soft money" are inevitably less favourable than those in other university positions but they should be worked out in full recognition of the requirements of the Centre and its operational constraints (including its competitiveness) and by analogy with persons doing similar work in other private and public institutions, not solely by analogy with other university staff (except, perhaps, in the case of academic and research appointments).

- Comprehensive, vigorous marketing is vital to the success of any commercial enterprise and a commercial, academic language centre is no exception. Resources must be available to enable such marketing to occur and to promote all the centre's activities. However, both the centre and its host institution must also accept that, in the academic context, especially to attract students into graduate courses and research higher degrees, to win research contracts, and to market the centre's consultancy services, the regular academic activities (such as publishing and conference presentations) are vitally important. Such activities not only make known the academics, the centre, and their institutions but they also demonstrate the worth of their research and their other skills by subjecting them to the scrutiny of the wider field. Any notion that such activities add to a staffmember's personal prestige but contribute little to the centre or the host institution is quite erroneous and, without them (and hence without resources being allocated to support them), the academic aspects of a centre's programme cannot long survive.

- The full corollaries of establishing a self-funding centre must be followed through, especially if one of the aims is to cross-subsidise and expand research. The host university cannot cream off substantial revenue, impose procedural requirements that add to the centre's costs but not to its revenue or cost-effectiveness, and yet still expect the centre to operate profitably, to cross-subsidise research and development, and make unfunded contributions to the university in the form of an advisory service, committee work, and student recruitment.

- If a centre is to operate under a commercial mandate, it should not only be charged for the services it receives from the host university (e.g., for marketing, facilities, or administrative support) but it must be recompensed for services it provides (e.g., advisory services or the bridging of high-profit, full-fee paying students into university award courses).

- There is considerable inconsistency, in Australia and perhaps elsewhere, on the part of government and the administrators of the major research and development funds. On the one hand, universities are set up to undertake research and, therefore, it is understandable that infrastructure costs and some salaries are not allowable charges in applications for research funding. On the other hand, universities are being obliged to generate more funds, they set up self-funding entities for that purpose, but, being self-funding, those entities are unable to bid successfully for research funds because of the cost structures that they are obliged to follow. In any case, the funds' argument that universities are already funded for salaries and infrastructure and that it is "double-dipping" to include those costs in research applications is not valid in the case of centres like CALL that have to find all their own resources and also pay administrative and capital levies as payment for rent and other services. This conflict needs to be resolved either by allowing self-funding centres to include more of their real costs in their submissions or by universities' realising that centres can cross-subsidise research and development activities only if they can make and retain a sufficient surplus on their other operations to be able to do so and only if the host university recompenses it for the services it receives from the centre.

- The strength of a centre with a diverse mandate is that more profitable activities can help to support less profitable ones or ones that, like research, are highly desirable and essential elements of a university but may be unable to cover all their own costs. The other important strength comes from the interaction between the different components of a diverse centre with, for instance, the language programmes existing in a strong applied linguistics context and the applied linguistics interacting with the daily practice of language teaching. Mutual support between the different elements of a centre or cross-subsidisation between more and less profitable activities is not possible if the host institution demands that each individual activity within the centre be financially self-sufficient. Again, the purpose of the centre and the full corollaries of its funding arrangements must be taken into account in determining the centre's budgetary and management procedures and parameters.

- Universities often still seem to be naive in the game of commercial competitiveness and to believe that the very title of "university" or "professor" will win contracts irrespective of the fees charged. In CALL's experience, having lost contracts because of unrealistic charges insisted on elsewhere in the university administration, universities must be realistic in their approach to costings, at least in the area of applied linguistics, whether that realism be in relation to the charges to outside bodies or the payments demanded from centres.

- The lack of financial reality of many university personnel is equally evident when it comes to centre projects within the university. CALL is required to be self-funding and to pay substantial levies to the University. In contrast, Schools in the university are funded for their infrastructure, support services and staff and do not pay rent or capital and administrative levies. Yet, academics unused to the reality of university costs have often accused it of charging excessively (even when the price is calculated at cost-recovery) and the Centre has lost out in competitive bids with other university elements which undercut it because they are not obliged to recover full infrastructure or salary costs. Two issues need to be addressed if a centre is to provide services within its host university: first, the host university cannot impose requirements on the centre that do not apply to or are not accepted by Schools and still expect the Centre to compete financially with other elements. Second, few university personnel in regular faculty and administrative positions seem to comprehend the real cost of education or that those real costs are paid by someone somewhere. If such persons are to be put into positions where they are judging the centre or its competitive bids, they must be trained to understand real costs.

- If the vitally important academic maintenance and development of language centre staff and a "think-tank" role are to exist in a self-funding language centre, the centre must either receive a substantial core grant or be able to generate and retain sufficient of its own revenue to be able to support these activities. In addition, the university must accept that activities such as personal research and writing and conference attendance and presentations are not luxuries but are vital activities in developing and maintaining academic excellence and in creating a reputation for the centre that will attract research and consultancy contracts and will attract students (especially graduate students) into the centre's programmes.

- Without discretionary funds because profit-margins are very low, because the host university extracts substantial funds from the centre, or because the host university fails to recompense the centre for services provided, it is virtually impossible for a self-funding centre to develop a meaningful strategic research plan since, without discretionary funds applicable to research, it can undertake only those projects for which it successfully bids. In such circumstances, a strategic plan becomes no more than a wish list and the systematic development of research expertise and a research niche for the centre are difficult, if not impossible, to achieve and maintain.

- As already discussed, the decision-making process in the centre and through the university hierarchy must be expeditious and with as few layers as possible. While it is necessary for new ventures to be thoroughly scrutinised, especially where foreign legal, financial and taxation issues are involved, nevertheless, if commercial centres are to be successful, decisions have to be made rapidly, with full information certainly and with proper regard for what is a reasonable and competitive price structure, but normal commercial timelines must be accommodated.

- While quality assurance processes are important, they must be relevant in content, procedures, and costs to the requirements and constraints of a self-funding centre and with minimum duplication. In Australia, ELICOS programmes, for example, already have to meet quite stringent national requirements through the National ELICOS Accreditation Scheme (NEAS) and, if the university's own internal performance review processes are also required, the centre has to bear the cost and time of two systems. In a regular School funded by university grant, when administrative decisions such as to introduce an elaborate performance review process are made, there is an implication that the grant is increased or, in some other way, allowance is made for the additional workload. That is not the case in a self-funding, commercial centre whose procedures and revenue are not altered by extraneous decisions made elsewhere in the university. Again, the source of the difficulties that thereby arise for a centre lies in the blanket application of procedures irrespective of the particular situation and needs of the centre without account being taken of the additional costs that the centre has to cover and, eventually, has to pass on to its market (with adverse consequences for its financial viability and competitiveness).

- The facilities within which a centre has to work must be appropriate to its purpose, of reasonable cost within the range met by the centre's private and other competitors, and of acceptable standard. They must also meet the expectations of the client, remembering that many of the institutions from which overseas students come to ELICOS and other programmes have facilities that are of very high standard even if the educational programmes and the teaching standards that occur in them might be of lesser quality. Language centres cannot continue to attract students if, because they might sit outside the mainstream of the university's traditional teaching programme, they are assigned lowest priority for teaching and office space or are assigned rooms that no other element in the university would use.

The experience of the Centre for Applied Linguistics and Languages demonstrates that wholly self-funding, commercially orientated language centres within a university's normal structures can be successful both financially and in terms of the academic and research reputation they generate. However, the requirements of such centres are different from those of a regular School or Faculty and the corollaries of being a self-funding, commercial, entrepreneurial but academic centre must be followed through in particular with regard to the centre's management, decision-making, and financial arrangements. Such accommodation poses significant challenges to university administration and requires that, whatever the management arrangements for the rest of the university, the centre's needs will probably be different and the administration, both in the centre and in the host university, will need to be sufficiently flexible to accommodate the centre's distinctive academic and commercial needs.

Postscript

In 2001, Griffith University announced funding for a dedicated teaching block of ten classrooms for CALL (available late 2001) and a new building to house the Centre's administration and laboratories (available late 2002).

The Centre for Applied Linguistics and Languages (CALL)

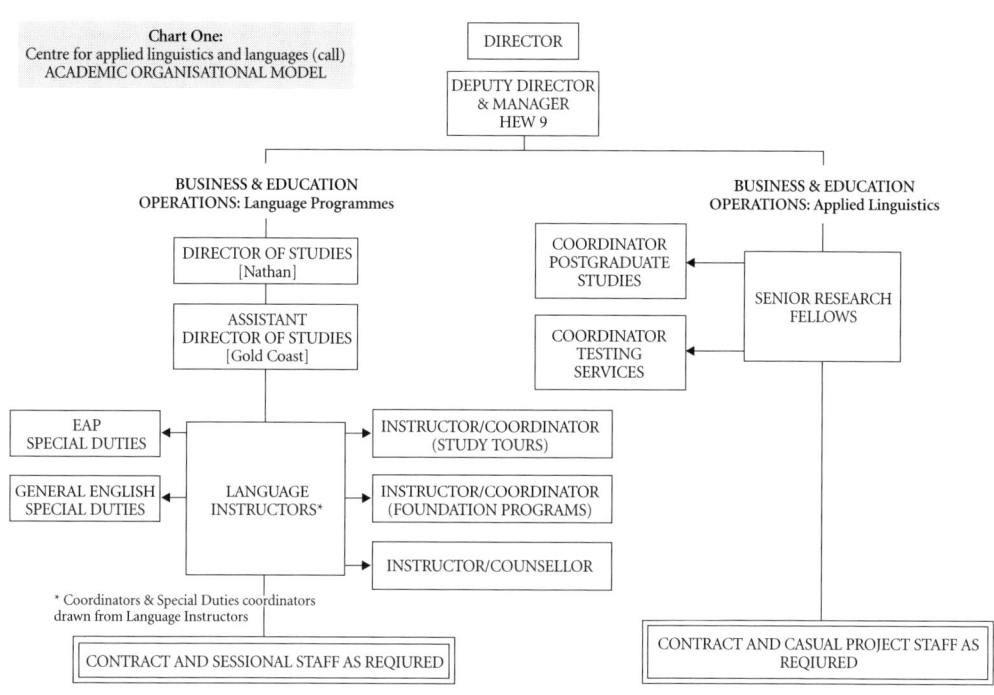

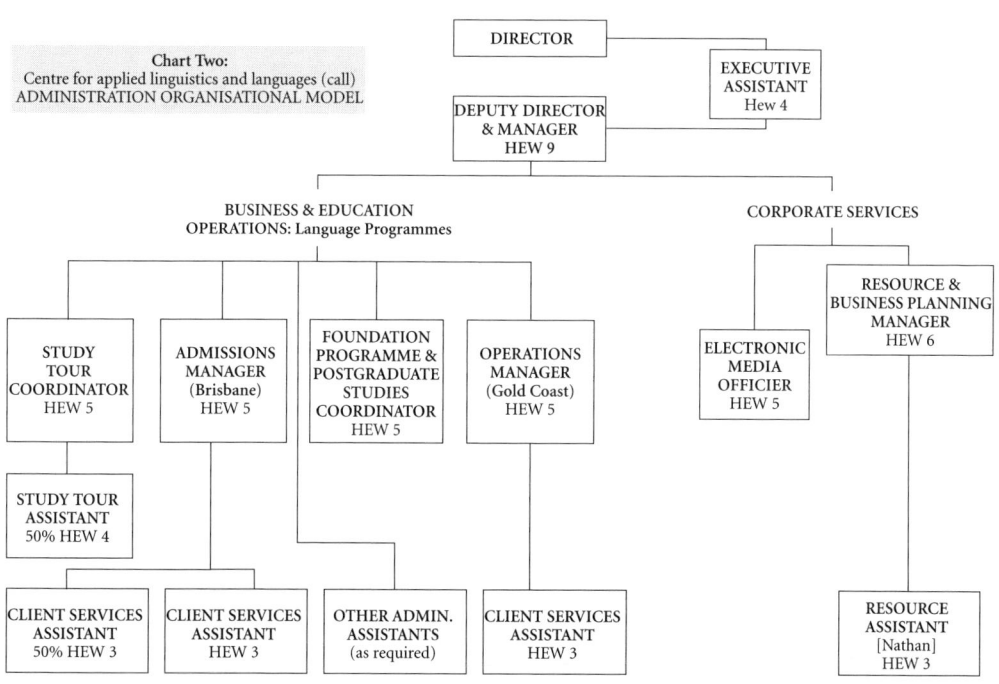

CHAPTER 7

A comparative view of five language centres

1. Preamble

   The preceding chapters have provided five contrasting models of language centres on four different continents. This chapter aims to bring together, necessarily very briefly, the main similarities and differences and so to lead in to the final chapter which draws out key issues for the management of language centres. Reference here is only to dominant characteristics of each centre.

2. Essential nature of each centre

   Two of the centres discussed are international centres with an international role and established by multi-government organisations, the European Centre for Modern Languages (ECML) and the Regional Language Centre (RELC). Both ECML and RELC have an important role in teacher education or teacher upgrading as well as in the provision of advisory services related to the quality of language programmes. Two are essentially national centres, one of which is government-funded and stands alone, the Centre for Information on Language Teaching and Research (CILT), while the other is university-based and largely donor-funded, the National Foreign Language Center (NFLC). Whereas CILT's major role is as a clearinghouse and information centre, NFLC's predominant concern is language policy. One centre, the Centre for Applied Linguistics and Languages (CALL), is self-funding, established by and located at a university; it is diverse in its interests, which include the teaching of languages (especially English as a second language) and research, consultancy and teaching in applied linguistics.

3. Backgrounds and origins

   All the centres were established in response to some perceived need or opportunity in their locality. NFLC is distinctive in being directly concerned with influencing language policy in the United States both through its leverage function and the vital think-tank role that has determined a great deal of what it has done and the structures it has set up. CILT, ECML and RELC were all established in order to improve the quality of language teaching in their areas of responsibility. CILT seeks to achieve this for Britain largely through its clearinghouse and information roles realised through its library, documentation services, publications, and conferences of various sorts. ECML was established to assist with the implementation of the policies emanating from the modern languages projects of the Council of Europe but its primary function on establishment was to assist the newly independent countries of the former Eastern bloc countries to upgrade their language teaching and adapt it to the conditions of the "new" Europe they were entering. RELC's principal role is to provide advanced training for language teachers and so to improve the quality of language education in the SEAMEO group of countries. CALL was established to respond to somewhat different needs and opportunities: needs and opportunities that were evident in Australia in the latter part of the twentieth century when education began to be promoted as a major Australian export, so creating the opportunity to provide English classes to overseas students and creating the need to provide English classes for non-English background students wishing to enrol in Australian educational programmes (especially university degree programmes). In addition, at the time CALL was established, there was strong interest in the development and implementation of language policy in Australia and language research and development were given high priority for Federal and State government funding (a priority that largely disappeared, along with the funding, after the election of a conservative Federal government in 1996).

The common feature underlying all of the initiatives to establish and develop the centres is the escalating move towards globalisation found in most areas of everyday life (but especially in industry, commerce and education) with the result that there has been a growing realisation that all societies need skills in a variety of languages and that many more people need to develop an understanding of other cultures; not least, opportunities have arisen for entrepreneurial programmes to attract students from other countries to learn English or other languages. In the case of CILT, ECML, and RELC, the need for language skills is strongly recognised in their regions and the centres' roles are largely to assist in the effective implementation of policy established by governments; they are not so much concerned with policy-making or exerting leverage (except to the extent that these are the natural though indirect result of raising practitioners' levels of skill) as with policy implementation. In CILT's case in contrast to the other two centres, awareness of the need for the Centre came, not least, from the realisation that, on the one hand, language skills were important but, on the other hand, that a rapidly decreasing number of British students were choosing to learn a language. In the case of NFLC, realisation of the need for language skills in the United States is less acute, policy is less responsive to the needs of globalisation, and the Center's role is to identify the need and bring it to the attention of the policy-makers, researchers and teachers: again, the think-tank and leverage roles were of basic importance in the Center's establishment. CALL's situation is different again in that it is primarily a self-funding university centre which seeks to capitalise on the recognised need for language skills principally outside of its own country but, through its research, development and consultancy activities, it has also sought to increase local and national awareness of the need for language skills in Australia, it has sought to provide tools to facilitate the development and implementation of language and language education policy, and it has responded to the needs of its host institution by offering language advice and providing English language courses to bridge overseas students into the University's award courses.

4. Geographical and administrative locations

The **geographical location** of each centre reflects its role and purpose. CILT, ECML and RELC are all located at key communications and transport hubs for the regions they serve, specifically in London, Graz and Singapore respectively. ECML and RELC are readily accessible from all parts of their regions. CILT's headquarters are in London, again a communications and transport hub, but it has also established branches around Britain that are further supplemented by the network of Comenius Centres enabling any person in Britain to have easy access to CILT's services. The locations of the other two centres have been determined by other factors. NFLC, as a centre concerned with language policy, is appropriately located in the national capital, giving it ready access to national policy-makers in the Congress and bureaucracy. CALL is a university centre and its main office is, therefore, located on the host university's main campus but, in order to extend the clientele it might attract and in order to service the University's most distant campus, CALL has also established a branch in commercial premises on the Gold Coast, within five minutes of the University's Gold Coast Campus. Thus, its geographical locations were determined by the need to remain part of the University, the desire of many overseas students to study on campus, the need to service a part of the University in another city, and the possibility of attracting some students into a non-campus location (especially one located in a major tourist resort).

The **administrative location and governance** of all the centres is quite different. The most independent is NFLC which, though located within the Johns Hopkins University for most of its existence, is essentially independent of it and is governed by a National Advisory Board which the Center itself appoints. Nevertheless, as NFLC has had to learn since late 1998, actual independence is subject also to financial arrangements and a change in the way in which a major donor was willing to provide funds has led to NFLC's having to re-consider most aspects of its operations, including its geographical and administrative locations. The least independent of the centres is, undoubtedly, CALL which, like NFLC, is located geographically and administratively within a university but, unlike NFLC, CALL is an integral part of the host university's structure, the Director answers to a Pro-Vice-Chancellor, as do Heads of Schools, and the same rules and procedures apply to CALL as to any other element within the University (except that CALL is self-funding, pays levies to the University, and receives no funding from it). RELC and ECML seem to operate largely autonomously though, in each case, they were established by and answer to a multi-governmental organisation. RELC ultimately answers to the SEAMEO organisation through a Governing Board appointed on the recommendation of each SEAMEO member country's Minister for Education. Similarly, ECML is a permanent institution of the Council of Europe and is governed by a Governing Board consisting of one representative from each of the Council's member countries that are signatories to the agreement establishing the Centre. CILT is, effectively, an instrument of the British government which, though it seems to operate autonomously, is governed by a Board of Governors appointed by the Secretary of State for Education and Employment. Again, despite CILT's considerable independence, a large part of its funding comes from the government with corollary implications for its viability and for how it operates.

5. Purpose and mission

The most distinctive of the five centres in terms of purpose and mission is CALL, which, as a university centre, is essentially an academic centre even though it is required to generate all its own revenue and to operate commercially. It is diverse in its mission, covering both the development and implementation of language programmes (especially in ESL) and research, consultancy and teaching in applied linguistics, the applied linguistics courses ranging from short non-award courses to Ph.D. research degrees. The purposes and missions of the other centres are defined more in terms of meeting the needs of their region than in the general promotion of applied linguistics. Thus, NFLC, CILT and RELC all include as part of their missions the aim of improving language education, cross-cultural communication, or the national capability in languages in, respectively, the United States, Britain and the SEAMEO countries. CILT, RELC and ECML are all very specific in identifying as a major task support for language teachers and the development of their expertise through training programmes and information services.

It is significant that all these centres have clearly defined goals and a clear limit to their roles. CILT, ECML and RELC are specifically concerned with improving the quality of language education in their specified regions (Britain, Council of Europe member countries, and the SEAMEO group of countries respectively) and NFLC focuses, especially, on language policy in the United States. Though CALL's interests are diverse, its role is limited, first, to serving its host university by bridging overseas students into degree programmes and by providing courses, research and consultancy services in applied linguistics, and, second, to goals as defined in the revenue-generating projects won. In other words, even though all these centres may directly or indirectly advise on and influence language policy in their countries, they do not control or seek to control language policy-making and its implementation but rather to assist in and enhance its implementation (especially through improved language education and more competent teachers) or, in the case of NFLC, to provide advice which policy-makers might draw on to develop more informed policy. Two of the centres, ECML and RELC, target for training those teachers or other personnel who can have a "multiplier" effect, i.e., they are key persons whose influence extends beyond their immediate circle of activities and who will further disseminate the knowledge and skills they acquire through the centre. In these ways, the influence of the centres is extended widely but indirectly through the quality of the training or advice they provide rather than by seeking to assume direct control over language policy or language education in their regions of influence.

6. Activities

Though there is some commonality in activities across the centres, the actual array differs according to each centre's mission and purpose and each has some activities that differ from the other centres. The preceding chapters, organised according to the nature of each centre, have considered activities under a broad set of headings covering language policy, leverage, think-tank, services, research, publications, conferences, information and clearinghouse, and examples of projects.

The NFLC is the centre most directly concerned with *language policy and its implementation*, which is its principal focus of attention. CALL states that language policy is one of its principal interests but its involvement depends on particular contracts won and on the personal advisory activities of individual staff members. CILT, ECML and RELC have the responsibility of assisting teachers towards more effective implementation of the policies of Britain, the Council of Europe, and the SEAMEO group of countries respectively. In other words, their involvement in language policy is either indirectly through the individual activities of their staff, projects that might be assigned to them (e.g., the Languages Lead Body activities that were housed at CILT), or as one of the outcomes of the training given to teachers and others. In the latter instances, their effects, though indirect, can be considerable and, to the extent that they are one step removed from government policy-making, the centres are probably a little less vulnerable to changes of government and government policy than was, for instance, the National Languages and Literacy Institute of Australia, which had sought a more integral role.

Similarly, the concept of **leverage**, which is so central to NFLC's activities and has considerably influenced the nature of the projects that NFLC has taken on, is less directly appropriate to those centres (CILT, ECML, and RELC) whose primary function is to enhance the implementation of policy through better trained teachers and higher quality programmes. Nevertheless, again, the fact that the centres provide through their training programmes higher skills and greater knowledge for teachers and others (including current and future decision-makers) gives them a significant indirect leverage role. In addition, as staff of language institutions of national and international significance, individuals on the centres' staffs frequently have the opportunity to exert considerable individual leverage when their advice is sought or offered. For CALL, any leverage exerted comes either from the activities of individual staffmembers who lobby, advise or act as individuals on advisory committees and councils or as an outcome of particular projects that are won and undertaken. Some leverage also arises from the publications that most of the centres produce or their individual staffmembers write for journals, conferences, publishers, and other outlets.

Only the NFLC was set up with the specific role of acting as a **think-tank**, a role that complements its language policy and leverage activities. For such an activity to be possible, a centre requires a certain amount of discretionary funding, either in the form of untied core funding or surpluses from other activities. In all centres, funded projects, whether research or consultancy, provide the opportunity for some think-tank role related to the particular issues in the project. However, a more general and creative think-tank activity is less feasible where a centre (such as CALL) is dependent on course fees or funds tied specifically to competitively won projects: in both cases, margins are low and, if the host institution also creams off substantial levies and fees, then there is little opportunity for the contemplation and general discussion that a think-tank role demands. In the case of CALL, the main contribution to think-tank activity comes about through the provision of research and study leave for tenured academic staff which, in the Centre, is only the Director. Think-tank activities have been an important part of NFLC's profile though it remains to be seen to what extent the changes in its funding arrangements that occurred early in 2000 towards more project-based grants will allow think-tank activities to continue. In the other centres (CILT, ECML, and RELC), again there is no direct think-tank role though it can be seen to occur as a spin-off largely from the training programmes and information services that these centres provide.

All the centres provide a range of **services**, which differ according to the nature of the centre and its responsibilities. These include, variously, provision of conferences, teaching programmes, consultancies, fellowships, publications, and information and clearinghouse activities, all of which differ according to the mission and purpose of the centre. Both RELC and CALL are also involved in provision of testing services in one form or another.

All of the centres organise **conferences**, seminars and meetings of various sorts according to the role of the centre. In the NFLC, various types of formal and informal conferences and meetings provide important means by which the Center carries out its think-tank and leverage roles. For CILT, ECML and RELC, conferences, seminars and workshops also constitute important means by which they provide continuous education for language teachers and assist with development in specific areas. CALL, as a university centre, is less involved with the mounting of conferences though it has its CALL Seminar Series intended to offer some training opportunities and the dissemination of information on projects undertaken in the Centre.

Research is a major activity for NFLC and, as a university centre, for CALL. For NFLC, research provides a means by which it can identify and respond to national need but it also uses its fellowship schemes to bring in researchers from around the world, both to increase its own level of research activity and to contribute to the think-tank. CALL has had a substantial research and development profile but, as a self-funding centre, its research programme depends on what contracts it can win or the bids to research agencies that are successful. CILT, ECML and RELC do not have research as a major part of their mission and terms of reference but they all have undertaken specific projects that involve research activity. CILT also has an important research clearinghouse role. ECML finances some research but, again, specifically to support the contexts and programmes it was established to assist. Staff of RELC are encouraged to be involved in research even though the Centre's primary aim is the upgrading of teachers.

Information diffusion is an important activity for NFLC, CILT, ECML and RELC. Conferences (NFLC, CILT, ECML and RELC) and teaching programmes (CILT, ECML, RELC and CALL) are two means by which these Centres diffuse information on applied linguistics and, to some extent, their webpages are also used for this purpose (especially in CALL's case where staff papers are often available through the web). In addition, all the centres provide publications of one sort or another for the purpose of information diffusion. NFLC has an array of formal publications, CILT's main publications tend to be of the newsletter variety and are very effective in that they are quite numerous, are produced quite frequently, are written in an informal and easy-to-read style, and so can quickly disseminate a lot of news in a variety of fields relevant to language teaching. Its main research role (other than the hosting of major projects such as the Languages Lead Body) is also realised through publications which collate and disseminate research information and review journal publications. ECML publications appear in the name of the Council of Europe and consist especially of reports of conferences, workshops and commissioned projects. RELC also has an impressive array of publications from conference reports to practical bulletins for practising teachers, to more formal books and the *RELC Journal*. For CALL, as a self-funding centre, in-house publishing is more difficult since, at best, publications are long-term in their generation of revenue, a factor which fits with difficulty with the requirement for every activity to cover its costs as it goes along. Consequently, as noted above, CALL has used its webpage to make some of its staffmembers' writing more widely available, its staff publish in national and international journals and present at conferences, and it occasionally publishes monographs. In addition, it produces reports on the projects it undertakes though such reports are very often not available for public dissemination or, those that are, can rarely be turned into publishable monographs because of funding considerations (in particular, the fact that few project grants actually go so far as to envisage the cost of formal publication and the project staff have to move on to the next funded project in order to maintain a revenue flow to justify their salaries).

CILT, ECML, RELC and CALL all provide **teaching programmes** of one sort or another. While CILT and ECML seem more concerned with conferences, seminars and workshops, RELC and CALL also have on-going courses. In RELC's case, the main focus is on language teacher training programmes at various levels with a lesser emphasis on the teaching of languages themselves. For CALL, however, the teaching of languages (especially English as a Second Language) is the largest source of revenue though it also provides non-award, graduate certificate and Ph.D. programmes in aspects of applied linguistics.

7. Interactions/links

All the centres have established links either as a result of the way in which they were established or as a part of their activities. NFLC and CALL are located within universities, though CALL more integrally than NFLC, and, as a result, it is constrained by the host University's rules and procedures. CILT has located some of its branches at universities though it seems not to be constrained in any way by them. RELC has cooperated with universities in offering some of its courses. CILT, ECML and CALL were established by other bodies, with which they necessarily have strong links of various sorts. CILT is essentially a government body, having been established by the British government, largely funded by it, and the Centre works for the more effective implementation of the nation's language programmes. ECML was established by the Council of Europe and assists with the more effective implementation of the Council's policies. Those policies and various modern languages programmes are developed by the Strasbourg-based Modern Languages Project, with which ECML necessarily has strong links. CALL was established by Griffith University, it is an integral part of the University, it bridges overseas students into the University, it provides a testing service used extensively by the University, and it raises the University's profile in applied linguistics through its courses, research, consultancy activities, and publications. Since CALL serves the University, it has been important for the Centre to create links with the Schools within the University into which it bridges students. All the centres have also sought to create other links through their governing bodies or advisory councils by including on those bodies persons who then become the link into, for example, government departments, industry, or ethnic communities. This sort of linkage is important to all the centres for differing reasons: for all, these linkages help to raise each centre's profile with potential funders or sources of information; for NFLC, they assist with its leverage role; for others, they are important in order that the centre be aware of the needs of the teachers or the governmental and other organisations that their programmes serve; and, for others, such linkages have the potential to provide access to projects and funds. Perhaps the most effective and extensive linkages are those built up by CILT, which enable it to extend its activities considerably with numerous persons helping to further its goals without being a part of the Centre, controlled by it, or drawing significantly on Centre funds.

8. Staffing

Those centres which engage in extended teaching programmes (specifically CALL and RELC) tend to have the larger staffs. On the other hand, as was noted above, CILT seems most effectively to have used its networking to minimise its staffing but maximise its output by facilitating the involvement of persons throughout its extended network of linkages. In all cases, the size of the staff reflects the activities and funding base of the centres. A centre such as CALL, which is self-funding and dependent on student fees and projects for revenue, has the flexibility to take on or dismiss staff according to its level of activity. However, it is always caught in the "vicious circle" of having to generate project submissions and prepare for programmes or projects before it receives funding for that activity. Centres such as those established by governments or multi-governments such as CILT, ECML and RELC always have the option of making a case for an increased or decreased staffing level either in order to generate a project or to carry it out. However, they are also dependent on those bodies' willingness to accommodate the new requirements and on their willingness or ability to see, value and accept the new objectives inherent in a new activity. NFLC's staffing level partly depends on its level of project activity but also on the success of its arguments to donors for core funding and, like government-related centres, it is dependent on the willingness and ability of the donors to perceive and agree to the goals that the NFLC sets for itself.

In most cases, the level of staffing depends on the level of activity of the centre and the revenue it either generates or can argue for from the body to which it answers. In this regard, ECML seems to be most fortunate in that, under its founding agreement, the host nation, Austria, has agreed to provide both the facilities and a secretariat at its own expense. Other centres such as CALL and NFLC are entirely reliant on the revenue they generate through student fees and project grants (in CALL's case) or through donations and project fees (in NFLC's case). CILT, which receives a substantial though decreasing proportion of its revenue from the government, seems to have been exceptionally successful in devolving its operations to other centres and branches around Britain where many of the staff are provided locally at little or no cost to CILT itself. RELC, which also is required to generate an increasing proportion of its revenue, has made use of other activities (especially some return from the RELC International Hotel) to support its activities and, hence, its staffing.

Those centres that are stand-alone in their administration are also likely to operate more cost effectively with regard to staffing. NFLC, CILT, ECML, and RELC seem better able to determine the terms and conditions under which their staff are employed than is CALL. As an integral part of its host University, CALL is required to observe the same staffing procedures and conditions as the rest of the University even though, as a commercial entity, it has to compete with private and semi-private institutions that are able to employ staff on lesser conditions and, hence, more cheaply and without such elaborated (and costly) quality assurance and performance review procedures. Its staff also carry similar obligations for committee membership as do staff elsewhere in the University even though such activity constitutes a real cost against CALL's own revenue. On the positive side, contract staff of a centre integrated into a larger university may have some greater security of employment since, as staff not just of the centre but of the university as a whole, if the centre were to collapse, their employment would still be assured unless the university were to invoke redundancy provisions. Redundancy provisions bring some financial compensation to the employee, which is also why centres such as CALL have a high proportion of casual staff (employed and paid on an hourly basis with little or no security of employment).

The terms and conditions under which staff in centres are employed and the level of staffing differ considerably from one centre to another depending on the centres' functions and terms of reference. The feature that most staff in the various centres seem to have in common is a strong commitment to their field, a strong sense of purpose and of the value of what they are doing, and a willingness to forgo better pay and conditions in the interest of that commitment.

9. Facilities

For those centres obliged to be wholly self-sufficient for revenue, the provision of facilities is a significant burden. In NFLC's case, its move from a location in the Johns Hopkins University to an association with the University of Maryland in 2000 was partly motivated by the cost of the former facilities. Though CALL is integrated into Griffith University, it is required under Federal government regulations to pay capital and administrative levies on its students that amount to a substantial rent for campus facilities over which it has minimal control and which are not of as high quality as the commercial premises it also rents off-campus. The fact that its student enrolments fluctuate and sometimes expand very rapidly, that ELICOS classes are based on ten week modules rather than the one or two semester courses of the rest of the University, and that CALL's activities are seen as peripheral to the core teaching programme of the Schools mean that access to facilities is a continual problem.

ECML, CILT and RELC seem to have found the best solutions to the problem of provision of facilities. As noted above, the establishment terms of ECML place an obligation on the Austrian government to provide suitable facilities. In CILT's case, as already noted, astute use of facilities around the nation has been made, sometimes without cost to CILT itself, and encouraging a widely scattered clientele to have access to the Centre and to identify with it. RELC has taken advantage of both the tourist market and the number of students and other visitors who come to the Centre by establishing an international hotel in the same building with the hotel profits contributing to the Centre's revenue.

10. Budget

The most distinctive of the centres is undoubtedly CALL, which is required, under its terms of reference, to be wholly self-funding, to pay *per* (student) *capita* levies and other fees to its host university, and to operate as a commercial, academic centre. Its revenue is from student fees and project grants with the level of its funding closely related to the level of its activities. The evidence from CALL is that it is possible to operate a centre commercially, generating all its own revenue but, if the basic but expensive and non-revenue generating activities required to develop and maintain academic excellence are to be possible, the full corollaries of being commercial and self-funding have to be followed through into normal commercial practices. The most important of these include the proper costing of activities, the necessity of building up a surplus to cover periods of lower or less profitable activity, and the need to ensure that due financial recognition is given to all the centre's activities so that it is paid for any services it renders its host institution and does not just pay for services it receives. While NFLC is self-funding in the sense that there is no other organisation that accepts responsibility for some of its income, it has relied on donor grants for core funding but also depends on project funding, sometimes from donors (as in the case of its fellowship schemes) and sometimes from research bodies or government. The major change that occurred in its operations in 2000 was the result of some of its core funding being lost or at least becoming project-based.

The highest level of funding security seems, superficially at least, to rest with those centres which are, directly or indirectly, backed by government or multi-government. This is the case for CILT, ECML and RELC though, in the case of CILT and RELC, there is considerable pressure on the centres to generate an increasing proportion of their revenue from student fees, services or projects. Centres funded in this way usually have, on the one hand, the opportunity to make a case for additional revenue for particular projects, for a planned expansion or new activity, or to cover a budgetary shortfall of some origin. On the other hand, they are also very vulnerable to changes in the political climate and, as CILT has had to fight on a number of occasions and as the National Languages and Literacy Institute of Australia found to its sorrow, no matter how large the centre or how effective its operations, it is always vulnerable to a change of government, to a change of policy by the same government, or to a change of whim by a Minister. All three of these centres also generate part (in the case of CILT and RELC, a large part) of their revenue from other activities such as courses or projects. In CILT's case, as noted earlier, it has successfully organised itself so that, on the one hand, it has a relatively small central secretariat and, on the other, it makes effective use of devolved branches and related centres, a large part of whose funding is met by partners. RELC has been, perhaps, most innovative in the use of an International Hotel, built over its centre premises, to generate revenue (in addition to the use of course fees and projects).

11. Constraints and opportunities

In all the centres discussed, the growing importance of globalisation in the societies they serve suggests many growing and diversifying opportunities. The main constraints on all centres is the inevitable one of finance: without exception, every centre could increase its level of activity with additional finance though that is not to say that, in most cases, they are under-funded for the work that they do. In most cases, there is a relationship between the work undertaken and the funds available, especially in those centres (such as CALL and NFLC) where the funds are generated from student fees or project funding but, in all the centres, some budget flexibility comes from the sale of services or from project funding. In this regard, CALL is probably the most limited because of the absolute requirement that it operate commercially, generate all its own revenue from student and project fees, and pay substantial levies and fees to the host university. The worst impact of this combination of requirements is to constrain the Centre's ability to engage in those non-revenue generating activities that are fundamental to the academic development and maintenance of its staff. Its research activities, which were very considerable during the first six or seven years of its existence, have also been constrained more recently both by the University's discouragement of cross-subsidisation between Centre activities and, in particular, by the lack of language-specific research funding following the election of a conservative Federal government in 1996. Its other major constraint, which is not evident in the other centres reviewed, is the limited availability of teaching space at its main, on-campus, branch, a limitation which, in 2000, has forced it to cap its student numbers and so has limited its capacity (and the University's) to take advantage of the rapidly expanding market for overseas students following the Asian economic downturn of the late 1990s. Though NFLC does not operate under a commercial constraint, its partial dependence on donors especially for core funding makes it vulnerable to their whims, as the changes forced on it in 1999–2000 illustrate. The main constraints that operate on the other three centres come from the fact that they are answerable to and at least partially dependent on governments, which can influence what they do and how they operate by controlling finances or making decisions about the operations in which they can engage and the priorities they should set. In that regard, despite the financial constraints that they have to confront, NFLC and CALL have considerable freedom to determine their activities so long as they are able to generate sufficient revenue from them or, in NFLC's case, they can be covered within its core funding. Overall, despite some inevitable limitations that arise from the availability of funds whatever the basis of their revenue, one has to conclude that the strong worldwide interest in the development and use of language skills, given further impetus by globalisation, has ensured that there are many opportunities for all the centres to continue to make major contributions to the development of the societies within which they operate and which they serve. Any limitations on them will come, not from a lack of opportunities, but from external decisions that might influence how they operate, whether that be the result of financial requirements or decisions about their roles and functions.

12. Uniqueness and impact of the centres

Each of the centres reviewed in this book is unique and each has had a significant impact within its own context. CALL is unique in being a wholly self-funding academic centre required to operate commercially. In that regard, its uniqueness and its impact relate to the fact that it illustrates the tension that increasingly occurs as universities, used to operating in a certain traditional way in which academic excellence could take priority over economic rationalism, are forced to bring the two together. It illustrates the tension between commercial exigencies and academic excellence with which it is as much concerned as any traditional university department. It has had to work through the accommodation and compromises that will have increasingly to be made if universities are to cope with the increasing demands of economic rationalism and the demand that they generate more of their own revenue. NFLC is unique in the ways in which it was founded and, for most of its existence, has been funded. It is unique in its core (and highly successful) leverage and think-tank roles that have been possible only while it remained independent and received substantial donor-based core funding. ECML owes its uniqueness and its impact to its role in the implementation of the languages policies and programmes of the Council of Europe, policies and programmes that are not only fundamental to the creation of the "new Europe" but, because of their solid theoretical foundations and creativity, have strongly influenced the development of applied linguistics, language policy and language education worldwide. CILT and RELC are unique because of the roles that they have fulfilled in their regions, the former in Britain during a time when language education was, first, under threat and, more recently, has had to confront new challenges to adapt to the demands of Britain's integration into continental Europe. CILT is also unique in the skilful way in which it has devolved its operations around Britain at minimal cost and with maximum input from the clients it is designed to serve. RELC has achieved a major leadership status, not only in the SEAMEO group of countries that it was designed to serve, but throughout the Asian-South West Pacific region. RELC is also unique in having, if not overcome, at least minimised the financial constraints by the innovative use of commercial premises, viz., an international hotel built over the Centre itself and serving it both in generating revenue and in providing accommodation facilities for its students and for other visitors.

Chapter 8

Issues to consider in establishing and developing a language centre

1. **Preamble**

In Chapter 1, language centres were defined as units formed to gain synergy in the area of language education and applied linguistics from bringing together in appropriate facilities enthusiastic, well-qualified personnel working together in pursuit of the goals set for the centre. They were described as coordinating activity and focussing resources towards set goals in the area covered by applied linguistics. In the next six chapters, we looked at five language centres and then compared and contrasted their features. In this chapter, the intention is to draw out from the preceding discussion key features of language centres for consideration, in particular, key features crucial to their establishment and on-going management. In so doing, it is hoped that guidance may be provided for persons interested in the establishment and management of language centres, at least to the extent that key issues are highlighted for consideration. Just how any issue should be handled will depend on the particular circumstances of the centre or proposed centre, its context of operation, and its purposes, roles and functions.

2. **Roles, functions and purposes**

The roles, functions and purposes of language centres are as diverse as the centres themselves. As we have seen in the centres discussed in earlier chapters, their common purposes include the development of applied linguistics, the improvement of language education, and the implementation (sometimes the development or monitoring) of language policy in the institution, nation or region that they serve. They may or may not include a language teaching programme. The strategic approach of language centres is to bring applied linguistic expertise together to provide mutual stimulus, gain synergy, undertake or stimulate research, rationalise the provision of costly language learning equipment and materials, and improve the quality of language education whether that is conducted by the centre itself, by the host institution, or in the wider community.

Over the years, the prime focus of attention of language centres has shifted in tandem with the increasing globalisation of human activity and the consequent changes in the principal focus of language education (not least towards a greater awareness of and focus on general and specified purpose proficiency and its development). Initially, centres such as CILT or the Language Centre at the University of Essex were dedicated to the improvement of language education, that being seen in the context, very often, of fairly traditional notions of what language teaching was about. Nowadays, at least for centres such as those reviewed in this volume, the prime purpose of a language centre is to **respond to globalisation** and to the need for language education to provide the skills necessary for interaction on a global scale, whether in vocational, political, recreational or cultural contexts or as a result of migration or technological change. This determining focus of language education today, that has, in turn, affected the dominant focus of language centres, is encapsulated in the terms of reference of the Nuffield Languages Inquiry in Britain, terms that equally encapsulate the mission of many language centres today whether their prime focus is responding to the needs of their host institution (e.g., CALL), their nation (e.g., CILT or NFLC), or their world region (e.g., ECML or RELC):

> In this age of technology there is a globalisation of markets and a merging of cultures. These changes are creating a global interdependence, which brings opportunities and constraints in its wakes. Communication is key, and we have to ask ourselves if our linguistic capacity … will prove adequate to sustain us in economic, political, social and cultural terms. (Nuffield Languages Inquiry undated, c. 1998: 4)

The prime purpose in establishing a language centre is, as observed earlier, to gain synergy, focus and resource rationalisation by centring applied linguistic activity in a particular centre, focussing on those functions and goals that are set for the centre when it is established. In addition to rationalising resources, some centres are created with a particular set of activities so as to provide **cross-subsidisation** from more profitable to less profitable but, nevertheless, important activities. Potentially profit-generating activities such as teaching programmes (e.g., language courses or courses in applied linguistics) might, for example, be used within the centre to cross-subsidise other desirable activities such as research, staff development, "think-tank" activities or centre expansion that are incapable of directly generating revenue or require an initial injection of funds. So, for instance, some centres, such as NFLC, obtain core grants that enable time to be directed to the fundamental academic development of, and stimulus to staff through discussion and "thinking time", activities that are, themselves, not profitable or even revenue-generating but are essential for the on-going maintenance and development of the centre's expertise and its sensitivity to current issues as they affect the nation or nations to whose needs the centre is intended to respond: the "think-tank" activities of NFLC or RELC are of fundamental importance to each Centre's activities and its ability to respond to the needs of its nation or region but they are not directly revenue-generating and have either to be funded out of profits generated by other activities or funded by a core grant. In other centres, revenue-generating activities with a profit potential (such as the sale of fee-based language programmes) are taken on in order to cross-subsidise research. The Centre for Applied Linguistics and Languages (CALL) provides one such example though other factors intrude to make it difficult for it to generate sufficient profit to support a viable research programme: those factors include the need to be totally self-funding, the competitiveness of the field, the need to invest resources in future developments in order to keep the commercial activities viable in a changing market-place and changing world economy, and, in particular, the substantial levies and fees paid to the host institution. Cross-subsidisation can occur and can be effective in supporting research and development but the centre's controlling body must accept the reality of commercial activity with its marketing and infrastructure costs, and the suppressing effect of competition on margins, and must ensure that its own legitimate financial interests do not drain the centre of funds that would otherwise be used for cross-subsidisation of the other non-commercial activities the centre was created to carry out.

In some institutions, a language centre has been created as one of the means by which to **improve the quality and practical relevance of language teaching** in the institution. Often the desire is to break away from approaches traditionally associated with university language departments (a focus on grammar, translation and literature) in order to focus more on the development of high levels of language proficiency and cultural understanding, and vocationally relevant language skills through special purpose language development. The corollary of such a move is often that the traditional department can continue to pursue the more academic and esoteric goals with a small body of students who have higher proficiency levels or more esoteric interests while those students who want practical language skills for vocational purposes or to complement other studies undertake their language courses through the language centre.

Resource rationalisation can also be achieved by concentrating language teaching in a language centre since a language centre that cuts across other departmental or faculty divides is better able to employ applied linguists with good training in methodology, curriculum design and assessment, whose skills can be applied to all the languages on offer; such a centre serving a number of departments and languages is also better able to provide the expensive language teaching and research equipment and software (e.g., for multimedia language laboratories) than can individual language departments. In addition, such equipment, together with the applied linguists' skills in curriculum design and methodology, allows the establishment of self-access learning facilities and more economical and effective diversification of course offerings. In this way, a language centre can diversify the languages available and provide a greater variety of general and specific purpose language courses better able to meet the needs of students with strong vocational interests or wanting language courses to complement other studies (e.g., a double degree in Chinese and law). Though none of these initiatives are impossible in a traditional language department, they are facilitated in a language centre with its human and financial resource rationalisation and the greater readiness of qualified applied linguists to break with language department traditions.

Such innovation is well illustrated in the description of the University of Cambridge Language Centre available on its webpage and related documentation (e.g., see http://www.langcen.cam.ac.uk). This centre provides advice to language faculties on the design of their language courses especially for "the many students whose professional life will take place in the context of Europe". It also provides advice on methodology and undertakes research and development focussing on the best use of learning technologies. The Centre provides multi-media materials for 120 languages and modern facilities for group and individual study. It adopts a philosophy of language learning based on "advising" that emphasises social interaction and the meaningful and purposeful use of language. What is important to the present discussion is that, though this centre has not taken over responsibility for teaching the language programmes in Cambridge, it has collected in the Centre significant applied linguistic expertise. This enables it to advise the language departments, undertake research to improve the quality of language learning, and develop innovative programmes reflective of current psycholinguistic and applied linguistic knowledge. In particular, this helps to ensure that courses are of practical relevance to the needs of the students, their programmes and their future vocations. Finally, the grouping of language learning facilities in the Centre means that higher quality facilities, equipment and materials can be provided to maximise the effectiveness (and cost-effectiveness) of language study at Cambridge. The description provided on the Centre's webpage makes it seem unlikely that equivalent expertise, facilities, equipment and materials could realistically be provided in each separate language department.

Some universities, under pressure to find alternative revenue sources for a variety of purposes, establish language centres specifically to **generate revenue**: the main founding purpose of the centre is to directly and indirectly increase the institution's revenue base. Such revenue may be generated in different ways and used for different purposes with various implications for the centres themselves, how they are managed, and their relationship to the host institution:

– Perhaps the most readily defensible use of revenue generated by a centre is to fund research and development activities within the centre itself. This in turn has a favourable impact on the host institution through its research quantum,[1] its reputation, and its ability to attract high quality students.

---

1. In the Australian system, this is Federal Government incentive money fed back annually to the university (and thence to each element) in recognition of the university's (and hence element's) research activity as represented by such things as grants won, refereed publications, and "research higher degree" completions.

- Universities are invariably jealous of their reputations and many of their procedures are set up specifically to enhance the institution's reputation. A centre that generates a strong publications list, has an impressive array of research activities, is substantially involved in community service activities, or is much sought after for consultancy services brings credit to the university, a credit which most institutions are ready and able to exploit to attract additional research and consultancy revenue and higher quality students. In this way, even though a centre's profits may not feed back directly into the host institution's coffers, the indirect effect can be considerable.

- The host institution may receive revenue from the centre to add to its own general revenue or to fund some specific project (e.g., to fund capital works). Thus, for instance, Griffith University receives substantial student fee-based levies from CALL that are split between the university's capital works programme and "administration", including contributions to library resources, to computing services, and to areas of the university's administration. Its Office of Research also receives a percentage-based levy on all research and consultancy contracts that are signed. In addition, during some of the time that CALL was "hosted" by a Faculty, that Faculty received the research quantum generated by the Centre.

- Profits may also be directed to cross-subsidising other activities within the university but outside of the centre, e.g., when CALL was first established it was intended (and written into its constitution) that it would provide revenue towards another centre in the host faculty that, otherwise, was quite unrelated to CALL. In addition, the host faculty on various occasions sought money from the Centre to supplement its own income or to contribute to its building programme. Even though it would seem to be quite legitimate for an institution to set up profit-making centres or other operations in order to increase its revenue, considerable care is needed if such revenue is seen to be used for general operations, thus supporting staff in regular academic positions: if, for example, the bulk of the centre's profits are generated through language teaching programmes and if the language teachers are employed on less favourable conditions than other academics (as is generally the case), then the impression may be given that staff employed on less favourable working conditions are being used to maintain the better conditions of academics in regular faculty positions.

- In some instances, the benefit to the host institution or host faculty may come from selling services to the language centre. If the language centre is set up to be commercial and self-funding, it would seem to be legitimate that it pay for the services used and this may give the host a small additional revenue. However, it is essential that such fee-based arrangements be two-way if they are to be equitable and if the centre is to operate on a properly commercial basis: a situation where the centre, as a commercial operation, is charged for services received but is expected to provide its own services free of charge to the host institution while still meeting normal commercial requirements for profitability is quite unreasonable and has an adverse effect both on relations between the centre and the host institution and on the centre's viability.

– If a centre is commercial, successful and generates considerable cashflow (e.g., from student fees or advance project payments), substantial interest can be earned if those funds are invested on the short-term money-market. If that interest is retained by the host institution (as has been the case with CALL and Griffith University), it constitutes a not inconsiderable additional revenue to that institution. However, it is also a revenue that, in a truly commercial operation, would legitimately go to supplement the revenue of the centre itself. Sometimes host institutions reap double benefit by deriving interest from unspent funds held for the centre while charging interest if the centre goes into debt at periods of low cashflow or when it seeks an injection of funds for establishment or expansion purposes. Such a strategy increases the host's revenue but risks undermining relations with the centre and its capacity to operate commercially.

– Where a language centre offers language programmes that are pre-requisite for entry into the host university's award courses, the centre can be seen as making a very substantial contribution to the university's commercial revenue by bridging students into the more profitable award courses. Thus, for instance, where a university's language centre offers pre-sessional English language courses for overseas students prior to their entry into the university's award courses (known in Australia as ELICOS or English Language Intensive Courses for Overseas Students), the centre serves an important and financially valuable bridging role into the university. In the case of CALL, for instance, over half the ELICOS students go on to other university courses. Whereas, in CALL, ELICOS students pay between $2,650 and $11,925 for their English courses depending on whether they stay for ten or forty-five weeks, they will pay between $8,000 and $30,000 a year for their award courses, depending on their field of study. In addition, whereas ELICOS courses are high-cost with intensive teaching for 25 hours a week, the presence of overseas students in award courses adds little to their costs and the student fees are largely profit for the faculty or institution. Thus centres offering low-profit ELICOS courses bridge many of their students into relatively high-profit degree programmes, thus making a substantial financial contribution to their host institutions. In some centres, the host institution acknowledges the magnitude of this contribution to its revenue by subsidising some of the centre's costs, commonly, for instance, meeting the salary and related costs of the Centre Director.

Many language centres have some direct or indirect interest in **language or language education policy**, either helping to develop language or language education policy, being involved in monitoring it, or facilitating its high quality implementation. Such language policy involvement may occur at the institutional, State, national or international levels. All of the centres reviewed in earlier chapters are involved at some level in language or language education policy. NFLC exists to observe the American language situation and offer advice on language policy at the national level in the

United States; CILT is not directly involved as a centre in policy development though its training and facilitation roles clearly give it a considerable indirect input and its activities are very much directed at improving the implementation of the *de facto* language policies and language education programmes in Britain; ECML is specifically not involved in development of Council of Europe language policy (a task for the Modern Languages Project based in Strasbourg) but it is very much involved in facilitating the implementation of the Council of Europe policies, not least through the provision of training to senior personnel and teacher educators from the participating countries; RELC's role in South East Asia and, specifically, in the SEAMEO group of countries is similar to that of ECML in Europe; and though CALL is a university centre, its academic staff have strong interest in language and language education policy and have carried out many projects in this area (projects ranging from measurement of literacy standards across Australia with implications for literacy policy to specific advice on language education to Education Departments and curriculum boards in Queensland and other States).

In fact, if a nation adopts a language policy, it is quite essential that some organisation (appropriately, a language centre) have the role of coordinating that policy, monitoring it, and providing feedback and recommendations on the policy to whoever is charged with its development and maintenance. If language policy is to be relevant and maintain its relevance, it must be seen to be responding to the needs of the society (or the institution if it is an institutional language policy), the success of the policy and its implementation must be monitored, and any changes that occur in the nature of the society (or the institution and its student body) must be identified and implications drawn for the language or language education policy. As identified in the initial document[2] that eventually led to the establishment of the National Languages and Literacy Institute of Australia, an important task for a national language centre is

> To identify, in consultation with appropriate professional and governmental bodies, areas of concern with respect to language use, language learning and teaching, and language research; to collect and coordinate information about Australia's language needs and resources and about all aspects of modern languages and their teaching; to make this information available for the benefit of education; to assist agencies of government with the formulation of language-related legislation and policy; and to contribute to the solution of relevant problems (especially involving language learning) in Australian society. (Ingram 1978: 12)

---

2. Unfortunately, in the present writer's view, NLLIA eventually came to deviate considerably from the original proposal in ways that, in retrospect, contributed to its early demise, not least because it attempted to become too large, to take responsibility for too much of the field of applied linguistics and language education in Australia, and thus became too costly, too bureaucratic, and too antipathetic to autonomous institutions and education systems in which the NLLIA's centres and other units sat and to which they had to answer.

Though no national language policy exists in the United States, the roles and functions of the NFLC are not dissimilar from most of the description above (see Chapter 2). Though it is not termed a "centre", the Modern Languages Project of the Council of Europe, based in Strasbourg, France, serves a similar purpose for the Council of Europe.

Though the nature and structure of language policy is a topic that goes beyond the scope of this book (but see Ingram 1993 and 1994 for a discussion of the nature of language policy), it is relevant to the present discussion to note that, if a language policy is to be systematic and relevant to the society or institution that it is intended to serve, it must grow systematically out of a clear and comprehensive understanding of the nature and needs of that society or institution. An appropriately systematic and needs-based policy must be developed, not just by an informed individual, a government department, or a group of academics (even applied linguists) but with strong input from persons able to sample opinions and needs across the community that the policy is to serve. Language policy, especially national language policy, must be based on a strategic view of the society or community and of the future. The Nuffield Languages Inquiry in Britain has recognized this need in setting out its terms of reference and calling for input from all sectors of society:

> This Inquiry provides a long overdue opportunity to take stock of our national capability in languages…
>
> We intend to range widely. …We shall want to be sure, to the extent we can, that the teaching of languages in the UK is effective, timely and imaginatively harnessed to society's wishes.
>
> The Inquiry must in consequence engage with all sections of the community. …
>
> …What is needed is a coherent national view of the future, in which strategic thinking will seek to build on our successes while addressing the remaining chronic problems. Such a task cannot be undertaken by any single sector, but needs to be a partnership between the many interests and stakeholders involved.
>
> The essential players include government, the business world, language learners and teachers at all levels, language minorities in this country, the media and our many institutional and national partners in other countries. *The Nuffield Languages Inquiry* will create a focus which will bring together these sectoral interests, while remaining independent in its judgement. (Nuffield Languages Inquiry undated, c.1998: 2–3)

Equally, a language centre that aspires to monitor language policy or to respond to the needs of a society, community or institution must establish procedures and structures that facilitate the identification of the needs and opinions of that society and community. All of the centres discussed in this volume have adopted strategies designed for this purpose: all of them have governing boards or advisory councils composed of representatives from across the community they serve. In the case of RELC, for instance, the governing board has representatives from all the SEAMEO countries.

NFLC has gone further than most centres in that it has a governing council that brings in representatives from American education, government and industry but it also has a diverse system of fellowships designed to bring in people (mainly applied linguists of one sort or another) from around the United States and from around the world who can contribute to the NFLC their knowledge of the nation, of the world, and of language policy.

3. Scope of language centres

Earlier chapters in this book examined in some detail five centres around the world and so provided, through actual examples, some detailed models of language centres with terms of reference that differed somewhat in their scope. Here we shall briefly consider some general issues in relation to the scope of language centres.

One of the most basic questions to consider is just how widely embracing a language centre, especially a national language centre, should be. There are several issues to consider in determining what a suitable size for a centre might be. On the one hand, it is a *sine qua non* that any centre must be large enough to have the human and other resources to be able to carry out the tasks assigned to it. It also needs to be large enough, with sufficient well-qualified staff with a diversity of expertise, skills and interests that it achieves the synergy referred to above that comes from bringing together a variety of experts to focus on the goals of the centre. Equally, it needs to be sufficiently large that, not only is there sufficient professional and support staff to do the work set for the centre, but there is sufficient staff available to back up those persons working directly on the prime tasks of the centre by developing project submissions, publicising the centre and marketing its expertise, making professional contacts, and carrying out the whole range of tasks needed if the centre is to gain some financial security and flexibility by generating some of its own revenue. The greater the requirement that the centre be self-funding, the greater this task is and the more important it is that specific staff be employed to do this rather than have the academic, research or teaching staff having to take time off their prime duties to generate revenue and engage in publicity.

It cannot be too strongly stressed that a centre needs to be sufficiently large to fund staff to carry out all the essential duties required to support the centre in achieving its goals: academic, research and teaching staff, senior management and other support staff with specialist skills should not be put into situations where they fritter away those skills or spend expensive professional time in doing things that, for instance, lower paid support staff might do. It is always tempting, for example, to try to minimise staff costs by reducing the support services available in a centre but, in reality, it is frustrating for professional staff to have to give time to such activities, it distracts them from their real functions and fragments their time, generally they lack the skills do the clerical, financial or marketing tasks as efficiently and effectively as qualified administrative support persons, and it is false economy to have more highly paid staff doing work that can be carried out more cost-effectively by lower paid staff.

On the other hand, a centre that is too large may become administratively unwieldy, it is costly to run and, if it is government- or institution-funded, the more expensive it is the more vulnerable it will be to fluctuations in political, economic, or institutional priorities and funding cuts. Perhaps the most seductive danger for a centre is to aim to be large enough to take over the whole responsibility for applied linguistics or language education in its institution, nation, or region. In most cases, such aspirations are self-destructive and are certainly destructive of the sorts of roles and functions of language centres discussed in this book: such a centre becomes too unwieldy, it loses focus, like any autocracy it becomes more concerned with its own survival and power than with the quality of the operations it was intended to support, and, in losing distance and failing to separate the expert advisory roles from the functional tasks, it diminishes and weakens the vital advisory role that many centres (especially national and international centres) are created to provide. In addition, the efforts needed to sustain the centre's power creates a large and costly bureaucracy that demands such effort from all members of the centre that it reduces the real work of the centre. Furthermore, the efforts needed to create and sustain such a centre's power may cause conflict with many of the field units that it seeks to control (e.g., units in autonomous universities or educational institutions that also answer to other authorities such as their host institutions, their own boards, or government departments). The result of this is that much effort is lost in disputation between the "centre" and its hierarchy, on the one hand, and the real workers in the field units on the other while the synergy that is fundamental to the success of any centre is also damaged. Thus, where a "centre" becomes too large, it can be in danger of losing focus or of turning its focus onto things that are not supportive of its essential mission. In the present writer's view, some aspects of the short history of the National Languages and Literacy Institute of Australia (NLLIA)[3] illustrated some of the dangers and some of the issues to be considered in considering the scope of, especially, a national language centre.

The NLLIA (which, significantly, was re-titled Language Australia) commenced operations in 1989 and sought progressively to extend its responsibility for all or most

---

3. Statements made in this volume in relation to the National Languages and Literacy Institute of Australia are, of course, made from the perception and perspectives of the present writer who, as noted elsewhere, wrote the initial paper that eventually led to the establishment of the Institute [Ingram 1978]. For most of the life of the NLLIA, he was also Director of one of the founding research centres of the Institute, the Language Testing and Curriculum Centre (LTACC), which he administered in Griffith University as a companion centre to the Centre for Applied Linguistics and Languages (CALL). LTACC's funding was always insufficient to cover infrastructure costs and so CALL helped to support it by providing infrastructure (including administrative) support services and facilities. Other persons involved with NLLIA may have had different perceptions of the Institute.

applied linguistic research that went on in Australia. The original motivation for this seemed to be to make the Institute large and, therefore invulnerable as an integral part of the language education and research system in Australia. The practical effect was, in part, that the Institute sought to exert an increasingly strong control over the entities out in the field (mostly in autonomous universities) that made up its elements both to ensure its control over applied linguistics across Australia and to favourably affect its own revenue; on a number of occasions, for instance, the NLLIA tried to get universities where it had research centres to sign agreements that would have made them franchisees of the Institute. On other occasions, if a different element of a university with an NLLIA centre sought and won a research or consultancy grant independently of the NLLIA, the NLLIA reacted angrily claiming that the project should have been sought through it, NLLIA should have received the same levies as one of its own centres would have paid, it should have some level of control, and it should hold intellectual property rights: inevitably such actions caused considerable antagonism and even anger towards NLLIA from institutions hosting its research centres or other units and made it extremely difficult for those centres or units to operate answering, as they had to, to two competing masters. Inevitably, the Institute's size and ambitions did not protect it, following a change of government in Australia, it lost most of its funding in the latter part of the 1990s, and, with its demise, virtually all of the language-specific research and development funding also dried up.

An all-embracing model for a national language centre is most undesirable for many reasons:

– Size is no guarantee of survival for a government-funded organisation. On the contrary, the more expensive a government-funded organisation is, the more likely it is to be targeted for cut-backs or abolition of its funding. Recent Australian history has shown that even highly profitable government-controlled Australian icons such as the Commonwealth Bank or QANTAS Airways, the telecommunications carrier Telstra, and large government-funded social security services such as the Commonwealth Employment Service can and will be privatised, abolished, or told to find their own resources. (In the Australian system, requiring a research-based entity to self-fund is tantamount to abolition since virtually all research and development activities in education and language policy in Australia are government-funded.)

– Universities, especially Australian universities, are fiercely independent and believe that their academic and administrative autonomy, which is protected by the legislation that establishes each one of them, is fundamental to their academic independence and role and is absolutely sacrosanct. Any action that reduces that academic autonomy is met with strong counter-action. Consequently, the history of NLLIA was a history of long and painful attempts by the Institute to have universities sign contracts for annual funding or for particular projects which, the universities believed, reduced their autonomy, reduced their intellectual property rights, and extracted fees or royalties for the Institute. In reaction, universities minutely dissected and amended contracts to protect themselves and the interests of their elements and their staff from what were seen, rightly or wrongly, as the predatory efforts of NLLIA. In some instances, the wrangling over contracts took so long that projects had to proceed in any case in order to meet the requirements of government grants and the contracts ended up being signed either shortly before the projects' completion or not at all.

– In a competitive situation, the addition of another layer of bureaucracy within the language research structure adds considerably to costs and approval times. In the case of the NLLIA, each centre, its host university, and the Institute each had to charge overheads of one sort or another to cover their operations. In such circumstances, the ability of centres to compete in cost terms becomes greatly reduced while the approval times for project submissions and reports become protracted.

– In order to achieve its control over applied linguistics and potentially language education in Australia, the Institute established not only contracted research centres in universities but also other units of various sorts, including "networks" in areas such as literacy and child ESL which had small units in many institutions and which, even though the funding was minimal, sought to bind the institutions or at least the host faculties to NLLIA and subjected them to the same stringent reporting, control and levies as the research centres encountered. Thus, to demonstrate its integral relationship with languages and language education in Australia and to exert influence over them, the Institute spread its tentacles increasingly widely. In such circumstances, much effort is lost in trying to maintain and enforce the centralised structure of what is inherently a disparate, diversified system of autonomous entities and, to the outsider such as politicians, it is easy to target for cost-savings the large and complex research bureaucracy that they see.

– It can be anathema in such a centralised or "totalitarian" research structure for outside entities to compete with it or to undertake activities that it could perform since it demonstrates to the political paymasters that the expensive bureaucracy is not essential and other entities can carry out its functions without it. To preserve itself, therefore, a national language centre of totalitarian intent is likely to try to prevent outside bodies taking on its functions or to absorb them if they do. Thus, if a university with an NLLIA centre also had a department or other element working in the area of applied linguistics, the Institute seemed to expect that all project bids in that institution would be lodged through the Institute, with corollary implications for control, intellectual property, and levies. In one major university, for instance, with an NLLIA centre, when a senior staff member in an element not related to NLLIA won a major project for the academic management of a major English language test, NLLIA asserted that the bid should have been made by its centre, and that it had the right to influence the project, to hold intellectual property rights, and to receive levies on the revenue. When the University did not accede to these demands, the Institute first reduced and then cut altogether its funding to its centre in that university. As distressing and divisive as such action might be, it is the almost inevitable corollary of a national language centre's seeking to exert ownership over all of the nation's language education or applied linguistics or even of all its relevant research.

– Another danger of the sort of situation just described, the centralisation of research and research funding in a single bureaucracy, is that some of the basic requirements of a vigorous, academic and research area can become undermined. In particular, freedom of thought, speech and research is likely to be lost and the synergy that we have argued is essential to a language centre becomes dissipated. Freedom cannot exist where units receive funding only so long as they remain in agreement with the funding hierarchy in the controlling centre but, if that hierarchy has control over who receives what research funds, then the field units that are dependent on the funding are unlikely to voice contrary opinions. There is also a serious danger that a belief will grow up that, to maximise their funding, the units must publicly express their approval of the work of the hierarchy of the organisation and that those who fail to do so or who take action that the hierarchy might claim, rightly or wrongly, to be contrary to its interests will lose their funding. In such a climate, objective and dispassionate research and objective and dispassionate selection of research priorities becomes impossible.

– One of the strongly negative effects of this sort of operation is that an expensive bureaucracy and its corollary bureaucratic procedures (or "red tape") are needed in order to keep control of what is happening out in the field in the numerous centres and other units that make up the centralised research organisation. In the case of the NLLIA, a complex and costly reporting system evolved that required frequent national meetings of representatives of all its units and a maelstrom of reporting and red tape, which re-directed much time, effort and resources away from research into "planning" and reporting. In a centralised bureaucracy, such procedures are, undoubtedly, necessary in order to maintain the bureaucracy and enable it to report to its funders but it can also carry the undesirable corollary that units that devote their time and resources to their research and fail to participate in the bureaucratic maelstrom will be in danger of losing their funding because they are loosening their ties to the central bureaucracy.

– Any totalitarian organisation that, potentially or actually, can demand that researchers either conform or lose their funding is always at risk of adopting undesirable practices; it is too easy, in the interest of maintaining the autocracy and, hence, in justification, the research funding, for it to demand "loyalty" as shown when its members pay allegiance to the hierarchy and sublimate their views to those of the hierarchy rather than argue their own point of view or freely undertake their own research and writing. Such a situation is contrary to the basic requirements of research and academic life in any democracy.

– When research and development funding for a particular field is all channeled through one organisation, the entire field is put at risk: if that one organisation is abolished or has its funding cut, the whole field is likely to be starved of funds. This, in fact, occurred in applied linguistics in Australia from the mid-1990s when, in contrast to previous years, funding to the Institute was reduced and eventually virtually abolished and little dedicated money was made available elsewhere for language-specific research and development.

In summary, in a democracy, it can never be considered good that a single organisation take over an entire education and research system. Diversity of choice, independence of decision-making, and the rights of all people and institutions to decide, within reasonable limits, their own actions and express their own opinions is fundamental. Equally, a vital academic research area demands that there be diversity in that research, that a variety of researchers and research units be pursuing their own independent research, exploring basic issues, developing new approaches, and applying research findings to the development of language education practice: it is undesirable that all of that be controlled by one organisation, limiting diversity, freedom of research and, potentially, freedom of thought and decision-making to that approved by the one "centre". For an expert centre to provide advice, to stimulate and to assist is highly desirable: for it to take over and make all the decisions and direct all the activity is highly undesirable and potentially destructive of the very field it was established to support. In an ideal world, a benevolent dictatorship might possibly be an effective and efficient way to get things done and to achieve set goals but it is a system that is inherently flawed: if the dictatorship should lose its benevolent qualities, if it should start to demand higher and higher dues (whether financial or in the form of respect and obedience), or if it should become self-serving with the goal of maintaining its own control, then it will inevitably lose its focus on those functions it was established to perform.

Rather than be all-embracing, the successful examples of language centres discussed in this book demonstrate that, so long as the basic requirement of synergy is met, size, *per se*, is not so critical an issue as that the centre be clearly focussed, with a clearly directed role and function, and with a specific and all-determining purpose. In the case of CILT, ECML and RELC, the principal purpose is to improve the quality of language education in their country or region by providing an information service and clearinghouse, by offering training programmes, and by providing advice or assistance in curriculum development. In the case of NFLC, the principal purpose is to provide advice, especially to government, on language policy and to undertake funded projects in specific areas such as Chinese syllabus development. In all cases, the aim of these centres is to provide assistance in order to improve what others are doing: not to take over their activities as part of itself. In the case of CALL, as an institutional centre, the principal purpose is to promote applied linguistics but it has to be large and diverse enough to be able to generate revenue in support of its own operations, to generate revenue for the university by bridging students into university programmes, to cross-subsidise and engage in research and offer consultancy services, and to assist to develop the field of applied linguistics both in the university and beyond through research, consultancy services, and its own (full-fee-based) teaching. As an institutional centre rather than a national or international centre, its role is quite narrowly delimited.

Lambert confronted this same issue in making the case for a national foundation that eventually became the National Foreign Language Center. The issue is also discussed in the chapter on NFLC but, in the context of the present discussion, it is worth noting Lambert's comment in relation to the coordination of "overseas linkages" (such as exchange programmes and overseas internships). He emphasises the need to find an appropriate balance between productive diversity, on the one hand, and centralised policy-making and productive coordination, on the other:

> We are not suggesting that in the area of overseas linkages, any more than in the support of research…, our system of productive pluralism should give way to a single czar in charge of all exchanges, nor that our exchange policy should be bent to a single purpose. It would be useful, however, if the Foundation were to take a more than occasional look at what the full range of transnational exchange and training programs is with respect to a particular country or set of countries, private as well as public. (Lambert 1986: 113)

Consequently, Lambert recommended a centre that would be limited in size and scope but have a major "think-tank" and policy advisory role. This "balancing act" is of great importance and provides strong justification for centres to be relatively small, independent, with limited jurisdiction and specific goals, and able to provide advice to governments and others independently of the actual projects and programmes themselves.

4. Governance and management

The **governance and management** models adopted by language centres vary considerably though most have, as their common feature, a governing or advisory body that sets priorities, approves programmes and strategies, and represents interests from across the area to whose needs the centre is established to respond. Lambert has described this feature in recommending an advisory council for what was to become the National Foreign Language Center:

> To establish the priorities for and to supervise this proactive program, a distinguished national advisory group should be established, comprising research scholars and representatives of universities, major international business firms, national research organizations and government agencies … (Lambert 1986: 99–100)

The various models adopted by the centres reviewed in this book differ in each case and are discussed in their respective chapters. CILT and NFLC have advisory or governing councils that reflect the community to whose needs they respond, as reflected, in NFLC's case, in the Lambert quote above. ECML and RELC have governing boards that represent the multigovernmental organisations that have founded and fund them. In the case of CALL, the one university centre described in this book, the two roles of governance and advice are met through a dual structure: governance is from the centre through the university hierarchy to the University Council while there is also an advisory committee that represents the university and potential clientele (industry, education systems, the ethnic communities, and students).

The critical issue is that the governing body and any advisory body should be relevant to the requirements of the centre, should be aware of the distinctive management needs of a centre, and should be capable of helping the centre to be aware of the needs and opportunities to which it should respond. Centres such as CILT and NFLC[4] that are not integrated into a larger institution and are able, to a large extent, to determine what and who constitute their governing bodies are less fraught with the danger of ignorance or irrelevance than a centre such as CALL within an established university administrative framework. Indeed, as noted in its chapter, CALL has frequently had to struggle with erroneous decisions undoubtedly made in good faith but imposed inappropriately on the centre contrary to more informed advice from Centre management. Early in its life, for instance, the Centre was required to pay 40% of its revenue into a joint venture marketing agency despite advice from the Centre that this would plunge it into debt and was inconsistent with its requirement to be fully self-funding. On another occasion, a triennial review instructed the Centre to undertake more *qualitative* research in language assessment and make research appointments accordingly rather than the *quantitative* research that it was supposedly undertaking even though anyone familiar with language testing and the publications of the Centre's research staff would have known that much of their work in language assessment was qualitative, based around the International Second Language Proficiency Ratings (Ingram and Wylie 1978/1999).

In CALL's case, the problem is two-fold: first, it is a language centre with the distinctive requirements of language centres for which the governing body should have some familiarity with applied linguistics; and, second, it is required to be wholly self-funding, to operate commercially, and to live at all times within the revenue that it itself generates while, at the same time, meeting the industrial, performance review and other requirements of any element within the university. In the CALL experience,

---

4. Note that, at the time of writing, NFLC was hosted by the Johns Hopkins University but the University had no control over it, did not fund it, and had no financial responsibility for it. For all practical purposes, NFLC is independent. See Chapter 2 for a fuller discussion. In 2000, NFLC changed its affiliation to the University of Maryland, though its independence remained assured.

academics or administrators used to working in a large institution or government department where they can access funds from some remote "pot of gold" by making a strong argument in support of a course of action, research activity, piece of equipment, or other expenditure rarely comprehend the requirements of a commercial, self-funding centre where the final decision as to whether something can be done, equipment purchased, a new management procedure introduced, or some other expenditure made depends on what revenue can be generated either by the proposal itself or in surplus from other activity. It is rare that such persons, when appointed to the Centre, are able to accommodate to the new way of thinking and decision-making under, at best, twelve months in the Centre. This has profound implications for staffing and management: the Centre has, on occasions, lost outstanding staff members because they could not accommodate to these management and funding requirements and the corollary need for flexibility in the duties they undertake and their ways of operating. Most of the adverse management decisions imposed on the Centre from outside have resulted from the same incomprehension.

The point is not, in CALL's case, that Griffith University or the Faculty within which it was originally established has been antagonistic or incompetent: rather, the nature of institutional bureaucracies is that individuals or committees at different levels are required to make decisions and do so on the basis of whatever knowledge or understanding they have within the contexts to which, as experts, they have been appointed and mostly operate. The problems occur when they are required to make decisions in fields in which they lack expertise or in management contexts with which they are unfamiliar. Centres such as NFLC or CILT that are more or less "stand alone" and can wholly or largely determine the nature of the governing body to which they answer are likely to experience more informed and sympathetic decision-making than centres integrated into some larger structure established for different purposes with persons of different expertise at the decision-making nodes. The problems for CALL, especially in its early years, arose partly from the fact that it has been at the forefront of the new "commercial" management exigencies that increasingly confront most Australian and many other universities: the governing structure to which the Centre has had to answer has been largely traditional even though it is now having to adapt to the sorts of changes that CALL, as a self-funding, academic centre, has already had to accommodate. A clash of governance and management expectations is inevitable.

In summary, it is highly desirable, whatever governing body a centre has to answer to, that its members be relevant to the task, that they have some knowledge of the field and some practical understanding of the management requirements of the centre, or, if they are purely managers or if, as usually happens within a university, their expertise lies elsewhere, that they be willing to listen to expert advice from the centre or from other relevant advisers.

Each centre has to establish its own **internal management structure**. This will differ according to the needs of each centre: each of the centres described in this book, for example, has its own distinctive internal management arrangements. The critical issues are similar to the foregoing: the structure must be relevant to the needs of the centre and persons in management positions must have the skills, knowledge, understanding and awareness needed for the position they occupy. Again, that understanding, knowledge and, desirably, experience must not only be of the relevant academic issues but of the particular *modus operandi* that the centre has to adopt according to the terms of reference under which it is required to operate. In other words, their knowledge and skills must encompass not only relevant areas of applied linguistics but also the management issues for the particular type of centre: if the centre is to be self-funding and commercial, for example, the issues are different from those involved if the centre is grant-funded by government, donors or an institution.

It is also desirable that those undertaking management or clerical duties have the appropriate training and be employed to do the tasks that are relevant to that training: as commented earlier, it is often tempting to fill a centre with academics or teachers who then, supposedly to economise on support staff, carry out their own administrative support, typing, filing, photocopying or printing, financial management, marketing, and so on. However, academics or teachers rarely have the skills or the time for such tasks, the tasks can be carried out more efficiently and expeditiously by people with appropriate clerical, marketing or other training, and, in most cases, support staff, who generally are on lower salaries with lesser working conditions (no study leave entitlements, for instance), can perform those duties more cheaply and cost-effectively.

Decision-making in a centre is often best carried out in ways that differ from those commonly found in university departments, which, at least in universities in the British, Australian and American traditions, favour a participatory or democratic decision-making process with a suite of committees at various levels that make the decisions. There are good reasons to foster such an approach. Not least, because all wisdom does not reside in the senior management of a centre any more than in any other organisation, there is advantage in having input to decision-making from as broad an information base as possible to help to ensure that the centre remains sensitive to the diverse needs of its generally wide-ranging clientele. In addition, the more the people who work in a centre feel that they are involved in the decision-making, the more "ownership" of the centre they will feel and the readier they are likely to be to work in the interests of the centre and its goals.

For these reasons, some of the centres have quite an elaborated internal management structure and the larger the centre and the more dispersed its operations, the more necessary it becomes for a decision-making process that involves the staff of the centre. As the chapter on CALL outlines, CALL, with a staff of 60 or more on two campuses almost one hundred kilometres apart and with overseas activities, has developed an elaborated internal management structure under which staff have the opportunity to be involved in different committees, to elect their representatives on those committees, and to elect representatives on the senior body, the CALL Committee. In the case of NFLC, where staff levels are quite small, there is little need for an elaborated structure since there is ready interaction amongst all staff and all staff can feel involved in the decision-making process as a result of the everyday interaction with their colleagues.

However, a commercial operation that has to be able to compete with similar operations in other universities or in private schools has different requirements from a regular School or Faculty in a university. First, decisions have often to be made rapidly, projects accepted or submissions lodged at very short notice, and there is need for mechanisms that enable that to occur. Second, the issue discussed earlier of how staff accommodate to work in a commercial, self-funding operation is also relevant: if decisions are made that are contrary to the basic terms of reference of such a centre, the means must be available to override them. Third, an elaborate committee structure can be very expensive to operate: it is time-consuming, staff time has to be paid for even when the staffmembers are sitting in non-revenue generating meetings, and budget possibilities and constraints must be considered in establishing the decision-making structure. Fourth, centres, by their very nature, often exist on "soft money", where the revenue comes from the sale of student places and grants for research or consultancy projects, and the revenue level may fluctuate from year to year and even within any year (e.g., in Australia, ELICOS numbers tend to be lower in the first part of the year and to increase towards the end leading up to the start of the new academic year). Consequently, both general expenditure and staffing have to be managed in accordance with overall budget requirements and cashflow patterns. Because of the revenue fluctuations, centres tend to have a larger than normal (for universities) percentage of casual staff, including staff on less than full workloads. In many instances, such staff work across two or more institutions in order to build up their workload and salary and the decision-making process has to take into account the probability that staff are working for one or more of the centre's competitors: there will often be matters that would normally go to a committee for input or decision that should be regarded as commercial-in-confidence and so cannot be subject to the same democratic processes as are commonplace in the administration of a university School or Faculty. Fifth, commercial exigencies for the centre as a whole often necessitate decisions that individuals with their narrower perspectives may see as not in their immediate interest: salaries provide one example but other issues such as whether a particular project is undertaken or whether a particular employment pattern is pursued may also require an objective decision by a senior manager taking account of commercial exigencies rather than a more democratic resolution. In brief, while there are strong arguments in centres, as there are in universities, in support of some degree of democracy or shared decision-making in the internal management of a centre, there are other issues that need to be considered that may mean that a participatory decision-making process has to be modified. For these reasons, in the case of CALL (though also supported by the principles underlying the structure introduced to

Griffith University in mid-1997), responsibility for all decision-making ultimately rests with the Centre Director and the various committees are officially considered to be advisory to the Director even though, whenever practical (which is the majority of instances), the committees' recommendations are respected.

As the issues discussed thus far suggest, it is essential that the **terms of reference** of a language centre be clearly spelled out, be coherent, and be agreed when the centre is established or very soon after. Ideally, this would occur before the centre commences operations (as it was, to a large extent, in the long process that led to the establishment of the NFLC as outlined in Chapter 2 in this book) but, in practice, it is generally necessary for key staff, expert in the field, to be appointed to provide their advice before these documents can be elaborated. If they are produced in advance without input from experts but by the founders who may have some good ideas concerning the need for the centre but no knowledge or expertise in applied linguistics or of centre management, the terms of reference are likely to suffer from the sorts of problems just discussed and fail to provide sufficient or appropriate guidelines for the centre's operation.

These documents take different forms in the centres discussed in this volume. In some instances, they take the form of a constitution: in CALL's case, this was developed by the university prior to the centre's establishment and the appointment of key staff, it was approved by the University Council, and subsequent amendments also have had to pass through the University's due processes, ultimately to be approved by the Council. CALL is also bound by all (or most) of the other University procedures and documents. It was originally a centre within a Faculty and was bound by any decision the Faculty chose to make but in recent years it has been a "stand-alone" centre within the Arts Group with the Director, like a Head of School, answering to the Pro-Vice-Chancellor for the Arts Group. In other words, it is a Centre but, for many practical purposes, it has the status of a School (though not the allocated funding, since it is wholly self-funding) and is bound by the same array of University regulations and documents as is any other element within the University. In other cases, the centres discussed have such documents as mission statements, statements of goals and objectives, vision statements, and "blueprints" or "five year plans". These documents, whatever form they take, constitute the terms of reference and operational guidelines within which any centre must operate and which, if adequately enunciated, can circumvent some of the problems referred to earlier arising from the distinctive nature, roles and functions, and *modus operandi* of language centres.

The **geographic and administrative locations** of language centres have important implications for how they operate and for their management. The geographic location is determined by such factors as ease of access to the clients, the ease with which potential clients can access the centre's services, the cost and quality of the facilities, the relationship the centre is able to establish with the host institution or owner of the facilities, the cost, quality and suitability of the services available in that location, and their effect on the centre's efficiency and cost-effectiveness.

The geographic location should obviously be selected to facilitate the provision of the services and the performance of the tasks assigned to the centre, as is evident in the discussion of the locations of most of the centres described in this book. Centres designed to influence language policy, like NFLC, are appropriately located in the capital where there is readier face-to-face contact with the nation's policy-makers who might also be given some "ownership" of the centre by, for instance, being appointed to the governing body or other committees of the centre. Where centres are designed to serve a region rather than an institution or one country (e.g., ECML and RELC), it is important that the location facilitate communication with and access to the member countries: thus ECML's location in Graz is said to be at a communication crossroads for Europe but, perhaps more importantly, it facilitates contact with the newly independent countries of Eastern Europe, which it was particularly established to serve in its first years of operation. RELC is located in Singapore because of the centrality of that location, the fact that it is a major transport and communication hub for South East Asia, and the advanced development it offers in such areas as human resources and technology. In some instances, it is strategic to have the centre in more than one location in order to facilitate access to its services by the intended clients or to take advantage of additional facilities or some aspect of the other locations. Thus, for example, CILT has its main office in London, presumably for reasons of ready access from around Britain and proximity to the founders and policy-makers, but it has also established main branches in Scotland and Northern Ireland, which facilitates access to its services by teachers in those areas further from London and gives a base for CILT in three of the four countries that compose the United Kingdom. In addition, these bases enable CILT to access additional resources through, for example, the Scottish Office and the institutions within which the branches are based. CILT is further devolving its services through the network of Comenius Centres being established across Britain thus further facilitating access to its services by teachers and others. In CALL's case, a branch has been established on the Gold Coast, a hundred kilometres from the centre's main Brisbane base on Griffith University's Nathan Campus for several reasons: first, further expansion on the Nathan campus was inhibited by lack of space and the quality of the facilities available, second, there was pressure on the Centre to provide services for the university's Gold Coast Campus, and, third, by opening a branch in high quality commercial facilities in Australia's premier tourist and holiday resort, it provided attractions that broadened the range of clients attracted to its student programmes. In addition, CALL is in the process of establishing one or more joint venture operations in key market areas overseas in order to expand the range of clientele it can service.

Despite the benefits that CILT and CALL have sought by opening other branches, it is not an easy decision to spread a centre over more than one location and the implications of doing so must be fully taken into account if it is to be successful. First, the additional cost of opening other branches (including, for example, rent, communications, consumables, equipment, and staffing) must be justified by the improved services offered, the increased revenue that can be generated, access to clients and access by clients to the centre, and the greater effectiveness of the centre in terms of the tasks it has to carry out. Second, when a defined operation such as a centre is split up over different locations, that fundamental feature of a centre, the synergy discussed elsewhere, is more difficult to maintain, and steps need to be taken to ensure that staff located away from the main branch identify strongly with the centre as a whole and work in harmony with it. Particular attention must be paid to maintaining communications, involving those staff in the decision-making processes of the centre, and encouraging their participation in any social activities designed to meld the staff into a coherent and compatible group. Sometimes, where distances, transport and personnel make it practical, there is advantage in having some staff, especially senior staff, spend some of their time in each branch. Thus, for instance, the Director and especially the Manager of CALL regularly spend days working from the Centre's Gold Coast Branch, various centre meetings are held at either branch, staff from one branch are regularly sent to the other to familiarise themselves with the operations there, to replace staff on leave or involved in some assignment, and staff positions on Centre committees are filled from both branches and elected, not as branch representatives, but by and representing all Centre staff.

As communications become easier and more economical with the advent of computers, videoconferencing, and the internet, a centre's geographic location and the need for branches to be scattered around the countryside become less significant though, as is evident from the discussion above, not all of the reasons for establishing branches can be met in this way. Often, the visible presence of branches such as those of CILT around Britain or of CALL near the most distant of Griffith University's campuses is important in terms of clients' identifying with the centre and, in the case of CALL, with its host institution. Thus, for instance, one reason for CALL's opening a branch at the Gold Coast was to help to ensure that students passing through its English language programmes there would go on to study at the University's Gold Coast Campus rather than at a Brisbane university or inter-state.

Wherever a centre is located geographically, the critical issue remains the ease with which it can access its potential clients and the ease with which they can access the centre. For this reason, nowadays, it is essential that centres pay particular attention to the quality, ease and effectiveness of their communication systems, especially their telecommunication system, email and webpage. This is especially important if one of their tasks is the provision of clearinghouse and information services (as with CILT and RELC) but it is also important in terms of making information about the centre available to clients and the general public. Increasingly, it is through the webpage that these things are achieved and so it is important that a centre advertise its webpage address, that it make as many of its services (especially information services) available through its webpage as is practical, and that it provide as many links as possible from its webpage to other services useful to the clients. It is also useful to provide on the webpage reciprocal links to other relevant organisations where the links will help to make the centre better known and more widely accessible. Not least, since the webpage is more and more becoming the "front door" of organisations, it is important that it be well designed, attractive in appearance with plenty of visuals (but with the option for clients to use it "text only"), with easy and rapid movement around the site, that it reflect the character of the centre, and that it provide as much information about the centre as can be made publicly available (including such things as the centre's mission statement, constitution, terms of reference, its projects and programmes, its current strategic planning documents, staff profiles and publications, and reports of earlier projects). Where a centre is selling its services, whether that be courses to students or consultancy services to other clients, it is important that potential clients be able to carry out all that they need to do to access those services through the webpage. Students should be able to lodge enrolment application and other forms through the webpage, pay fees by credit card, receive acknowledgement and confirmation of enrolment, and engage in all the initial and on-going enrolment formalities as simply as possible through the webpage. This requirement and all the other communication needs mean that the webpage should also provide the opportunity to communicate by email with the centre even though the clients may not themselves have an email address. Though many of these requirements are self-evident and just commonsense, one still encounters many webpages which do not meet them and it is often difficult to convince relatively conservative host institutions unused to being entrepreneurial or client-sensitive that they are needed.

Whether a language centre should be geographically located on the campus of another institution or in its own facilities depends on the relationship that can be established with the host institution. In the case of a university centre such as CALL, the first choice is usually to be on campus since many students prefer that location for reasons of prestige or of continuity if they are going on to further studies. Similarly, in terms of marketing a centre's other services, the identification with the university that comes from that location may be advantageous. However, whether these advantages outweigh the possible disadvantages will depend on individual circumstances, the agreement that is made with the host institution, and the obligations and expenses that the location incurs. In some cases, being located on a university campus (especially if staff are nominally staff of the university) carries obligations to participate in the administrative and other activities of the university. These might include such things as involvement in the university's committee system, provision of gratuitous advice on language issues to other elements in the university, participation in the institution's performance appraisal and quality assurance processes, and so on. While, on the one hand, there might seem to be some advantage in this involvement in informing the university about the centre and keeping the centre aware of its most immediate market, the financial implications for a self-funding centre can be very heavy indeed:

for example, whereas the cost of committee involvement for regular faculty staff is met through the university's allocation to each element as part of their normal work requirements, in the case of a self-funding or unsubsidised centre, staff time equates to money that has to be recouped from student fees and project charges. Hence such involvement can be a heavy financial drag on a centre and can so inflate the costings of the centre's programmes and projects that it reduces its competitiveness. This problem is further exacerbated if the host institution charges for services it renders to the centre or charges, as do most universities, an administrative levy on all projects the centre gains without, in turn, paying for the services received from the centre.

In the case of NFLC, which is located in premises owned by The Johns Hopkins University, there seems to be no interference with NFLC activities, minimal costs and no committee obligations. This university was chosen by the Center's founder, Richard Lambert (see Lambert 1987), because the nature of its programmes made it unlikely that there would be conflict or competition between the two organisations and there was some mutual advantage of prestige in the one being associated with the other. CALL has the best and worst of both worlds, occupying both on-campus and off-campus premises, since, in addition to the campus location of its main branch, its Gold Coast branch is off-campus in commercial premises in Southport that are purpose-designed, of very high quality, convenient to a full array of commercial services in the same building, and with a superb outlook over one of Australia's major tourist resorts. Being off-campus, the Gold Coast branch pays smaller levies to the University with the result that, when full, it will be somewhat cheaper on a *per capita* basis to operate than the on-campus branch. On the other hand, the Gold Coast rent is fixed whatever the student numbers whereas the student levies at the main branch are *per capita*-based and the financial advantage lies with being on-campus while student numbers are small and projects, which also pay "university overhead" charges are few. All in all, there is no simple answer to any question about the most desirable geographic location for a centre: one can only weigh up purposes, needs and costs and seek the most cost-effective compromise.

The issue of the administrative location of a centre raises similar issues to those discussed thus far. In particular, it raises issues of the centre's independence in decision-making and its relationship to the host institution, which leads to similar issues as already discussed in relation to the management of centres and the relevance of the knowledge, skills and understanding of any persons in line-management and filling a decision-making role over the centre.

To be entirely independent or autonomous in its decision-making, a centre desirably would be fully self-sufficient, "stand-alone" and operating with its own governance and administrative structure. In practice, even though centres like CILT, RELC and NFLC seem largely to be autonomous, all centres require funding (unless they are fortunate enough to manage their own endowment or to be able to generate enough revenue from marketing their services) and whatever funding or establishment body is involved will generally want some say in how the centre operates or will at least require the centre to account in some way for the funds received or generated. Consequently, even in the best of circumstances, it is difficult for a centre to avoid some intrusion from other bodies in its management and operations and university centres like CALL, integrated into a university's academic and administrative structure, must accommodate to the university's requirements. The NFLC, even though it is located within a university, probably goes further than most in arriving at a system that gives it a very high degree of autonomy. As noted in Chapter 2, its founder, Richard Lambert, negotiated an arrangement with the Johns Hopkins University that gave NFLC a useful geographic location with virtually no university interference in the running of the centre. Beyond the university, however, there seems to be some interference from some of the donors who provide core funding since they require that the Center account for the funds received, they require regular reviews of the Center, and some donors have shown themselves not unwilling to question how the Center operates, the types of activities it engages in, and the success of its advocacy: in the course of 1999, for instance, one major donor moved from providing core grants to providing project-specific grants, reflecting, amongst other things, the donor's scepticism about language policy and its desire to see more specific returns from its investment.

In favour of being located administratively within another larger organisation such as a university is that that organisation may support it in various tangible and intangible ways in return for such things as the kudos of association or from the more tangible increase in its research and consultancy profile as a result of the work carried out in the centre and which, in the Australian system, brings a return to the university through the "research quantum" (funds paid to the university by the government in recognition of its level of research involvement). The former seems to have motivated Stirling University to provide, free of cost, the facilities for CILT's Scottish branch whereas the latter was a significant motivation for CALL's establishment in Griffith University. Centres benefit from being located in the larger institution in several ways: by the prestige that may be associated with the university, by being able to make use of facilities, utilities, and equipment in the university without having to purchase them from elsewhere (e.g., conference and meeting rooms and, sometimes, infrastructure items such as electricity, mail services, cleaning, library facilities, technology support services, access to the university's server, and accounting and auditing services). Sometimes some of these or other costs may be "lost" within the university's larger budget (e.g., security services, mail sorting, and so on) while some costs such as rent may, as already seen, be related to activity level with the total space occupied being flexible and related to, for example, student numbers rather than being fixed at a pre-determined level for pre-determined space.

However, the advantage of the support that may come from a centre's being administratively located within a host institution may, like its geographic location, come at a considerable cost, not least because, in today's economic and accountability climate, few institutions are willing or even able to offer such support gratuitously. On the other hand, the actual costs to the centre of the obligations arising from its location in the university's administrative system (such as the time the centre's staff spend in university committee activities or in fulfilling reporting obligations) may be unfunded, difficult to on-charge, and expensive. In CALL, for example, because the Centre staff are considered to be university staff, they are required to go through the same arduous and frequent performance review processes that other staff in the university are required to undergo but, whereas other Schools effectively have these costs paid for (through the university's grant to the School), CALL has to meet the costs from its own resources, i.e., from student fees and project charges. Similarly, because CALL is within the university, there is a tacit requirement for its staff to be available for the regular university committee work integral to university academic administration or, if they do not so participate, they are vulnerable to criticism and to accusations of not having demonstrated their administrative ability when it comes to securing promotion or even tenure. Clearly, such obligations that arise from centres being administratively located within a larger institution incur substantial costs of time and, hence, money, these costs have to be recouped from the centre's revenue, and can significantly affect its profitability and competitiveness. As with decisions about its geographic location, decisions about the administrative location of a centre can only be made by weighing up the benefits and costs of the location against the terms of reference of the centre.

The **facilities** available will to no small extent determine the location of a language centre. If a centre is located independently of another institution (e.g., ECML, CILT and RELC), it has to provide all of its facilities for itself. This clearly increases the cost of establishing and maintaining the centre quite considerably and centres use a variety of means by which to cover that cost. In the case of RELC, an international hotel has been established above it to generate revenue as well as to provide accommodation for the large numbers of visiting students and staff that come to RELC continually through the year. The costs of CILT's principal facilities are presumably included in its base grant but it has also sought the cooperation of other organisations to host its Comenius Centres and its main branches: the University of Stirling hosts CILT's Scottish Branch, apparently at no cost to CILT itself. Because its on-campus facilities have been inadequate, CALL has, on several occasions, sought to negotiate with private investors to construct a building which would provide the centre with the facilities it requires and house a hotel or student residence to provide most of the return to the investor. Since the residential facilities would largely be filled with CALL's own students and CALL operates all the year round (in contrast to the traditionally shorter teaching year of most Australian university programmes), the revenue generated would be quite substantial and would be augmented during the academic year by an intermingling of other students encouraged to reside there to provide an English-speaking environment for the English language students.

Being located within another institution, a university for example as is the case for NFLC and CALL, can, if a suitable agreement is worked out, give ready access to the range of facilities in that institution and reduce the initial and potentially very substantial outlay that provision of a full range of facilities incurs. However, nowadays, it is rare to find situations like that of CILT's Scottish branch in Stirling University where the institution is willing to grant the facilities at no charge and, as already observed, the rent, utilities and maintenance charges can be very substantial and prompt centres to look for more economical locations off-campus. NFLC pays rent of the order of $US165,000 annually to The Johns Hopkins University for their fairly limited premises and the occasional access they require to conference halls in university buildings (David Maxwell, NFLC Director in a personal discussion, 21 July, 1998). CALL pays capital and administrative charges to Griffith University based on student numbers to cover rent of its main (Nathan) branch and access to computer laboratories, the library, and the other facilities and services on-campus. Its Gold Coast branch occupies purpose-designed premises in an outstanding location in commercial premises on the Gold Coast, the premier holiday and tourist resort in Australia, space that one would expect would be (and is) very costly but which, student-for-student, is less costly, when full, than the facilities on-campus. Though the Centre has considered moving its main branch off-campus in order to obtain better quality facilities, more space, and lower *per capita* rental costs, it has not done so because many of its clients want a university location and having one branch on-campus and one off in excellent facilities enables it to appeal to a wider range of clients. In brief, the decision as to where a centre should locate itself in order to have access to the facilities it requires both regularly and intermittently, whether it should take advantage of space on an institution's campus with flexible access to a wide range of facilities, or whether it should establish itself off-campus is a complex decision that can be made only on consideration of the range of factors discussed above: the facilities available, comparative costs, accessibility of facilities needed intermittently, and marketability or appeal to the clients.

What facilities are required will depend on the nature, role, function and mission of the particular centre though there are certain features in common. All centres require adequate (preferably individual) offices for academic, research, and teaching staff, appropriate space for administrative staff (including individual offices at least for senior management), a secure room and safes for the Finance Officer, a reception area, waiting room (or other suitable space) for visitors, library and resource-holding facilities, storage rooms or other space with appropriate shelving and cupboards, confidential counselling rooms if the centre will be receiving students, small and large meeting rooms, and either appropriate conference rooms or access to them nearby (the nature of these depending on the types of events the centre will be mounting). If the centre has a teaching function, appropriate classrooms will be required including multimedia laboratories, an autonomous learning or self-access laboratory, and technical support facilities if the centre engages in language teaching. In addition, the research that the centre is to carry out will also influence the facilities that are required. Computing facilities must be designed to maximise the efficiency of the work of the office and intra-office communication but also to facilitate external communication with the centre's clients and information sources and be suitable for research and teaching purposes.

In all centres, if the important synergy of the centre, as discussed earlier, is to be realised, there must not only be places where small and large meetings can be held, but there should be an appropriately large commonroom with easy chairs and tables designed to enable staff to relax informally over lunch and teas and to hold occasional receptions and parties. If the centre has a teaching function, then similar facilities should be available for students either within the centre or nearby and there is need for larger space for orientations and graduations, student meetings, and student relaxation. Though sometimes these facilities are seen as luxuries that receive the lowest priority and may even be dispensed with altogether, they are essential for reasons of synergy and informal communication amongst the centre staff. The more dispersed staff are in a centre (e.g., using offices and other facilities across a campus or in two or more branches), the more important it is to provide such facilities and, even if the branches are in different parts of the country, to ensure that there are social and other activities that bring them together at times, preferably face-to-face but at least electronically if costs prevent frequent face-to-face gatherings. Again, such events and the facilities to enable them to occur on a regular and frequent basis are not luxuries but essential to ensure the synergy that is one of the basic reasons for the creation of a language centre.

Staffing is an area of considerable concern in establishing and maintaining centres. Some issues were referred to earlier in discussing management, especially the need for staff to have relevant skills for the tasks they are undertaking whether that be in teaching, research, consultancy or the provision of support services. It was also emphasised that it is essential that staff appointed to a centre understand and be willing to accept the constraints on the centre and the distinctive ways in which it has to operate. All this means that it is important that centres have the autonomy to select their own staff or at least, if others (the host institution, the funding agency, etc) are to be involved, that they understand the nature and requirements of the centre.

There are also some distinctive issues involved in staffing a centre. In addition to understanding the role, functions, constraints and requirements of work in a centre, staff must have the sort of flexibility referred to earlier so that they can turn to other things until, for example, their research funding is sufficient to justify their salaries. Obviously they also require qualifications appropriate to the duties they will perform in the centre and, very often, they require a sufficient level of idealism that they are willing to forgo the conditions of employment available in a regular academic position in order to be able to pursue the more specialised and often influential activities of the centre. It is an ironic situation that, on the one hand, centres, by their very nature, require staff with a high level of expertise in aspects of applied linguistics and, therefore, they must employ highly qualified, well reputed staff, staff of the sort that could readily win senior positions elsewhere in universities. On the other hand, the funding basis for most language centres is less secure than for a university and they may rely heavily on "soft money" generated from student fees and competitively won projects. Even centres such as RELC and ECML, which have the security of funding that comes from being backed by strong multi-governmental organisations, may be subject to transient political whims and NFLC is dependent on donors who do not always understand its distinctive nature and may wish to impose their own views on its operations. Consequently, few language centres are able to offer the degree of security and the ancillary benefits (tenure, study leave and long service leave, for instance) that universities provide for their staff (especially at the senior levels that staff found in language centres would probably enjoy in regular faculty positions). Of the academic staff in CALL, for example, only the Director has tenure or is entitled to study leave, conditions enjoyed by even quite junior lecturers in regular School and Faculty positions in Griffith University. On the other hand, where centres do provide such benefits, they impose a heavy financial burden, again considerably reducing the centre's cost-competitiveness with other institutions or private consultants. Consequently, centre staff need to be willing to work longer hours, generally with employment conditions inferior to those of regular staff in a university, and to do so willingly in order to pursue the goals of the centre.

As emphasised earlier, a proper balance is required amongst the staff taking into account the role, functions, and tasks of the centre. In particular, there must be a proper balance between academic, teaching and support staff to avoid the false economy of having academic and teaching staff perform clerical and other administrative tasks that can readily and more efficiently and cost-effectively be carried out by support staff.

Increasingly, one of the conditions associated with employment is the willingness to participate in **quality assurance** processes. Activities such as performance reviews are now commonplace in universities, especially in Australia where they have come to be formalised as part of industrial productivity agreements. On the one hand, in education establishments where productivity and quality assurance are difficult to demonstrate, it would seem desirable to introduce arrangements that are often quite complex, aimed at addressing both the measurable and the intangible elements of quality and productivity in education. Where this is done in a university, it is possible to make arguments to funding bodies that justify the increased administrative costs entailed in establishing such arrangements and in insisting that staff give time to them. Such processes may well be justifiable in centres that are wholly government-funded and where funding can be increased in order to accommodate them. However, in language centres that have to find some or all of their own revenue by selling student places, winning competitive grants, and competing for other projects, these costs can be very damaging indeed to the budget and can greatly reduce the centre's competitiveness with other organisations such as private schools and private consultants. In addition, one has to question whether, in such circumstances, a fully elaborated performance appraisal system implemented at fixed and frequent intervals is necessary since there are strong constraints on such a centre to be productive in order to maintain its competitiveness and to maintain its quality since otherwise it will lose clients: in a wholly or partially self-funding centre, quality and productivity are rapidly reflected in the maintenance of business activity. It is not a sufficient justification for the imposition of these procedures on a language centre that they are requirements of a host institution: rather, as with many of the other management issues discussed here, whatever quality assurance (including performance appraisal) and productivity procedures are put in place, they must be relevant to the nature and operational constraints of the centre and not, through excessive idealism, reduce the centre's productivity and competitiveness.

These issues relate quite closely to the need in most systems for language centres, like most other organisations, to be subjected to regular *review and evaluation*. Again, on the one hand, if a centre is self-funding, commercial and entrepreneurial, its success can be demonstrated quite objectively in the number of students it attracts, the projects it wins, the consultancies it carries out, and the research and publications it generates. In such circumstances, other than internal monitoring and review that any responsible management undertakes on an on-going basis, one has to question whether the cost in time and money of external reviews merely imposed as a regular formality is warranted. If the cost of external reviews is warranted, then the founding and/or funding bodies should ensure that funds are specifically allocated for this purpose and that they do not become yet another revenue-negative element that the centre has to fund from its student fees and project charges.

On the other hand, some reviews are vitally important and determine whether the centre will continue or not and in what form. In the chapter on ECML, for instance, there is reference to the fact that it was established for an initial three year period at the end of which it was to be reviewed and a decision taken as to whether it should continue or not. The donors who fund the NFLC have often required that its performance be reviewed before renewing their substantial funding of the Center. In CALL's case, the University Council motion establishing the centre and approving a constitution included a clause requiring a triennial review of the Centre's operations principally, it would seem, because similar reviews are required of other centres in the University that operate very differently, with a different management and funding base, and with less, objective evidence of the centre's success or otherwise than occurs in CALL's case.

Whatever the justification (or lack thereof) for a review, it is essential that it be carried out by ethical people, able and willing to look dispassionately at the centre's performance, credits and problems, able to provide informed advice, and able to make a fair evaluation of the centre's performance. It is also essential that the review team be able, willing, and have enough time and resources to be able to explore all issues raised with it. The simplistic "cop out" that some review panels use that any statement made to them must be included in the report, whether it has been verified or not and whether the integrity and competence of the person making them have been assured or not, is highly irresponsible. This has occurred on two occasions in CALL reviews conducted by the (generally antagonistic) host Faculty with the outcome being reports that were replete with factual errors, reflected adversely on the competence and integrity of the review panel rather than on the Centre itself, and, on one occasion, almost led to litigation until the host university itself intervened and removed the Centre from the Faculty. On both occasions but especially in the second review, the panel had undoubtedly been influenced by statements made to it by individuals who, either at the time or soon afterwards, were no longer working for the Centre but it is negligent on the part of a review panel simply to accept statements made to it without verification and without giving any staff criticised the democratic right to respond to accusations before the evaluation is finalised and the report made public.

Again, in order that evaluations be made fairly and from an informed basis, it is not only essential that the review panel be ethical and have appropriate skills relevant to the work of the centre, but that the founding and other key documents providing the terms of reference of the centre (as discussed above) spell out the goals and objectives to be achieved and that any strategic plan for the period over which the centre's work is to be evaluated also spell out the goals to be achieved and the criteria against which success is to be judged. Most of the centres discussed in this volume provide in some form, more or less elaborated, such goals and criteria and present them on their webpage. Other examples of such criteria were given in the initial document arguing for a national language information and research centre in Australia (Ingram 1978: 44–45).

The funding basis, **budget and budget process** of a language centre play a major part in determining how it operates and how it is managed and staffed. It goes without saying that the level of the budget must be adequate to enable it to undertake the tasks assigned to it under its terms of reference or founding documents and that what it can achieve and whether it can achieve the goals and carry out the tasks assigned to it will be determined in no small measure by the resources it has available to it. If the founding organisation does not fully fund the centre, then it has to find funds elsewhere by approaching donors (the principal funding basis for NFLC), by generating some or all of its own revenue by the sale of student places or other services (the sole funding basis for CALL), or by some combination of these three sources (as is increasingly the case for CILT and RELC).

A variety of *funding models* exist to cover the costs of language centres and each of the centres discussed in this book is different. The models tend to lie along a continuum from fully government- or institution-funded to fully self-funding and commercial. Here we shall consider a few models along this continuum.

In some instances (CILT, for example), a centre may be funded by **government or institutional grant**, presumably through a regular budget process in which the centre puts in a submission for funding for the next period, argues for what it aims to do and for the money required, and then eventually has an amount approved. In this model, there is also advantage if the centre generates some of its own revenue through project bids, fee-based conferences and meetings, the sale of materials, and the sale of services (e.g., the organisation of conferences for other organisations or consultancy services to industry). In CILT's case, for example, though it is largely government-funded, there is strong encouragement for it to generate up to half of its revenue. The advantages in generating some of its own revenue and not relying wholly on government handouts is that centres generally gain more flexibility in determining what they do as well, of course, as reaping the advantages of a higher annual budget.

Overall, a wholly or largely government- or institution-funded model has a number of advantages over other models, including a flexibility in terms of costs and activities that, for example, a fully self-funding centre lacks: as discussed below, a fully self-funding, commercial model makes it difficult to carry out projects that may be highly desirable but that cannot generate enough revenue to cover their costs (e.g., work with depressed minorities where it is not possible to charge full costs even though their case for assistance may be very strong). This model also leaves the centre open to argue for funds to enable a think-tank role to be carried out or for normal academic development activities (reading, discussion, conference attendance, or personal academic writing and publishing) to be catered for in the centre's infrastructure costs. There is also an immediate prestige that attaches to a centre if its work is seen as sufficiently valued by government or by its host institution that they are willing to put funds into the centre and if it is accepted that such funding is justified in the interest of the society or community which the government or institution is intended to serve (e.g., see Ingram 1978: 38–40).

The main disadvantage of the grant-based funding model is that the centre is vulnerable to changes in the political or institutional climate and funding can fluctuate considerably for such reasons without any relationship to the quality of the centre's work or the needs it meets. Governments and government budgets are subject to an array of political pressures (elections, media "beat-ups", fluctuating balances of trade, world economic conditions, stock and currency market perceptions, and so on) and this uncertainty qualifies even the most secure of government-funding arrangements. Since governments tend to work on an annual budget process, such uncertainty also makes it difficult for a centre to make long-term plans that are funding-dependent since the funding level might change. This is often the case (and certainly occurs in the Australian context), even where longer plans and corollary commitments are made based on three- or five-year plans that have been approved by government or institutions since such plans are also generally subject to the annual budget process and, in the case of government, to parliamentary expenditure committees. Even CILT, a highly successful and respected centre, has had to cope with the uncertainty that comes from reliance on government funding since it has, several times, been threatened with closure when the political climate of the day demanded cutbacks in government expenditure. The fate of the formerly vigorous National Languages and Literacy Institute of Australia, which largely lost its funding at the time of a change of government in Australia in 1996, illustrates the uncertainty that accompanies the benefits of the government-funded model. Another disadvantage of the grant-based model can be that the accounting procedures required for government or institutional purposes are often more complex and, therefore, more time-consuming and costly to carry out than is warranted for a budget of the size and nature of a centre. While such procedures may be fully justified for a large institution or government department, they can constitute an irrelevant drag on a centre's budget unless the funding authority allocates resources specifically to enable the process to occur. Finally, a centre that is dependent on government disbursements has more difficulty in critiquing government policy and implementation and in providing objective advice than a centre that is funded through an autonomous university or is wholly or partially self-funding. At best, no matter how objectively they try to conduct themselves, observe, critique and offer advice, government-funded centres are always open to accusations of being too close to government, of being afraid to speak out for fear of losing funding, or of offering self-interested advice.

Another institution-funded model is one where the centre is not funded to cover all its costs but staff already employed by the university are allocated a "centre" without the requirement to generate funds other than for particular projects. In this model, such centres, sometimes called "**allied centres**", are little more than a grouping of academics and researchers of like interest who gain some mutual support and generate some synergy by being part of a group and "belonging to" (even if not employed by) the centre. Some additional revenue may also be allocated to such centres for minimal support services beyond those normally available through each academic's Department, School or Faculty but the main source of additional revenue comes from projects that are won through the routine research funding processes or from consultancies that are offered to or won by members of the centre. In this model, there is no constraint on centre members to do anything more than what they do in their normal academic employment (they do not have to generate their own salaries, for instance), and the centre is little more than a grouping of like or "allied" interests. Such a model is commonplace in many universities and, in fact, is the model that operates for the majority of the allied centres that exist in Griffith University. Such centres are very different from CALL, which fits the "commercial" model discussed below at the opposite end of the funding-model continuum to the government- or institution-funded model.

In two cases reviewed in this book (ECML and RELC), the funding model is similar to the government- or institution-funded model except that it entails **funding**

provided by a multi-governmental organisation. In many ways, this model may provide more stability of funding since changes in the political whim in one country may be counter-balanced by changes or stability in the other countries or in the organisation as a whole. In this sort of model, unless the multi-governmental organisation itself can mediate, there may also be an increase in pressure on the centre as a result of the differing demands from the various governments. In the case of the two centres reviewed that operate under this model, ECML and RELC, there would seem to be certain advantages in comparison with other centres. The Council of Europe (ECML's founding body) has shown itself to be more strongly supportive of progressive language policies than some of the individual countries that compose it. SEAMEO (RELC's founding body) also has shown itself strongly supportive of language education, as have the associate members, many of which provide financial support in the form of subsidies, language specialists, conference support, and funding for visiting lecturers. Again, the strength of this model is that the centre has open to it the option of making a case for increased funding or funding for special purposes and special projects, e.g., ECML receives funding to support improved language education in the newly independent countries of the former Soviet bloc. Under this model, the option is also open for additional revenue to be raised by charging for services that go beyond those covered by the core grant or to raise funds for special projects in other ways: so, for instance, in support of language education in SEAMEO countries, RELC seeks joint projects with institutions in developed countries that pay some or all of the project costs. RELC also undertakes projects beyond its funded five-year plan provided that the requesting government or institution covers the cost.

Another funding model is the **donor model** based on receiving major grants from philanthropic bodies. This is the model under which NFLC has operated for most of its existence and further information is provided in Chapter 2 of this book. NFLC has received core grants from such bodies as the Ford Foundation while other donors have funded scholarships or specific projects. The Andrew Mellon Foundation, for example, has supplied funds for the Center's main fellowship scheme and the Center was able to use the interest on that money to fund its Adjunct Fellow scheme.

The donor model has some advantages over the government-funded model. First, NFLC has been able to make some long-term arrangements with donors so that it has a degree of stability in its funds that is not found under the first model above where centres rely on annual disbursements from governments or government-dependent institutions. Second, though the centre seeking the funds has to compete with other organisations seeking similar support, its approach is to an organisation that exists to disburse funds for worthy purposes, the negotiations are with persons whose role is to respond to worthy organisations, and one would expect that, in general, the negotiations would be less arduous than with politicians and government bureaucrats. Third, where the donor requires periodic reviews, the review team is likely (if not inevitably) to be more sympathetic to the centre's cause and more easily able to get their recommendations adopted than are bureaucrats faced with a maelstrom of government departments, budget processes, expenditure committees, Senate Committee hearings, and so on. Fourth, a donor is likely to be able (as is a government department) to insist as a condition of the donation that interest on its money be used for the centre's purposes and not be creamed off by the host institution: this increases the value of the donation, as the NFLC has shown by using the interest on one major donation to fund its prestigious Adjunct Fellowship scheme. Such an arrangement is not possible in CALL where the host university has ultimate budget control and retains interest generated on Centre funds. Fifth, philanthropies are generally set apart from the education system and a centre funded by donors is likely to be and to be seen to be more independent than one funded by government and so it is better positioned to observe, critique and advise objectively and without fear or favour.

The donor model is attractive but also has disadvantages. One disadvantage is that it is not so readily available in some countries as it is in the United States. In Australia, for example, such arrangements are practically unheard of and substantial philanthropic donations in support of educational institutions are relatively rare. Second, donors and their review teams are not inevitably knowledgeable about applied linguistics or sympathetic towards language policy, may make judgements on erroneous bases, and, in being less publicly accountable, they are likely to be less open to persuasion or a change of mind when such judgements are made. Third, not unlike politicians, many foundations and other donor bodies may be keen to see objective results that they can trumpet through the press and media for whatever purposes they may have and this may well limit the range of activities that they are willing to fund. Thus, for instance, such bodies may be more attracted to projects with defined goals and objectively quantifiable outcomes even though the more fundamental issues of language policy and language education planning may, in the long term interest of language education, be more important and more appealing to a centre. The same reason may make a donor less willing to provide core grants untied to particular projects and this may leave the centre in the same academically precarious position as is referred to in the discussion of the commercial and self-funded model below. Fourth, one effect of relying on donors is that, similarly to centres that rely partly or wholly on project funding, a large amount of time has to be devoted to seeking out donors, writing submissions, meeting with their representatives, and meeting accountability and reporting requirements. Such processes, like project submission writing, are costly of time and resources and may inhibit a centre's ability to carry out its other tasks or to be innovative and able to undertake new initiatives.

Sometimes private investment funds may be accessed to support a centre through, for example, a joint venture arrangement under which another organisation, generally an investor of some sort, provides funds for some purpose in expectation of a return on that investment. The **investment model** may take various forms: for example, the investor may provide a loan that the centre pays off with interest, the investor may fund a building on which the centre subsequently pays rent, the building funded by the investor may be designed to provide additional space to be used by the investor for some other purpose (e.g., the investor's own office space, a commercially run conference centre, a tourist hotel, or student residences), or the investor may market the centre's programmes and receive a commission on all students recruited or project contracts attracted. There are many possibilities but the main advantage of such arrangements to the centre is that it receives a burst of venture capital that it could not otherwise access that gives a "kick-start" to the centre's establishment or to some development project.

The main disadvantages of the investment model include, first, that the profit on centre operations is rarely large enough to make an investment financially interesting to an investor though the security of putting money into, for example, a building on a university campus may sometimes be a sufficient attraction in itself. Second, investors may believe that they are buying more control over the operations of the centre in order to secure their investment than the centre itself, its founding body, or the host university is willing to concede. When CALL was initially established, for instance, the host university entered into a joint venture arrangement with a foreign marketing company to provide establishment funds, potentially to provide a building, and to undertake most of the marketing for the Centre's English language courses. It was not long, however, before the joint venturer sought to interfere in the academic decision-making process and, for example, to insist that unqualified staff be employed at lower salary levels to teach English so as to maximise profits. The university, in support of the Centre, refused to allow any interference in the academic decision-making process, the joint venture agreement was terminated, and the centre returned the investment with interest. In other instances, as discussed earlier under the donor model, unless the role of the investors and the extent of their intrusion into the centre's operations are clearly delineated, the objectivity of the centre's advisory services may also be put in jeopardy.

In brief, a joint venture arrangement leading to an injection of investment funds into a centre can be of great value but it also carries serious risks. It is a funding model that is well worth consideration but only if it is possible to arrive in advance at a clearly delineated agreement that envisages and clarifies the whole range of situations that can occur, spells out the initial and on-going responsibilities and obligations of all parties, ensures that the academic responsibilities of the centre are not intruded upon, and provides a clear dispute-resolution mechanism that can operate within the fundamental principles (e.g., the centre's mission and its autonomy in academic matters) within which the centre has to operate. Without such agreement (as CALL found), the investment model can lead to bitter wrangling (the larger the investment, the more bitter the wrangling) and eventually to the collapse of the agreement with serious funding consequences for the centre if it has to find ways to re-pay the investment.

Finally, at the opposite end of the funding model continuum from the whole-grant model is the wholly self-funding, commercial model as found in the Centre for Applied Linguistics and Languages. **Commercialisation** has become a popular means by which universities expand their services or increase their revenue and, at first sight, it provides a means by which institutions or governments can increase their support for language education without incurring additional expenditure. Under a commercial model, centres (or other parts of education, for that matter) are required to generate their own revenue in whole or in part, to behave as commercial entities, and to be entrepreneurial in order to promote and market their services to the clients. While there is considerable potential in this model, it raises serious issues for the management and operations of language centres even though, standing a little apart from the mainstream of the education system, they seem often to be thought of as prime targets for commercialisation. This is especially so for language centres in English-speaking countries in recent years since English has become such a high priority language for international business, commerce and industry and a pre-requisite for foreign students wishing to take part of their education in an English-speaking country. The fact that the sale of English language courses to overseas students has become such a valuable export industry and a valuable revenue source for universities (and other language schools) has enabled it to provide a funding basis, in whole or in part, for some language centres.

Though commercialisation can provide a successful model for a language centre (as the CALL experience demonstrates), there are a number of issues critical to success. First, there are the important implications for the management of centres already discussed in this chapter. Second, all the corollaries of running a commercial operation must be followed through so that, for example, the host or funding institution doesn't just pick and choose those that bring it revenue leaving the centre struggling to meet its commitments. The issue raised earlier of centre staff giving their time gratuitously to other unfunded university activities illustrates the point since this constitutes an unreasonable drain on centre resources and gives the university hierarchy a false notion of how the centre is performing financially. Third, the accounts should show the full extent of the revenue the centre generates (including any interest the host earns on unspent centre revenue) if a fair assessment is to be made of the centre's financial performance and if it is to properly operate as a commercial entity. In commercial operations, unused revenue or payments in advance can be invested to generate additional revenue but if the host institution, for example, holds all funds, takes all interest for itself, or prevents the centre from investing or reaping the rewards of accumulating positive cashflow, then it constitutes a serious breach of the normal commercial conditions under which the centre is required to operate. The contrast between CALL and NFLC well illustrates the point: NFLC has received substantial sums from the Andrew Mellon Foundation by which to fund its fellowship programme. It has been able to invest that money and the interest earned has paid for the Adjunct Fellow programme under which some dozen or so eminent applied linguists from around the world have been able to visit NFLC for, on average, a month each year making a substantial contribution to the level of activity in NFLC and contributing their considerable skills to the Center's work. In contrast, interest on CALL money held by the university (funds that frequently have amounted to more than a million dollars at any one time) are invested by the university on the lucrative short-term money-market providing a potential return of at least $50,000 a year, even with the low interest rates that prevailed through the 1990s, but none of that revenue is returned to the Centre. Similarly, for most of its life, the "research quantum" received by the university as a result of CALL's research and publishing activity was retained by the then host faculty, sums which, even calculated on an annual basis, were very substantial. To correctly assess a centre's financial performance and to enable it to operate on a proper, commercial basis, all such income should be included in the calculation of the centre's financial returns.

Fourth, any centre dependent in large part on project funding is in danger of losing some of its autonomy and of being thought to be less than dispassionate in any advice that it provides or any criticism that it may need to make, especially in a situation where, as in Australia, most of the research and development funding comes from government. It is at best difficult for a centre to observe, critique and advise "without fear or favour" (and even more difficult for it to be seen to be doing so) when the employment of its staff and the very survival of the centre may depend on its being able to win subsequent projects from the very government department or other agency that it may need to criticise. Even under a donor model this can be an issue since one would have to anticipate that few organisations willing to put up substantial sums for research and development projects would be wholly neutral and dispassionate about their outcome. This type of situation has occurred on several occasions in the life of CALL: once, when it was commissioned to carry out a project on the English language assessment of overseas students by Australian universities, the project officer in the particular government department that funded the project tried to persuade the Centre to report its findings in a certain way to support a particular point of view and the project ended in considerable acrimony when the Centre refused to do so. On other occasions, another centre (rightly or wrongly) felt itself to be at risk when its staff refused to participate in what they saw as sycophantic behaviour at meetings of the national umbrella institute to which the centre was affiliated and the research staff sometimes believed themselves to be under pressure to write up project reports in particular ways, feelings that they subsequently believed to have been justified as relations with that agency became soured, when what they believed to be false accusations appeared in an institute review, and research funding dried up. Clearly, the problem of maintaining the independence, integrity and objectivity of a centre when it depends on project funding from governments or other agencies is a considerable one: there would seem to be no final solution to it though it can be reduced if the centre can diversify its funding sources by engaging in other revenue-generating activity, by using a range of project-funding agencies, and by seeking core funding from several disinterested funding sources. Risk or not, it is obviously essential for reasons of academic integrity, ethics and the confidence that can be placed in the advice and other work of a language centre that it maintain the highest standards of professional ethics and seek through negotiation and agreement to minimise the dangers discussed here.

Similar questioning of the objectivity of a centre's advice may occur in situations where that advice, if implemented, could lead to projects or to an increase in other activity for the centre. This is often a danger where a wholly or partially self-funding centre has an advisory responsibility at an international, national, local or institutional level. It is illustrated in situations that have confronted CALL in carrying out its role of providing advice on language matters to its host university: if, for example, CALL gives advice to Schools within Griffith that the level of English language proficiency of overseas students should be increased, it could be accused of simply trying to get increased business from the greater number of students that will come to it for English courses. Thus the independence and objectivity of a centre's advice may be put into question in ways that do not apply where centres are able to rely on core funding grants (from philanthropic bodies or even government) that are not affected by any corollaries flowing from the advice given.

As noted earlier, commercialisation has other serious implications for academic activity to the extent that some academics argue that commercialisation and academic excellence are mutually incompatible (cf. Bostock 1998). The fact of the matter is that, if high quality academic activity (including research) is to be maintained, academics and researchers must have time to maintain their academic development through reading, thinking, exchanging ideas, attending conferences, browsing the internet, and so on. However, none of these activities are revenue-generating but, taking the staffmember's time, have to be paid for out of centre revenue. Unless they can be covered through regular core grants from the host institution, founding organisation, or donors, that cost has to be added to student fees and to project charges, again with serious implications for competitiveness. It is for such reasons that commercialisation and academic excellence are said to be incompatible. However, if the full corollaries of commercialisation are followed through without, for instance, legitimate centre revenue being taken off by the host institution and without the centre being expected to provide gratuitous support to the host institution while paying for any services received, such academic maintenance and development activities could be covered, are vitally important if the centre is to continue to offer high quality commercial services, and do occur in commercial industry-based research and development centres.

The range of activities that fall to a language centre with their very different revenue potentials (e.g., different types of language programmes, research, training in applied linguistics, and consultancies together with the essential support activities for these and the centre's overall operations) means that *cross-subsidisation* is both possible and necessary. Some activities that a language centre legitimately and desirably might undertake (information services and a clearinghouse, for instance) either generate no revenue or the level of fees that can be charged is too low to cover costs, or, like the development of a new course, may require a substantial initial investment in curriculum development, accreditation processes, staffing, materials acquisition, and marketing before they can become financially self-sufficient. The establishment of a new branch in another city or, even more so, in another country generally requires a very costly and prolonged investigation and establishment phase before the branch becomes operational and a further development phase before it becomes self sufficient, recoups the establishment costs, and returns a profit. Much research also falls into this category (especially in the Australian system where the principal research grants do not allow either infrastructure funding or full salaries for the chief investigators). For these reasons, it is highly desirable that centres be able to cross-subsidise within their budget so that activities that are well established or more prone to making a reasonable surplus (language courses, for example) can cross-subsidise highly desirable but less lucrative activities. If this is to occur, all those who work in the centre and the founding body and host institution must agree that cross-subsidisation is acceptable; most of all, it requires that the centre management and any body that they have to answer to realise that not all activities will, individually, operate profitably or even meet their full costs. Throughout most of CALL's existence, for example, the faculty that hosted it imposed a requirement that each individual activity had to cover its costs, which immediately made it impossible for CALL to bid for major research grants (such as those funded by the Australian Research Council) which do not allow infrastructure costs or chief investigator salaries to be included. The Australian Research Council's argument is quite reasonable, viz., that universities in Australia are government funded partly to undertake research and the inclusion of infrastructure and salary costs is therefore considered to be "double-dipping" but, for a wholly self-funding centre, it means that cross-subsidisation of research from other activities is essential or research cannot take place. Even if cross-subsidisation is permitted, of course, it becomes virtually impossible to achieve if the host institution or funding body, seeing moderate profits from some activities in a centre or naively believing that all commercial activities reap large profits, seeks to cream off centre "profits" for itself. Host institutions and founding bodies need to make a decision as to whether the centre exists to produce profits for themselves or whether it exists to carry out the tasks and mission for which it was founded and, in the case of centres with a research focus, whether the surpluses are to be lost in supplementary funding for the host institution or whether they are to be used to increase the centre's (and, by implication, the university's) research profile.

Again, the resolution of such conflicts rests on the need for the body establishing the centre to be clear about the centre's mission and goals and about how it is to be funded and managed, and, consequently, how it is to operate; equally, it must respect the implications and corollaries that flow from that. These matters should be spelt out in the basic strategic documents of the centre (the mission statement, constitution, etc) and all parties, the founding organisation, the host institution (if any), any possible investor, and the centre itself must be willing to respect them and to recognise the distinctive requirements of a language centre in terms of management, decision-making, budget and budget management.

For a centre to operate successfully, whether it is run on commercial lines or otherwise, it is essential that strict *budget and accounting processes* be observed. In the experience of the present writer, the normal accounting and budgetary requirements of a university are not sufficiently detailed to meet the requirements of budget-control in a complex, commercial operation such as a wholly self-funding language centre with a high turnover of programmes and projects. Where a centre has to operate under a dual system so as to meet its own requirements and also those of the host institution, there is a serious risk of duplication of effort (and hence of costs) and of errors as items of revenue or expenditure fall "between the cracks" between the two systems. In such circumstances, there is particular need for clarification of the requirements and of the processes to be followed with regular auditing of the accounts to ensure that errors arising from the complexities of a dual system do not occur.

Good financial management requires that there should be an overall financial plan or business plan for whatever period of time is used for strategic planning (in RELC's case, it is five years), an annual budget, and periodic budget projections so that at any point of time the senior management is able to see how the centre's finances are proceeding, how each programme or project undertaken by the centre is performing financially, what future commitments exist, and what the likely end-of-the-year outcome will be. How frequently the performance reports and projections need to be made depends on the nature of the funding and how much it fluctuates throughout the year. In CALL's case, where the centre is run on commercial lines and where the revenue comes from student fees and project contracts that come in throughout the year, strict on-going monitoring and reporting at frequent intervals (at least monthly) are essential. In CALL, a three-year business plan is prepared and translated annually into an annual budget, these documents being prepared with input from all areas of activity within the Centre. Through the year, monthly reports are prepared indicating the income and expenditure for each month and accumulating for the year, the cashflow situation, end-of-the-year and whole-year projections based on the current year's performance with analogies drawn from the progressive performance patterns from previous years and their cashflow and profit-and-loss positions, the debtor situation, outstanding orders, and anticipated income and expenditure for the rest of the year. This information (or as much of it as is relevant) is required for each programme and project in the Centre as well as for the Centre as a whole. Only with at least this level of detail (as well as other routine accounting and auditing information) can a commercial operation be monitored and adjustments made to the budget and to the centre's activities as the year progresses.

In most centres, it is desirable that a *Finance Officer* be appointed with appropriate qualifications to control the budget and handle the necessary bookkeeping, accounting and reporting. In brief, the duties of the Finance Officer should include at least the following:

– to develop, control and manage the business plan and annual budgets,
– to prepare annual projections and monthly reports,
– to receive revenue and pay accounts (or document their receipt and authorise their payment by the host institution if the accounts are handled at that level),
– to prepare costings for programmes and projects or any other activities in the centre,
– to propose an objective basis for the distribution of expenditure in relation to the revenue received (e.g., agreed formulae related to student numbers provide a practical, readily estimated and objective way by which to allocate expenditure for regularly recurring items in a language programme such as staffing, level of casual staff, materials acquisition, staff development, entertainment for visitors or students, equipment, student excursions or field experience, and so on),
– to negotiate fees for consultancy services provided by the centre or any of its staff (or, if the Finance Officer does not do this, then some other administrative officer should handle it and not the academic staff members themselves who rarely have the negotiating skills or the necessary dispassionate willingness to arrive at reasonable financial arrangements),
– to provide the centre director, senior management, heads of cost centres, and the governing board with all necessary financial information to enable the centre as a whole and each programme or project to be managed responsibly and within budget, and
– to develop a transparent budget spreadsheet (or spreadsheets) identifying all expected outlays and revenues, providing a clear indication of the funds available in all areas of expenditure (e.g., casual staff, materials acquisition, materials acquisition, course development, equipment, conference support, etc), and, as indicated above, the performance of each project or programme and the centre as a whole.

One of the difficult areas in a centre's costings is the handling of undistributed (or undistributable) costs. In the present writer's experience in Australia, there seems to be little comprehension of the real costs involved in running an educational programme, especially a fully self-funding language centre (this is perhaps hardly surprising since CALL is the only one of its kind in Australia which is academic, has a research focus, teaches English and other languages, and is expected to be wholly commercial and self-funding). In particular, it has to be realised that there are some costs that cannot be distributed easily to particular projects, particular programmes, or specific budget lines within projects and programmes and yet are integral to the running of a commercial, academic centre. Some of these have already been referred to but, in addition, there are common costs such as infrastructure support, marketing, equipment purchases, maintenance and replacement, and rent and other charges levied by the host institution. CALL's solution to this is to add an administrative or overhead charge (about 20%) to all project costings, a charge that has been arrived at over the years as providing a fair and reasonable estimate of "undistributed costs". Griffith University also adds a 10% "overhead charge" to all projects so as to cover the costs of the Office of Research, which is required to approve all project submissions and contracts as well as promote research and consultancy opportunities to the different elements in the university. In the United States, it has been accepted that an overhead charge is appropriate to cover the undistributed costs; the accepted figure for government-funded projects was, at one time, 69% though it is now 20% (David Maxwell, NFLC Director, personal communication, 21 July, 1998). Whatever figure is used, it has to be realised by the centre, by the centre staff, and by funding bodies that "undistributed costs" are real costs that have to be recouped and, therefore, charged.

5. Interactions and links

As already discussed in the context of the governance and management of centres, it is essential for most centres that they establish strong links and on-going interaction with other organisations, with professional associations and other bodies, and, in particular, with their potential clients and the communities they serve (whether that be at the international, national, state, local or institutional levels). This is especially the case if the centre is concerned with language policy (see Section 4 above and the sub-section on **language or language education policy** in Section 2). Such considerations, as already discussed, affect not only the role and function of language centres but also their structure and governance.

Nevertheless, it is also essential, as discussed above, that language centres have a certain amount of autonomy and independence in their decision-making so as to ensure that their distinctive needs can be met whether that be in terms of the research undertaken, the advice given, or their governance and management.

Language centres are established as centres of expertise, able to undertake research, provide consultancy services, and respond to the needs for language skills in the community at large. They can do so only if they are known and respected by the community which they are established to serve and hence all centres put some effort into achieving a significant public and professional profile, ensuring an appropriate status in their field and in the community, and achieving both public and professional visibility and credibility. For this reason, as we have already noted, some centres (e.g., NFLC) have found it advantageous to be located geographically and/or administratively in a university with an established reputation and status and others such as CILT, ECML or RELC immediately gain some status and profile from the fact that they are government or multi-government funded, serving purposes already accepted as important and in the national or multi-national interest by decision of the government (e.g., the British Government and CILT) or of the multi-governmental organisation (e.g., SEAMEO and RELC or the Council of Europe and ECML). In addition, most of the centres reviewed in this book put considerable effort into achieving and maintaining an appropriate profile and status. This is achieved in many different ways including

- by maintaining an attractive, user-friendly and useful webpage with links to other relevant and useful organisations;
- through publications that are academically respectable, that are useful to the profession, and that lend prestige to the authors and the centre;
- by hosting or providing workshops, seminars and conferences that address issues pertinent to the centre's mission and that are responsive to the needs of the communities the centres serve. (This is especially evident in the activities of the NFLC, the structure of its advisory council, its frequent and large-scale colloquia, and its more or less weekly "brown bag lunches" to which both Center staff and outsiders are invited. In addition, by attracting in potential clientele from the education system or from government to participate in colloquia and other meetings, the Center makes it more likely that they will come to see it as a centre of expertise and that they will, in turn, come to it for advice and projects when they have need. These issues are discussed at some length in the chapter on NFLC in the context of its structure, activities and governance and especially in an extended discussion on the notion of "leverage", how the Center can exert "leverage", and how it can identify the "points of leverage" to which it can most effectively contribute. Similar processes have added considerably to the profile, visibility, status and credibility of RELC through its annual RELC Seminars, its journal, which is widely read especially in Asia and the Pacific, and its various other publications of practical usefulness to language teachers not only in the SEAMEO countries but elsewhere in Asia and the Pacific — and probably beyond.)
- by attracting into the centre people from the local, national and international communities who come into the centre for some worthy purpose but who also "spread the word" about the centre. (These persons may include students who come in to undertake some course or other, visiting research fellows or visiting scholars, and persons invited onto the centre's advisory council or other committee or contracted for a project of some sort. Again, the NFLC under the design developed by its founder, Richard Lambert, has made effective use of this strategy: the NFLC's Fellowship and Adjunct Fellow schemes, for example, attract into the

Center applied linguists and sometimes others of status in their field and with a language interest who, by their association with NFLC, through their publications and business cards which acknowledge a link with NFLC, and through their own oral and published statements, lend credibility to the Center and considerably increase its profile.)

By establishing close contact with relevant professional associations, language centres can favourably affect their profile, status, visibility and credibility while also identifying and responding to particular needs. There is mutual value in this: on the one hand, the professional associations such as the Modern Language Teachers Associations represent the practitioners in the field who are immediately conscious from their daily activities of the needs to which language centres are established to respond and, in many instances (e.g., RELC or CILT), it is the teachers themselves that the centres have been established to assist; hence, involvement with the professional associations is likely to assist centres to identify and respond to needs and so to carry out their mission. On the other hand, professional associations, being funded out of membership dues and being managed essentially by volunteers who do it out of interest in and love for their profession, are continually hard pressed for resources, for personnel to do the work of the association, and for a permanent home for the headquarters of the associations in the face of continual changes amongst the elected officers. The present writer became acutely aware of these problems for professional associations during his eleven years as Secretary, Vice-President and President of the Modern Language Teachers Association of Queensland, his fourteen years as national President of the Australian Federation of Modern Language Teachers Associations, and his six years as a Vice-President and Regional Representative for South East Asia and the South West Pacific for the Fédération Internationale des Professeurs de Langues Vivantes.

Language centres, especially ones with State, national or regional roles, can greatly assist professional associations by providing them with a headquarters, a place to which correspondence can be directed, possibly an office and meeting rooms, and perhaps some administrative assistance with basic secretarial and other administrative services. The problem for both the centre and the association is that the cost of such things has to be met by someone and professional associations rarely have sufficient resources to meet them in full. If, however, through its core and other grants, by making a nominal charge to the association, or simply by "losing" the expenses in its larger budget, a language centre can provide such assistance to relevant professional associations, it greatly benefits its profile and visibility, it multiplies its links across the profession, and it can considerably increase its sensitivity to the needs that exist out in the field.

In the submissions that the present writer produced on a "national language information and research centre" in Australia that led eventually to the creation of the National Languages and Literacy Institute of Australia, an important role for the proposed centre was to provide "a permanent headquarters and secretariat for the

[Australian] Federation [of Modern Language Teachers Associations]" (Ingram 1978:1). The submission envisaged a very close relationship between the proposed centre and the professional associations (especially the Australian Federation of Modern Language Teachers Associations, AFMLTA, and the Applied Linguistics Association of Australia, ALAA):

> It is proposed that the AFMLTA and ALAA should have a considerable voice in the management of the Centre, that their secretariats should be lodged there, and that they should make some contribution to the running of the Centre. …
>
> There are considerable advantages in the Centre's being partially a centre for AFMLTA (and, hence, State MLTAs) and for ALAA rather than being a solely government-run organization … In particular, it is much better able to capitalize upon the energy, initiative and professional skills of a large group of enthusiastic and concerned language teachers and academics who already make major contributions to the development of Australian education through their professional associations. It also ensures that the Centre remain in touch with the reality of the schools and the needs of the society since, through the MLTAs, the Councils of AFMLTA and ALAA, the Assembly, and the Board of Management, practising teachers will directly influence the Centre's policies and activities. …
>
> In short, a *National Language Information and Research Centre* funded by the government but with significant involvement from the professional associations can benefit greatly in efficiency, cost-effectiveness, and the encouragement of and benefit from individual initiative. As a specialist and expert centre responsive to practical needs, it provides the ideal combination of highly developed skills, academic insight, practical concern, and awareness of social and practical realities. (Ingram 1978:43–44)

It should be noted that the NLLIA, when it was established, did not provide this sort of assistance to professional associations though, in its latter years, it did attempt to find ways by which to involve them in determining the Institute's research agenda. This lack of involvement was partly because the nature and level of funding for NLLIA probably did not allow it to offer secretariat services. It was also because, in a country as vast as Australia, it is difficult for professional associations whose executive members could be anywhere in the country to ensure that appropriate officers were based within everyday research of the Institute. It was also, however, because the attitudes of the Institute were sometimes perceived (rightly or wrongly) as inimical to the interests of the Associations as a result of the control the Institute seemed to want to exert over organisations involved with it, as noted elsewhere in this chapter, and because of unfortunate statements that Institute staff sometimes made, e.g., when an Institute representative objected to the presence of professional association representatives at a meeting on language policy because, the person asserted, only the Institute could make statements on language policy.

The issue of balance discussed earlier in the context of the scope of language centres is especially important in this context of the relationship between a centre and the professional associations that it might seek to assist or with which it might, in some way, be involved. Professional associations are independent, autonomous bodies designed to meet the needs of their membership and answerable only to that membership. Anything which undermines that independence and autonomy is inimical to the association, its decision-making and its effectiveness. If a language centre, because of the services it offers to a professional association, were to seek to exercise control over it or to ensure that, for example, it expressed only views in accordance with the views of the centre, the centre would be undermining the very nature, role and function of the professional association and would, undoubtedly, be met with profound antagonism. If a centre is to provide support to professional associations, it is essential that the correct balance be found between the nature and level of the support provided and the associations' independence.

It is not only with professional associations that language centres might establish links of some sort but with all aspects of the community and clientele to whose needs it aims to respond. CILT has taken a major initiative in the area of language and business and industry and has established a variety of relationships with them. Not least, it provided a headquarters for the Languages Lead Body and its branches and Comenius Centres seek to involve local industry in their activities and to respond to their needs. The NFLC has sought to involve industry leaders in its governing council. The National Languages and Literacy Institute of Australia at one stage established a unit specifically aimed at creating awareness in Australian industry of the value of language skills and cultural understanding and of responding to industry language needs. Unfortunately, this unit survived only a short time until its funding was abolished following an Institute review (the report, remarkably, questioned the relevance of industry needs to the language interests of the Institute) and it was forced to close down. The Australian Federation of Modern Language Teachers Associations then created a Special Interest Group on Languages in Industry to try to pick up some of the pieces but, with the very limited funding and infrastructure support that a professional association can provide, the impact of the Special Interest Group was, inevitably, minimal.

To sum up, the very nature of a language centre, especially one involved in any direct or indirect way with language policy and its implementation, demands that it establish strong links with the community and the clientele it is established to serve. It cannot stand apart and still expect to remain sensitive to the needs of the society and its potential clients and, for this reason, for reasons of practical relevance and sensitivity to need, it is essential that language centres establish strong links and strong channels of interaction with all aspects of the community and the clients it is intended to serve. In addition, the establishment of a national or international language centre or of centres that serve smaller communities (e.g., a State, a local district, or an institution) provides concrete demonstration of the fact that the language needs of the community are recognised but that recognition will be no more than a show unless the centre itself ensures that it is sensitive to them and that it meets the needs to which it is intended to respond; for this to occur, the centre must establish links and interact continually with the community and the potential clientele. The present writer, in recommending a national language information and research centre for Australia, wrote thus in 1978 but the general issues raised remain relevant today, at least in English-speaking countries (though with additional emphasis on the relevance of language skills to industry):

> There have, indeed, been many pious words, many expressions of support for second language teaching, even considerable realization of the needs it fills and the positive values that it has to contribute to Australian society. However, ...[a]ction is needed to show that Governments and other bodies are serious in their expressions of support for multiculturalism [nowadays, for a significant role for language skills and language education in meeting industry needs], and for second language learning; action is needed to give stimulus to language teaching; and action is needed to provide language education in this country with the resources that will make it efficient, effective and responsive to the nation's real needs. The formation of a *National Language Information and Research Centre* would be a major step in this direction. (Ingram 1978:4)

6. Activities

There is a vast range of strategies by which language centres pursue their missions, activities in which language centres could engage, and services that they provide; the five language centres discussed in detail in this book have different sets of activities and services even though there are certain common features across most centres. The usefulness and effectiveness of the strategies, activities and services found in any language centre can usefully be considered or evaluated only within the context of operation, the role, function, purpose and mission, and the funding model of that particular centre and, not least, according to its status as an international, national or institutional centre. This was done in the earlier chapters for each of the centres discussed in this book and here, where the focus is on language centres in general, only a brief listing of common activities and services provided will be considered.

At the national and international levels, centres are more likely to have catalytic or **stimulatory, advisory and training roles**, their activities being directed, catalytically, at stimulating applied linguistics and language education, seeking to promote their development and quality, providing advice throughout the system (to teachers, education systems and administrators, and to government), and having input to language policy. The work of CILT, a national centre, and of ECML and RELC, international centres, well illustrates this. By virtue of their role and of their relationship to government, such national and international centres are able to maintain a broad perspective over the needs of the society, of business, and of the education system (or systems) and so to identify desirable directions of development, provide leadership for the language profession, and respond to changing needs through policy and curriculum advice and training programmes for language professionals (cf. Ingram 1978: 4–5, 28, 30]. Institutional centres, as illustrated by CALL, are more likely to be involved with specific research and consultancy projects, providing language programmes, and advising their host institution on its language policies and implementation.

Language centres generally are not directly responsible for the systematic development of **language policy**, that being more often undertaken by government through its own departments or through such bodies as committees of inquiry established by government. So, for instance, the Australian Language and Literacy Policy was developed by Australia's Federal Education Department (DEET 1991, 1991a) and, in the late 1990s, the British Government set up the Nuffield Inquiry to examine language policy in Britain. NFLC well illustrates the advisory role of language centres in language policy: through its various publications, conferences, colloquia, and other meetings, it seeks to stimulate research, thought and development. Granted the dispersed nature of language policy in the United States, NFLC does not so much produce systematic language policy as identify need, exert "leverage", advise and lobby; though Federal and State language and language education policies are effectively developed by others, NFLC undertakes projects that may have decided impact on language policy (e.g., the large, contracted review commenced in 1998 of Title VI, the principal legislation under which the Federal Government supports language education in higher education in the United States, and the language needs study undertaken in the context of that review). CILT has no direct responsibility for language policy development (though individuals within CILT may be involved in it) but, through its information and clearinghouse role and its conduct of seminars, courses and other training activities, it stimulates the development and implementation of policy. The major international centres with a regional responsibility discussed in this book (ECML within Europe for the Council of Europe countries and RELC in South East Asia amongst the SEAMEO group of countries) are not involved in policy development but assist in the implementation of policy developed or supported by the multi-government organisations to which they answer: in the Council of Europe countries, for example, language policy is developed by the Council's Modern Languages Projects based in Strasbourg, France, while ECML is charged with, particularly, conducting conferences, meetings and training courses, and providing advice that will assist in the implementation of the Council's policies. By their nature and the restricted geographical extent of their responsibility, an institutional centre is not so much concerned with the development of formal policy as with provision of expert advice, the conduct of research, teaching award and non-award courses in applied linguistics and offering other training programmes, and teaching languages. However, some centres, like CALL, may take particular interest in language policy and its implementation and may seek to undertake particular projects in that area, or provide advice to government. Most institution-based centres would be involved in providing advice on language education policy and practice within the host institution. In CALL's case, in addition to frequent advice to Schools, individuals, and the university administration on language policies in the university (e.g., on desirable English levels for overseas students), the Centre has won a number of contracts to advise government departments on aspects of language education policy. The first contract the Centre undertook after it commenced operations in 1990 was to give a newly elected Queensland Government systematic advice that led to a new State language education policy for Queensland (Ingram and John 1990).

Even though language centres may not usually be directly involved in the development of systematic language policy, there are several ways in which they can contribute significantly to it. As noted above, they may be contracted to provide specific advice on language policy in response to specific terms of reference expressed in a specific contract, either by drafting a systematic policy to be amended and/or adopted by government (as CALL did in advising on a Queensland State language education policy) or by providing advice on some aspect of policy (as in the case of NFLC reviewing Title VI and providing a needs analysis of the American situation). As argued in the present writer's submission for a national language centre in Australia (Ingram 1978: 4–8; 45–46), there is also an important though intangible role for a national language centre in representing the government's and society's support for language education:

> In this context, a National Language Information and Research Centre not only can promote language learning but becomes a tangible sign of the nation's and government's determination to respect and foster the languages and cultures of its peoples and to respond to their national and international needs for language skills. Furthermore, such a Centre could do much to advise and assist in the formulation of a national language policy and national language education policy, in particular because it becomes a centre for the collating of the sort of information on which such policies can be rationally based. ...
>
> ...a national centre entrusted with the task of responding to the nation's language needs and promoting language teaching and learning provides tangible evidence of that worth and of the fact that ... [language teaching] is a profession which is soundly based academically and which is supported by a body of knowledge available to increase their effectiveness and to respond to their needs. (Ingram 1978: 4, 7, 8)

Thus, the existence of a centre such as CILT, ECML or RELC and their support by government provides a tangible sign of the importance attached to language policy and to language education.

If language policy is to be rationally based, systematic and coherent, it should respond to and grow out of the changing needs of the society and there is need for some organisation, typically a language centre, to **monitor the society, industry,** education, and demographic changes, to identify needs, to evaluate programmes, policy and other initiatives, and to provide advice to the appropriate authorities and to the profession through reports, conferences, seminars and other training programmes (cf. Ingram 1978: 4–5). This is well illustrated in the role that NFLC has adopted from the outset, a role which, as discussed in some detail in Chapter 2, has profoundly influenced its structure and activities. In one of his earliest papers on the need for a national foreign language centre (which, there, he referred to as a National Foundation), Lambert discussed the need for centralised planning with some organisation being available to monitor needs and to coordinate the piecemeal efforts he saw being taken to stimulate foreign language education:

> These many initiatives in the improvement of the national capacity to teach foreign languages are most encouraging. However, right at the beginning of this upsurge of interest and investment, it is extremely important that a central planning, initiating, coordinating, and implementing organization be put in place to assure that the scattered efforts in the area of foreign language education are cumulative, that they address the central agenda issues, and, above all, that they are effective and represent the best use of our national resources. …
>
> …Assuming such a catalytic role in the development of a more effective system of foreign language instruction would be a natural first priority for the proposed National Foundation … [which later became the National Foreign Language Center]. …
>
> A primary function of the foundation should be to provide central planning, coordination, and the necessary marginal resources to improve the nation's foreign language education system. (Lambert 1986: 12)

Lambert went on to discuss in some detail the agenda for such a national foundation, focussing on "points of leverage" in order to effect change in the foreign language teaching system to better meet the needs of American society and he proposed that the Foundation undertake needs and use surveys especially in key occupations where foreign language use would be most productive (Lambert 1986: 12–22).

Closely related to this common monitoring task for, especially national, language centres, is the **"think-tank"** role in which a centre continually examines, on the one hand, the society, its education, its demography, and all the strands of development and change going on within it and, on the other hand, the developments in the discipline of applied linguistics. Coming out of this think-tank activity, the centre is able to promote both applied linguistics and language and language education policy, on the one hand, and the implementation of policy in language education practice and the provision of other language services, on the other. The NFLC, as discussed in its chapter, is undoubtedly the pre-eminent example of a centre designed for this purpose.

The corollary of monitoring changing needs and of the "think-tank" role is, as Lambert argues (as in the quote above), that centres exert pressure for change in language education, i.e., that they adopt a **leverage** role, identifying key points where change might most effectively and efficiently be brought about in response to the needs identified for the society. In the centres discussed in this book, the leverage role is commonly found and takes different forms. Leverage may be exerted through formal submissions to government or institutions, through training activities (conferences, seminars, workshops, etc) directed at members of relevant professions, or by lobbying through press and media statements, formal submissions, or direct approaches to governments or other authorities. Such a role is not unusual amongst professional organisations but, if a language centre is specifically designed for this purpose, it will have salaried staff with some security of employment, who are articulate and have a broad vision of the society and of applied linguistics, and they will have the resources, support services, and access channels that make them better placed to exert leverage than are individuals or voluntary professional associations whose members often lack the time, the knowledge-base, the broad perspective, and the security to be able to be outspoken, especially when their representations may need to be critical of governments, institutions or other employers.

Most language centres, especially national and international language centres, have an important **information-gathering and dissemination and clearinghouse** role. CILT and RELC strongly illustrate this role, ECML is developing it, and, in the United States, the Center for Applied Linguistics in Washington DC has provided such a service both to the United States and worldwide for many years. These activities are listed in the chapters on the various centres described in this book. One of the common roles of language centres is to monitor the large and diverse language education system and the field of applied linguistics nationwide and worldwide, to gather information on these in its clearinghouse, and to make this information available to the profession (cf. Ingram 1978: 13, 15). The dissemination role is typically realised through the centre's publications (books, journals, newsletters, etc), abstracting services, consultancy services, conferences and other meetings, and, increasingly, through the maintenance of a strong and informative database and library services accessible through the centre's website and supplemented by links to other information sources. In some instances, centres may provide support to professional associations (and expand their own information dissemination and clearinghouse activities) by making available their printing and publishing facilities to the associations, possibly at reduced or no cost (cf. Ingram 1978: 20, 21).

The information and clearinghouse role is not only valuable in itself in informing and training the profession but it has an important role in empowering the profession. The efficiency and effectiveness of applied linguists, whether researchers, academics or teachers, depends very largely on their having available a strong knowledge base on which to draw in their work. A national centre with strong information-gathering, dissemination, and clearinghouse roles contributes greatly to this both intangibly by increasing the practitioners' realisation of the breadth and activity of their profession and tangibly by providing an information base on which they can draw to enhance their skills, inform their decision-making, and strengthen their professional independence. This is especially important in education systems such as exist in Britain, the United States and Australia where more and more responsibility for critical education decision-making (e.g., in curricula, syllabuses, work programmes and assessment) are devolved to the schools and to individual teachers (cf. Ingram 1978: 8, 13, 15).

In some centres, **language teaching** programmes are undertaken either in order to upgrade the quality of the teachers or other professionals in the centre's geographic area of responsibility or in order to generate revenue for the centre. RELC offers language programmes of different types for the former purpose while CALL, a wholly self-funding centre, offers fee-based language courses (especially in English for overseas students wishing to study in Australia but also in other languages on contract to government departments or industry) as a means of generating revenue and, in principle if rarely in practice, to cross-subsidise other activities such as research. As noted earlier, some language centres are, in fact, language teaching centres with their sole responsibility being to teach languages to students in the host institution, to persons from industry or the wider community, or to international students who have come to learn, generally, the local language. The roles, functions and management of language teaching centres raises some similar but also other different issues from the language centres discussed in this volume.

In most language centres, whether they are international, national or institutional, **language teacher education** is a major activity. At the least formal level (as with NFLC), this may take the form of conferences, seminars or workshops but in centres such as CILT, RELC and ECML, they form a major part of their activity with a regular programme of seminars and short courses on offer, often specifically targeted towards some particular area of need. ECML, for example, has a particular responsibility to update and upgrade language policy and the relevance and quality of language education in the "newly independent countries" of Eastern Europe. RELC provides not only frequent short courses and seminars (including its annual RELC Seminar, one of the largest conferences in the Asia-Pacific region), but it also provides regular award courses, especially at the graduate level, awarding Masters degrees and, at one time, doctorates in collaboration with universities. Though CALL is a self-funding centre outside of the mainstream academic programme of its host university, it also offers both non-award and degree courses both on contract to other institutions or agencies such as UNESCO and on an individual student, fee-paying basis. The award courses currently range from graduate certificates in such areas as language assessment, applied linguistics and second language teaching to the supervision of doctoral candidates in a range of applied linguistic areas related to language education. Its short non-award courses cover any area of applied linguistics and second language teaching where a market demand is evident and characteristically include, for example, aspects of assessment such as the use of the International Second Language Proficiency Ratings (Ingram and Wylie 1979/1999) and short introductory courses ("professional programmes") in aspects of applied linguistics, second language teaching, and language policy. Increasingly, centres are making their teacher education and other training programmes available through "flexible learning" modes. So, for instance, CALL's graduate certificates are taught in "flexible learning" mode using a combination of the internet and hard copy and, subject to certain conditions of supervision, even Ph.Ds are available at a distance.

The place of **research and development** in the work of language centres tends to differ according to whether the centre is international, national or institutional. As already noted, the main international and national centres such as CILT, ECML or RELC are less involved in research and development than in facilitating the implementation of policy and the improvement of the quality of language education in their region of responsibility. Nevertheless, they would all claim (especially CILT) to make an important contribution by stimulating research, by providing basic information and clearinghouse services, by convening meetings that lead, or contribute to, research and development activities, and through their think-tank and leverage roles. Though the NFLC carries out important research and development activities in support of its other roles, its research contributions are diversified through its fellowship schemes under which both new and experienced researchers are enabled to spend time at NFLC pursuing their own research and development agendas and contributing (even if more through conversation and discussion than through direct participation) to the NFLC's own agenda. The NFLC's own research and development agenda is very much seen in the context of its "leverage" role as it identifies areas where change is needed and can be achieved through more information, lobbying and the pre-requisite research and development. Lambert, in his paper foreshadowing the NFLC, wrote of the Center's research and development agenda thus:

> Without this evaluation and planning capacity, neither the Foundation nor anyone else can perform the crucial monitoring and agenda setting; and, except for the hunches and enthusiasms that have dominated policy formulation so far, there is no sound basis for directing national investment to the points of leverage where its impact will be greatest. …
>
> The Foundation should establish a proactive program of research support to direct research toward topics of great national importance, to fill in gaps in country or language coverage, and to carry out the evaluation and planning activities for the field as a whole. To establish the priorities for and to supervise this proactive program, a distinguished national advisory group should be established, comprising research scholars and representatives of universities, major international business firms, national research organizations and government agencies along lines similar to the National Science Board. Both private and public funds should be provided to support research on the topics selected by the group. (Lambert 1986: 99–100)

For centres that depend in whole or in part on project funding for their revenue (in contrast to centres that receive core funding from government or elsewhere), it is difficult to adopt a systematic research plan but rather, like CALL, the centre has to bid wherever and whenever grants are available and for whatever project is most relevant to the terms of reference of the centre and the granting body and so likely to be successful. In such centres, also, even though (unlike NFLC) funds may not be available to offer scholarships and fellowships, it is possible to have visiting arrangements (CALL calls them CALL Visitors) which impose minimal cost on the centre itself but which enable researchers on study leave or with other financial support to spend time in the centre working on their own research, writing papers, and contributing to the centre through interaction with centre staff and by acknowledging the centre in their papers. Such arrangements are stimulating for both visitors and centre staff, serve to raise the centre's profile, and give the visitor access to the centre's and host institution's facilities.

As discussed earlier in this chapter, it is important that a centre not aspire to control all of the applied linguistic research that goes on in the country or in its area of responsibility, as seemed to occur with the National Languages and Literacy Institute of Australia in the 1990s. The reasons for this were discussed earlier but, in particular, such a centralised model of research funding reduces the creativity of the field as a whole, it is in danger of focussing research around just those areas of interest to the one centre, and, as has occurred in Australia following the virtual disappearance of the NLLIA, if the centre should disappear, there is great danger that the research funding will disappear with it leaving the entire field considerably depleted of research funds. Though some centres may undertake research and development activities, for national centres it may be more useful to adopt a research stimulating, monitoring and information dissemination role and undertake only that research themselves which contributes directly to their other tasks.

One area of research and development in which most centres are involved is curriculum. Most centres, whether international, national or institutional, are involved in research and development in syllabuses, either in providing expert advice on syllabus design, in providing expert evaluation and development advice on new syllabuses, or in developing syllabuses themselves. Syllabus and curriculum development cannot be separated from methodology since most syllabuses explicitly or implicitly require a certain approach to methodology for their implementation and consequently most centres also play a major role in the development of methodology and in the training of teachers in methodology both in general and in that required for specific syllabuses (cf. Ingram 1978: 21–25). NFLC, for example, has taken the lead in the United States in advocacy for the "lesser taught" languages and has developed syllabuses in languages such as Chinese. CILT and RELC have contributed to syllabus development and provide substantial training for teachers in the development and implementation of syllabuses. ECML was founded with its major initial role that of assisting the newly independent countries with the development of their language policies and their implementation and, hence, with the development of new curricula and the training of teachers in methodology. CALL, as an institutional centre, has contributed substantially to syllabus development in Queensland through the work of several of its staff on State and national curriculum agencies and has, through national projects for which it was contracted, assisted in the development of national Asian language syllabuses by providing formative evaluation on syllabuses in such languages as Vietnamese, Chinese, Korean, and Thai and developing the assessment components of the syllabuses. CALL has also specifically researched methodology and syllabus design, for example, in the context of the fostering of more positive cross-cultural attitudes and in the use of "community involvement" to enhance language proficiency development.

Most centres have, as a major part of their activities, the provision of **advisory or consultancy services**. Such services are essential in centres whose missions include improvements in the quality of language teaching. Most of the roles referred to above, especially the clearinghouse and information dissemination roles, provide access for language teachers and others to advisory services but most centres, either through their basic terms of reference or through revenue-generating contracted projects, offer consultancy services (see Ingram 1978: 18–20). In some centres such as CILT and RELC, the principal (though not exclusive) focus of the advice is at the level of the implementation of language education policy and the on-going training of teachers. As already noted, ECML was established with the initial role of providing advice on the development of language policies and their implementation in educational programmes. NFLC is more involved in advice at the policy level though, again as already noted, it also is involved in the implementation of policy through syllabus development, specific research projects undertaken by its Fellows, and in such specialised areas as language assessment, the teaching of the (for America) "lesser taught" languages (such as Chinese, Japanese or Russian), and in the maintenance, development and teaching of the "heritage" languages, the languages of the American people.

It is clear that all centres focus much of their activity around specific **projects** and project funding, for some centres, makes up much of their revenue. This can be both a strength and a weakness for those centres. All centres realise their mission through particular projects, whether that be in the area of language and language education policy (such as the NFLC's review of Title VI) or in aspects of policy implementation (such as ECML's activities in assisting the newly independent countries to implement the language education policies of the Council of Europe or CILT's activities in assisting teachers to improve the quality of language education in Britain). In some cases, where centres receive substantial core funding, they are able to develop and implement projects at their own discretion and in fulfillment of their missions. In self-funding centres such as CALL, projects form an essential part of their revenue and it is essential that they monitor and bid for projects as they become available. However, while projects might make up a considerable part of the activity and funding of most centres, they have a serious "down side" since centres such as CALL that are heavily dependent on project funding have less strategic control over their own agendas because they are dependent on what is available and what they can win. In addition and as already discussed, they are faced with the ever-present problem of winning projects, with the costly exercise of continually preparing project submissions knowing that they will win only a relatively small proportion of them, and with the task of maintaining their professional and academic integrity, objectivity and critical independence despite having to continually win projects, perhaps from government and other sources that might, at times, wish to influence project outcomes but which, in other projects and in other roles, the centre may be obliged to criticise.

7. **Advantages and constraints**

In this chapter we have considered at some length the nature, roles, functions, purposes and management of language centres. A wide range of options in the establishment and development of language centres have been discussed. The essential feature that should permeate a language centre is the synergy that comes as a centre pursues certain defined goals through a coherent set of activities using staff with similar or complementary interests and abilities in contrast, for example, to many language departments in universities where there will, appropriately, be many disparate interests represented amongst the staff, many of whom may lack qualifications, experience or expertise in applied linguistics. Language centres are generally more focussed in their goals and activities, specifically focussed around applied linguistics and whatever are the key foci in the terms of reference under which the centre is established. In many instances, perhaps most and whether they be international, national or institutional centres, language centres generally have more autonomy than departments in determining their directions (within their founding terms of reference), in managing their budget, in staffing, and in their general operations.

Undoubtedly the greatest constraints and difficulties to be overcome lie in the area of the budget and the basis of their funding. In the majority of cases, language centres operate on a significant proportion of so called "soft money", rather than on a more or less assured grant within university funding. Nevertheless, it has to be said that, nowadays, at least in Australia but, in the experience of the present writer, in the United States, Britain and undoubtedly elsewhere, departmental funding within a university is anything but secure from year to year and its level is little less dependent on the department's performance and ability to attract students than is the revenue of a self-funding language centre attracting clients on the basis of the quality of the services it provides. Beyond this, the most serious constraints that occur on language centres are those that are imposed by governing bodies with little understanding of the constraints within which self-funding centres must operate, the speed of the decision-making that is essential in the context of commercial competition, the different conditions under which staff must be employed and be willing to work in order for the centre to be competitive, and the dangers that must be avoided in the potential (but not inevitable) conflict of interest between commercial interests and academic requirements. We also noted earlier the difficult but critically important need for a centre, which may have the role of observing, advising, and critiquing, to maintain its independence and insist on its autonomy and the objectivity of its advice. This need, if the centre is to maintain its academic integrity, is seriously (but not necessarily) put at risk if the centre has to survive on project and other funding from organisations such as government departments and agencies that might, potentially, be the subject of its criticism. Such difficulties can probably be reduced, if not wholly circumvented, if the centre has a multiplicity of funding sources and has the capacity itself to generate a substantial part of its income. Project funding, characteristically a major proportion of a centre's funding, also incurs the costly problem that the winning of projects requires first that considerable time, effort and skill (and, therefore, money) be put into submission writing, a great deal of which is seemingly wasted since no centre can confidently anticipate winning more than a small proportion of the projects it bids for and many funding agencies (such as the various State, Territory and Federal governments in Australia) demand that projects be advertised on the open market rather than be negotiated with an identified supplier. We also noted the critical balance that national language centres, in particular, have to achieve between, on the one hand, a desirable analytic, catalytic, coordinating and overview role of the nation's needs and activities in the area of language policy and language education and, on the other, the unacceptable, undemocratic and inevitably self-defeating dangers inherent in a centre's seeking to become, in Lambert's words, a "czar" (Lambert 1986:113), trying to assume full control over the field of applied linguistics and centralising policy, decision-making, funding and implementation on itself.

8. Conclusion

Language centres have played and can continue to play important roles in the ongoing development of applied linguistics and in assisting societies and institutions to meet their needs for language skills. However, if they are to do so, it is essential that they be well managed and that the full corollaries of whatever constraints or requirements are placed on them through their terms of reference be followed through.

At times, statements have been made that may be interpreted to be critical, sometimes highly critical, of certain centres or their hosts. However, if the issues discussed were to be interpreted simplistically in this way, it would be unfortunate. In most instances, the issue to be considered is how a rapidly spreading emphasis on commercial-like approaches to management in educational institutions, not least in universities, is to be managed and, in particular, how commercialism or economic rationalism and the traditional aims and management style of universities in particular are to be reconciled. Language centres as they have evolved are, in many instances, at the forefront of this confrontation. If universities are to survive the challenge of economic rationalism and the demand for a more commercial orientation without losing any of their vital tradition of academic excellence and independent thought, they could do worse than learn from the experiences of the sorts of language centres discussed in this book. It is essential that universities, like language centres, come to understand commercialism and its management requirements, that they realise what is required if academic excellence and commercial activity are to be compatible, and that they follow through the corollaries of commercially managing an academic unit.

The advent of globalisation has given a centrality to language issues, to language policy, and to language education. Language centres have developed with a pivotal role in enabling institutions and societies to manage globalisation and linguistic and cultural diversity, a role which has to be properly managed if the full potential of language centres is to be realised and their full contribution to the global society achieved. It is hoped that this book, which has sought to raise some critical issues in the roles, functions, and management of language centres, will assist in the development of language centres. It is hoped that, in raising those issues for consideration, it will help at least to make readers aware of the issues and help managers, host institutions and language centres themselves accommodate to the new demands arising from globalisation and social diversity, on the one hand, and the pressures on management from commercialisation and economic rationalism, on the other.

References

Bim, Inessa. 1995. "Changes in FLT training". In *Modern Language Learning in the New Europe: The Role of the European Centre for Modern Languages in Graz: Proceedings of the First Annual Colloquy of the European Centre for Modern Languages of the Council of Europe, 8 and 9 December 1995, Graz, Austria*, European Centre for Modern Languages, 10–12. Graz, Austria: Council of Europe/ European Centre for Modern Languages, c. 1996.

Bostock, William. 1998. "The Techno-Corporate University: A Global Paradigm". Paper to the conference of the Griffith Institute of Higher Education, *Re-Working the University*, Griffith University, Brisbane, Australia, 10–11 December, 1998. Mimeograph.

Brändle, Maximilian. 1996. *Languages in Continuing Education*. Brisbane: Centre for Applied Linguistics and Languages.

Brändle, Maximilian. 1993. *Adult Language Learning and Languages in Contact*. Brisbane: Centre for Applied Linguistics and Languages.

Brecht, Richard D. 2000. "Memorandum to NFLC Fellows, 21 September, 2000". Washington DC: National Foreign Language Center. Mimeograph.

COAG 1994: See Council of Australian Governments (COAG) 1994.

Council of Australian Governments (COAG). 1994. *Asian Languages and Australia's Economic Future: A Report prepared for the Council of Australian Governments on a Proposed National Asian Languages/Studies Strategy for Australian Schools*. Brisbane: Queensland Government Printer.

Council of Europe and Modern Languages. 1998. *European Centre for Modern Languages, Graz*. (Brochure with no publication details shown)

Council of Europe and Modern Languages. 1998a. *Modern Languages Projects, Strasbourg*. [Brochure with no publication details shown[1]]

Davis, Val. 1998. "Foreign language learning in the FE sector — a view from FEDA". In *CILT Further Education Bulletin*, No. 3, Spring 1998:2.

Department of Employment, Education and Training (DEET). 1991. *Australia's Language: The Australian Language and Literacy Policy*. Canberra: Australian Government Publishing Service.

Department of Employment, Education and Training (DEET). 1991a. *Australia's Language: The Australian Language and Literacy Policy: Companion Volume to the Policy Paper*. Canberra: Australian Government Publishing Service.

European Centre for Modern Languages (ECML). 1998. "Key Questions of Language Learning: Feedback of Prof. Hanna Komorowska, Prof. Georges Ludi, Prof. John L.M. Trim to the Tenth Meeting of the Bureau of the Governing Board, European Centre for Modern Languages, 10–11 September, 1998". Graz: Council of Europe/European Centre for Modern Languages. CC-ED/GRAZ (98) 60. Mimeograph.

---

[1]. This publication is the other half of the preceding one, turned upside down and back-to-front.

European Centre for Modern Languages, Graz (ECML). 1997. *1998 Programme of Activities*. Graz, Austria: European Centre for Modern Languages.

European Centre for Modern Languages, Graz (ECML). 1997a. *1997 Programme of Activities*. Graz, Austria: European Centre for Modern Languages.

European Centre for Modern Languages (ECML). c.1996. *Modern Language Learning in the New Europe: The Role of the European Centre for Modern Languages in Graz: Proceedings of the First Annual Colloquy of the European Centre for Modern Languages of the Council of Europe, 8 and 9 December 1995, Graz, Austria*. Graz, Austria: Council of Europe/ European Centre for Modern Languages.

Griffith University. 1999. *Griffith University Strategic Plan 1999–2003 Operational Plans 1999*. Brisbane: Griffith University.

Hawkins, Eric. (ed.). 1996. *30 Years of Language Teaching, 1966–1996. 30 Years*. London: CILT.

Huyghe, Tina. 1998. "National policy on foreign language learning: a case for a national framework to accredit non-specialist adult learning of foreign languages by the Open College Network". *CILT Further Education Bulletin*, 3, Spring 1998: 5–7.

Ingram, D. E. forthcoming. *Languages in Australian Industry*.

Ingram, D. E. 2000. *Foreign Language Employment Agenices with International Agencies in the United States*. Brisbane/Washington DC: Centre for Applied Linguistics and Languages/National Foreign Language Center.

Ingram, D. E. 1994. "Principles of Language-in-Education Planning". In *Glottodidactica*, XXII: 11–27. Poznan: Adam Mickiewicz Press.

Ingram, D. E. 1993. "Language Policy in Australia in the 1990s". Invited paper to the Pre-conference International Workshop on Foreign Language Planning, National Foreign Language Center, The Johns Hopkins University, Washington, DC, 20 September 1993. In *Language Planning around the World: Contexts and Systemic Change*, Richard D. Lambert, 69–109. Washington, DC: National Foreign Language Center, 1994.

Ingram, D. E. 1990. "Survey of National and International Information and Research Centres for Modern Languages". Survey paper commissioned by the Fédération Internationale des Professeurs de Langues Vivantes (FIPLV). Mimeograph.

Ingram, D. E. 1980. "Applied linguistics: a search for insight". In *On the Scope of Applied Linguistics*, Robert B. Kaplan (ed.), 37–56. Rowley, Mass.: Newbury House.

Ingram, D. E. 1980a. "To See, To Speak : Participate! Community Involvement in Language Teaching". *Unicorn*, 6 (3), August 1980: 276–283.

Ingram, D. E. 1979. "The Case for a National Language Policy in Australia". *Babel* 15 (1): 3–16.

Ingram, D. E. 1978. *A National Language Information and Research Centre: Submission to the Commonwealth Government from the Australian Federation of Modern Language Teachers Associations and the Applied Linguistics Association of Australia*. Brisbane: Mt Gravatt College of Advanced Education.

Ingram, D. E. 1978a. *An Applied Linguistic Study of Advanced Language Learning*. Thesis for the degree of Doctor of Philosophy, University of Essex, Colchester, England.

Ingram, D. E. and Glyn John. 1990. *The Teaching of Languages and Cultures in Queensland: Towards a Language Education Policy for Queensland Schools*. Brisbane: Centre for Applied Linguistics and Languages, Griffith University.

Ingram, D. E. and Elaine Wylie. 1979/1999. *The International[2] Second Language Proficiency Ratings*. Brisbane: Centre for Applied Linguistics and Languages, Griffith University.

---

2. The International Second Language Proficiency Ratings were known as *The Australian Second Language Proficiency Ratings* prior to 1997.

Ingram, D. E. and Elaine Wylie. 1995. *The International Second Language Proficiency Ratings — General Proficiency Version for English*. Brisbane: Centre for Applied Linguistics and Languages, Griffith University.

Ingram, D. E. and Elaine Wylie. 1995a. *The International Second Language Proficiency Ratings — General Proficiency Version for Indonesian*. Brisbane: Centre for Applied Linguistics and Languages, Griffith University.

Ingram, D. E. and Elaine Wylie. 1995b. *The International Second Language Proficiency Ratings — Version for Second Language Teachers*. Brisbane: Centre for Applied Linguistics and Languages, Griffith University.

Ingram, D. E., Elaine Wylie and Geoff Woollams. 1996. *The International Second Language Proficiency Ratings — Version for Teachers of Indonesian*. Brisbane: Centre for Applied Linguistics and Languages, Griffith University.

Ingram, D. E., Elaine Wylie and Hilda Maclean. 1995. *The International Second Language Proficiency Ratings — English for Business and Commerce Version*. Brisbane: Centre for Applied Linguistics and Languages, Griffith University.

Ingram, D. E., Elaine Wylie and Laura Commins. 1995. *The International Second Language Proficiency Ratings — English for Engineering Purposes Version*. Brisbane: Centre for Applied Linguistics and Languages, Griffith University.

Ingram, D. E., Elaine Wylie and Catherine Hudson. 1995. *The International Second Language Proficiency Ratings — English for Academic Purposes Version*. Brisbane: Centre for Applied Linguistics and Languages, Griffith University.

Ingram, D. E., Elaine Wylie and Peter Grainger. 1995. *The International Second Language Proficiency Ratings — Version for Japanese*. Brisbane: Centre for Applied Linguistics and Languages, Griffith University.

Jones, Stephen. 1998. "Modern Foreign Languages and International Cooperation in Education". *CILT Links*, 18, Spring 1998: 3.

Kaplan, Robert B. (ed.). 1980. *On the Scope of Applied Linguistics*. Rowley, Mass.: Newbury House.

Lambert, Richard D. 1994. *Language Planning around the World: Contexts and Systemic Change*. Washington, DC: National Foreign Language Center.

Lambert, Richard D. (ed.). 1994a. *Foreign Language Policy: An Agenda for Change*, Special issue of *The Annals of the American Academy of Political and Social Science*, 532, March 1994. Thousand Oaks, California: SAGE Periodicals Press.

Lambert, Richard D. 1990. "History and Future of HEA Title VI". Paper to the conference on the reauthorization of HEA Title VI convened by the National Association of State Universities and Land-Grant Colleges, University of Pittsburgh, 2 March, 1990. Reprinted in *Language and International Studies: A Richard Lambert Perspective*, Sarah Jane Moore and Christine A. Morfit (eds), 237–245. Washington DC: National Foreign Language Center, 1993.

Lambert, Richard D. 1986. *Points of Leverage: An Agenda for a National Foundation for International Studies*. New York: Social Science Research Council.

Lambert, Richard D. 1987. "The Case for a National Foreign Language Center: An Editorial". *The Modern Language Journal* 71, Spring 1987: 1–11. Reprinted in *Language and International Studies: A Richard Lambert Perspective*, Sarah Jane Moore and Christine A. Morfit (eds), 128–140. Washington DC: National Foreign Language Center, 1993.

Little, David. 1995. "New approaches and attitudes towards learning and assessment". In *Modern Language Learning in the New Europe: The Role of the European Centre for Modern Languages in Graz: Proceedings of the First Annual Colloquy of the European Centre for Modern Languages of the Council of Europe, 8 and 9 December 1995, Graz, Austria*, European Centre for Modern Languages, 13–19. Graz, Austria: Council of Europe/ European Centre for Modern Languages, c. 1996.

Lo Bianco, Joseph. 1987. *National Policy on Languages*. Canberra: Australian Government Publishing Service.

Moore, Sarah Jane and Christine A. Morfit. eds. 1993. *Language and International Studies: A Richard Lambert Perspective*. Washington DC: National Foreign Language Center.

National Foreign Language Center. 1998. *The National Foreign Language Center at The Johns Hopkins University: Overview*. Washington DC: National Foreign Language Center. Mimeograph.

Nuffield Languages Inquiry. undated, c. 1998. *Where are we going with Languages? A National Inquiry appointed by the Nuffield Foundation*. London: Nuffield Languages Inquiry.

Nuffield Languages Inquiry. 1998. *Where are we going with Languages? Consultative Report of the Nuffield Languages Inquiry*. London: Nuffield Languages Inquiry.

Regional Language Centre (RELC). 1997. *Blueprint 1997–2001*. Singapore: RELC.

Regional Language Centre (RELC). 1992. *Blueprint 1992–1996*. Singapore: RELC.

Regional Language Centre (RELC). 1987. *Blueprint 1987–1991*. Singapore: RELC.

Regional Language Centre (RELC). 1982. *Blueprint 1982–1986*. Singapore: RELC.

Regional Language Centre (RELC). 1977. *Blueprint 1977–1981*. Singapore: RELC.

Regional English Language Centre (RELC). 1972. *Blueprint 1972–1976*. Singapore: RELC.

Satchwell, Peter. 1998. "News from the Primary Language Network". *The CILT Primary Languages Bulletin* 3, Spring 1998:2–4.

Senate Standing Committee on Education and the Arts (SSCEA). 1984. *A National Language Policy*. Canberra: Australian Government Publishing Service.

Szépe, György. 1995. "Language policy for a wider Europe". In *Modern Language Learning in the New Europe: The Role of the European Centre for Modern Languages in Graz: Proceedings of the First Annual Colloquy of the European Centre for Modern Languages of the Council of Europe, 8 and 9 December 1995, Graz, Austria*, European Centre for Modern Languages, 20–25. Graz, Austria: Council of Europe/ European Centre for Modern Languages, c. 1996

Tench, Gill. 1996. "A Calendar of events". In *30 Years of Language Teaching, 1966–1996*, Eric Hawkins (ed.), 353–376. London: CILT.

Trim, John. (ed.). 1997. *Language Learning for European Citizenship: Final Report (1989–96)*. Strasbourg: Council of Europe.

Trim, J.L.M. 1997a. *Modern Languages: Learning, Teaching, Assessment: A Common European Framework of Reference: A General Guide for Learners*, Draft 1. Strasbourg: Council of Europe/ Council for Cultural Cooperation. Also on webpage of the Council for Cultural Cooperation (see below).

Trim, John. 1996. "A View from the bridge". In *30 Years of Language Teaching, 1966–1996*, Eric Hawkins (ed.), 321–330. London: CILT.

Trim, J.L.M. 1995. "The ECML in the context of the Council of Europe Modern Languages Programmes". In *Modern Language Learning in the New Europe: The Role of the European Centre for Modern Languages in Graz: Proceedings of the First Annual Colloquy of the European Centre for Modern Languages of the Council of Europe, 8 and 9 December 1995, Graz, Austria*, European Centre for Modern Languages, 9. Graz, Austria: Council of Europe/European Centre for Modern Languages, c. 1996.

Truchot, Claude. 1998. *Introduction to Language Policy: Methods of Analysis and Evaluation Fields of Intervention: Report, Workshop 12/97, 23–28 June, 1997, Graz, Austria*. Graz, Austria: European Centre for Modern Languages/Council of Europe.

Wylie, Elaine and D.E. Ingram. 1995. *International Second Language Proficiency Ratings: Master General Proficiency Version (English Examples)*. Brisbane: Centre for Applied Linguistics and Languages, Griffith University.

Webpages

Centre for Applied Linguistics and Languages, Griffith University (CALL):
   http://www.gu.edu.au/centre/call/

Centre for Information on Language Teaching and Research (CILT): http://www.cilt.org.uk

Council of Europe: http://www.coe.fr

Council for Cultural Cooperation: http://culture.coe.fr/

European Centre for Modern Languages (ECML): http://culture.coe.fr/ecml
   or http://culture.coe.fr/ecml/eng/gralist.html
   or http://culture.coe.fr/ecml/index_e.htm

Global English Newsletter: http://www.english.co.uk/newsletter/gen.html

National Foreign Language Center (NFLC): http://www.nflc.org/

Nuffield Languages Inquiry: http://www.nuffield.org

Regional Language Centre (RELC): http://www.relc.org.sg/

Southeast Asian Ministers of Education Organisation (SEAMEO): http://web.singnet.org

Index

A

ACCESS 134
Adjunct Fellow 17
advisory committee 121, 188
advisory council 188
agents of change 93
allied centre 114, 205
ALLP 112
applied linguistics 111
Arts Group 116
Associate Membership 89
Association of the European Centre for Modern Languages 72
AST 130
AusAID 131
Australian Language and Literacy Policy 112
Australian Study Tours 110, 130

B

Blueprints 92
Broadwater 115
Business and Education Operations 123

C

CALL Seminar Series 136, 165
CALL Visitors 137
CDCC 65
Centre de Ressources 4
centres of excellence 89, 91
characteristics 4
CILT Direct 53
CILT Information Sheets 55
CILT Links 55
COE 65
Comenius Centres 41, 49, 161, 219
Comenius News 55
commercialism 230
Committee on Research and Development in Modern Languages 46
Corporate Services Group 123
cross-subsidisation 211
curriculum 227
czar 19, 25, 230

D

discretionary funding 105, 164
donors 3, 34–35, 206–207

E

economic rationalism 230–231
ELICOS 112, 129
ELICOS Association 139
English Australia 139
English Language Intensive Courses for Overseas Students 112, 129
Enlarged Partial Agreement 70
European Commission 79
European Cultural Convention 66

F

FDTL News 56
fellows 22, 29
fellowship 17, 29
FFPOS students 109
First Annual Colloquy 64, 74, 76
Fund for the Development of Teaching and Learning 44

G

globalisation 160, 174, 231
Gold Coast Education Network 139, 141
governing board 188
governing council 188
Graz 71
Griffith University 113

240 Index

Griffith University English Language Institute 110, 131
Griffith University International Centre 151
GUELI 110
GUIC 151
Guidelines 99

H
heritage languages 30, 31
homestay 130, 144

I
IELTS 111, 133
Institute of Applied Linguistics 114
institutional centre 221
international centres 159
International English Language Testing System 111, 133

L
Language Australia 182
Language centres 1, 3, 173
Language Colleges 57
Language Export network 48
language policy 180
language resource centres 4
Language Teaching 55
language teaching centres 1, 4, 225
Languages Lead Body 40, 54, 219
Languages National Training Organisation 40, 54
languages other than English 134
levies 145
Lingu@netEuropa 49
LOTE 134

M
mission 174
Modern Language Teachers Association 217
Modern Languages Project 79, 179, 180
modern languages projects 47, 48, 64, 68, 69, 82, 221

N
NatBLIS 40, 53
National Asian Languages/Studies Strategy for Australian Schools 112

National Business Language Information Service 40, 53
National ELICOS Accreditation Scheme 119, 126
National Foreign Language Resource Center 13
National Foundation for Foreign Languages and International Studies 9
National language information and research centre 217, 218, 220, 222
National Language Resource Centers 5
National Language Standards 54
National Languages and Literacy Institute of Australia 26, 60, 179, 182
National University of Singapore 92, 94, 95, 102, 103
NEAS 119, 126
Netword 56
NLLIA 26, 182
Nuffield Foundation 45
Nuffield Languages Inquiry 42, 45, 174, 180

O
On est fou du foot 56

P
participatory decision-making 191
professional associations 217
proficiency 20

Q
Qualifications and Curriculum Authority 45

R
Recommendation No. R (82)18 67
Regional English Language Centre 87
Regional Schools Internet Project 98, 99
RELC Anthologies 99
RELC Building 104
RELC International Hotel 91, 104
RELC Journal 99
RELC Newsletter 99
RELC Occasional Papers 99
research quantum 176
Resolution (69)2 47
Resolution (94)10 71
Resolution (98)11 70, 72, 74
Richard Lambert 7, 9

S
SEAMEC 89
SEAMEO 89, 206
SEAMES 89
shared decision-making 191
Southeast 85
Southeast Asian Ministers of Education Council 89
Southeast Asian Ministers of Education Secretariat 89

special needs 58
strategic approach 173
submission writing 18
synergy 3, 80, 173, 181, 200, 229

U
university centre 109

W
webpage 194